SPY HANDLER

SPY HANDLER

Memoir of a KGB Officer

THE TRUE STORY OF THE MAN WHO RECRUITED ROBERT HANSSEN AND ALDRICH AMES

VICTOR CHERKASHIN *with*
GREGORY FEIFER

BASIC
BOOKS

A Member of the Perseus Books Group
New York

Books published by Basic Books are available at special discounts for bulk purchases
in the United States by corporations, institutions, and other organizations. For
more information, please contact the Special Markets Department at the Perseus
Books Group, 11 Cambridge Center, Cambridge MA 02142, or call (617) 252-5298
or (800) 255-1514, or e-mail special.markets@perseusbooks.com.

Designed by Trish Wilkinson
Set in Goudy by the Perseus Books Group

Library of Congress Cataloging-in-Publication Data
Cherkashin, Victor, 1932–
    Spy handler: memoir of a KGB officer : the true story of the man who recruited
Robert Hanssen and Aldrich Ames /Victor Cherkashin with Gregory Feifer.
        p.   cm.
    "A Member of the Perseus Books Group."
    Includes bibliographical references and index.
    HC: ISBN 13 978-0-465-00968-8; ISBN 0-465-00968-9 (alk. paper)
    1. Cherkashin, Victor, 1932- 2. Intelligence officers—Soviet Union—
Biography. 3. Espionage, Soviet—History—20th century. 4. Soviet Union.
Komitet gosudarstvennoæi bezopasnosti. 5. Intelligence service—Soviet Union
6. Spies—Soviet Union. 7. Soviet Union—Foreign relations. I. Feifer, Gregory.
II. Title.

JN6529.I6C49 2005
327.1247'0092—dc22

                                                                                    2004017609

PB: ISBN 13 978-0-465-00969-5; ISBN 0-465-00969-7

16   15   14   /   10   9   8

*To my family—my wife,
children and grandchildren—
to whom I have dedicated my life*

CONTENTS

PREFACE

Publication of this book comes against great odds, the result of a path on which I embarked at the height of my career. It eventually led me to decide that telling my story was important—for the debate over Cold War espionage as well as for my sake. In addition to my initial reluctance, I had to confront the fact that intelligence work doesn't lend itself to memoir writing. A political tool since ancient times, intelligence doesn't normally play an independent public role in affairs of state. Its essence is secrecy. For those like me who have spent their careers in espionage, publicizing its details goes against instinct and tradition.

Usually the public learns the identity of intelligence operatives only when something goes wrong. When operations fail, intelligence officials are often loudly arrested, exposed, or made the subject of a successful setup by the intelligence services of an opposing side.

My name became known in Russia following the arrests of CIA officer Aldrich Ames in 1994 and FBI special agent Robert Hanssen in 2001, both in the United States, several years after I retired from the KGB in 1991. The press in Russia and the United

States covered some aspects of my involvement in both espionage cases, but most reports lacked key details and misrepresented facts to fill in the gaps. Meanwhile, my experience (actually, my lack of it) in speaking to journalists who tried to interview me led to an even greater mess. American writers read their own preconceived notions into my words (I purposely left many details vague), while Russians came up with their own explanations. Eventually I stopped giving interviews to the media, and I'm only now ready to tell my full story.

For most of my career, I conducted operations against the Main Adversary—as KGB terminology designated the biggest strategic threat to the Soviet Union. Until World War II, that honor belonged to Great Britain, after which it went to the United States. I operated against both until 1965, when my efforts became solely directed at counteracting CIA activities against the USSR. During those dangerous years, U.S. and Soviet intelligence services often fought on the front lines of the Cold War.

I joined the KGB in 1952, just as that war was heating up and a year before Joseph Stalin died. I retired almost forty years later in 1991, days after the attempted August coup d'état against Mikhail Gorbachev that did so much to help bring down the Soviet Union. My career encompassed Russia's transformation from a totalitarian dictatorship to a country opening its arms to democracy.

I must warn readers expecting to read about James Bond–style exploits in these pages that I undertook none in my career. Intelligence consists chiefly of workaday routine and, with luck, rare successes. In my many years with the KGB, I met officers, spies and others who subsequently became well-known. But that came in the course of normal duties. I never parachuted out of an airplane, learned how to kidnap or assassinate or how to crack safes. I never took a course on espionage tradecraft. I joined KGB counterintelligence after studying foreign languages and was sent abroad to learn through experience. What follows is the account of a real KGB career.

I have changed some names and omitted others. I've tried to be as accurate as possible, but in such accounts it's not possible to reveal everything. Many of the agents I handled and operations I ran in my career have never been exposed. While I discuss them here, the real names of some must remain secret. I've drawn my story almost entirely from memory, and while I've done everything possible to ensure that the basic facts of each episode are correctly portrayed, some of the dialogue and actions describe events as they likely happened.

Although I make my views about the KGB, the CIA and Soviet and American politics and affairs clear, I tried to avoid falling into the trap of polemics. This account is not KGB propaganda. Other memoirs and tales of Cold War espionage carry disinformation either purposely or unwittingly gathered from interviews with intelligence officers still intent on misleading the other side. Serving and retired operatives often refrain from correcting bad information—making it seem that they agree—while disseminating more of their own skewed narratives to blur the facts. The nature of espionage makes a certain degree of that inevitable. I try to get beyond the circle of purposeful misinformation to simply tell my own story as I remember it.

I didn't undertake to write about myself in order to aggrandize my career or the KGB—enough fuss has already been made about my part in Cold War espionage. Aside from the new details in this account, intelligence professionals generally know who I am and understand the significance of my role in KGB history. I wrote for a general Western audience, which has shown more interest in the real facts—the good and the bad of intelligence history—than Russians have. In the past, I've been interviewed for several accounts of Cold War espionage. In most cases, my actions and words haven't been portrayed entirely correctly—not necessarily as a willful decision on the part of the writers, but because they didn't have all the information. Here is my attempt to correct the record.

I continue to care deeply for the KGB's reputation. My goal is to clear away some misperceptions about Soviet intelligence, to try to communicate that the KGB was staffed by human beings who made the same mistakes and held the same feelings others did. Most intelligence officers are able to separate their professional and personal feelings. The many years I spent working against the CIA were my contribution to the maintenance of my country as a great power. But that didn't mean I didn't respect Americans or enjoy the United States. I always believed Americans were trying to do for their country what I was doing for mine.

Finally, I don't intend this chronicle to be published in Russia, where intelligence professionals are now generally seen more as suspicious "spies" than dedicated officers serving the interests of their country. Many former KGB officers have published memoirs claiming to address public curiosity, where none really exists. Most of these books were vanity projects, presented as the official versions of events. Some of those accounts have tarnished my reputation and those of other former KGB officers, reflecting the politics at work in any bureaucracy. Instead of waiting for future historians to write more balanced analyses of the claims and counterclaims, I decided to tell my story now and enable readers to come to their own conclusions.

ACKNOWLEDGMENTS

Victor Cherkashin: I would like to thank my colleagues Yacob Medyannik, Leonid Shebarshin, Stanislav Androsov and all those in intelligence with whom I had the privilege of working and who did so much to help me in my professional life.

Thanks to my former opponents—Milt Bearden, David Major and Jack Platt—for their understanding and their candid analyses of the events in which we all participated. They demonstrated just how far beyond the designation of "main adversaries" we've moved.

Thanks to those who helped make the seemingly impossible come true by realizing the manuscript—including Trident Media Group's book producer Iazamir Gotta, for his professionalism and determination (his ability to keep coming up with reasons to convince me of the project's feasibility—and then keep it on track).

Thanks to Trident's Robert Gottlieb, my literary agent, who understood the rationale behind my life and believed in this project. Thanks also to Irina Krivaya, translator-coordinator, who spared no effort and maintained the lines of communication between those cooperating on the manuscript. Thanks also to Trident's John Silbersack.

Special thanks to Gregory Feifer, who managed to preserve my general tone and narrative direction, while making the book interesting to read. Gregory possesses a rare quality engendering respect and trust without his having to make extra efforts to display artificial enthusiasm. Without his interest in my professional life and the goodwill between us, we would have hardly been able to conduct the frank discussions necessary for writing the manuscript.

Gregory Feifer: I would like to thank Victor Cherkashin for telling his important story, which was a pleasure to write about. Thanks also for his openness and boundless patience with my many questions. Trident Media Group's Zamir Gotta put this project together and persevered in seeing it through. Thanks to him and Irina Krivaya for her scrupulous transcriptions and many other important duties. Thanks also to Trident's Robert Gottlieb and John Silbersack for taking me on and their savvy advice.

I'd like to thank those who helped with editing the manuscript, including George Feifer for his matchless line editing and Elizabeth Feifer for her merciless cutting. Special thanks to those who reviewed the manuscript and pointed out my many mistakes, including David Major and Connie Allen of the Centre for Counterintelligence and Security Studies, which also helped with photographs. Thanks also to Phillip Knightley.

Thanks to those who agreed to be interviewed, to my family and to all those who helped with advice and encouragement.

Thanks also to the editors at Basic Books for generating the final product.

PROLOGUE
Betrayal

1

I stood staring at my wife in the small foyer of our new apartment in Krylatskaya, the concrete-block residential district in the southwest of sprawling Moscow. I understood what she just said, but the news took a few seconds to register. Then I went back to my usual routine, taking off my coat and shoes and putting on my slippers. But any sense of normalcy had vanished. What she'd just told me concerned something I thought had been buried in a long-forgotten life. That past now rushed back like a thundering locomotive.

"Aldrich Ames has been arrested."

Elena repeated it slowly and gravely. I looked at her straight dark hair and handsome, furrowed brow. I'd seen the same expression many times over the years—it indicated she was controlling her emotions. She didn't have to repeat herself; my blank look should have assured her I'd understood correctly. "I saw it on the news tonight. I wanted to call you, but, well . . ." There was no need to mention our old habit of never saying anything of importance over the telephone, even three years after the collapse of communism, which forever changed our way of life.

I thought back to the first time Ames had surfaced between us, nine years earlier. At the time I didn't know his real name, and even if I had, I couldn't have told it to her. She heard about him for the first time on the news and put two and two together. She suspected that something major had happened back then in 1985 because of her work typing secret cable traffic between headquarters at Moscow Center and the KGB station, or *rezidentura*, in Washington, where I was head of counterintelligence. When I came home that April afternoon, she raised her eyebrows to question me and I replied with one deep nod. That was enough. We'd become veteran practitioners of silent communication by then.

Now, on February 23, 1994—two days after Ames was arrested— the name that had remained unspoken between us until that very minute was being broadcast to the entire world.

I was weary. The gray company Mercedes had dropped me off moments earlier at the row of high-rise apartment blocks where I lived. The buildings were a cut above the standard hastily assembled piles of concrete, with a clean entrance, neat blacktop and walkways instead of the usual potholes and muddy tracks. I had to wrap my coat around me against the invading cold and clammy late winter air.

I'd had a tough day. Running security at one of Moscow's largest new banks was a nerve-racking business. Overseeing the 150 men who guarded the bank's main office and various branches was only part of it. My larger job was helping steer the company through the cutthroat world of post-Soviet business at a time when criminal groups made themselves "partners" of almost every business in the capital—when they didn't seize them outright. Meanwhile, to channel profits from the mad grab for former state property, banks were springing up faster than any other type of company. Bankers were being assassinated almost weekly on Moscow streets. A company's survival in that murderous atmosphere required the kind of information a former KGB officer was well positioned to provide.

I'd barely had time to adjust to this new life of ours. Elena and I had been true believers in communism, and we shared the idealism and hopes of those around us. I'd always felt the difficulties and cruelty I saw—now in retrospect much easier to isolate and criticize—were a necessary part of the work it took to shore up our socialist state. When we were posted abroad, Elena and I always found the words and proof to defend Soviet achievements—to which we were doing our best to contribute in our own way. Nevertheless, it had been clear for years before the collapse that the Soviet administration had let down the Motherland. Things had to change—the state was so badly mismanaged, it had no choice but to crumble. But not in the way it did, with the robbery and lawlessness that formed the foundation of the new Russia.

I'd dealt with staff problems all day and had to negotiate with some crooked cops, but those concerns now vanished. I was thinking again as I would have in my past life. Making my way to my carefully wallpapered living room, I sat down on a brown velour couch. *How could Ames have been compromised?* Taking precautions, protecting our precious "assets," had always been the top priority—indeed the key to having him as an agent. My assurances to Ames on the matter made the difference between running a spy of average importance and one who felt safe enough to hand over some of the best counterintelligence information the KGB had ever netted. How did we fail to protect the man who'd been so crucial to reversing our fortunes?

Ames, who became one of our biggest successes ever, began working for us at a time when the KGB had been crippled by the

CIA and the FBI—although we had no idea of the scale of the damage until Ames provided us with that information. He enabled us to turn around and land one major blow after another on the United States. Thanks to Ames, we all but shut down CIA operations in Moscow.

Success like that was never planned. I thought back to when I was a young officer stationed in Lebanon. It took me many months to lay the groundwork to entrap one CIA officer—bugging an apartment he secretly used for his work, befriending his cleaning lady, tracking his moves around the city, taking secret photographs. Even then, the opportunity to use the information I gleaned came years later, when we found him working in West Germany. I traveled to Bonn to meet him, but in the end, he refused my recruitment effort.

Years later, I was still amazed at how it had happened so differently with Ames, how a former head of counterintelligence in the Soviet section of the CIA, with practically unlimited access to the secrets of American intelligence, *came looking for us!* Various sums have been reported about how much Ames was paid. We considered his efforts worth every penny of the $2.7 million he was actually allocated. As American news reports lamented, he gave us the names of more than twenty spies, selling out every U.S. agent operating on Soviet soil. The ten sentenced to death after his revelations earned him the title of the CIA's "deadliest spy." He also placed many other CIA officers at risk and helped undo a number of technologically advanced, multimillion-dollar covert operations in the Soviet Union.

My mind moved quickly back to the present, racing through possible reasons for Ames's exposure. Perhaps it had been just a matter of time until the inevitable happened. The likeliest cause was a blunder by Russian—that is to say, post-Soviet—intelligence. Plenty of circumstantial evidence in the past could have easily warned the CIA it had a major leak. But even the most obvious signs often don't lead to exposure. The arrest couldn't have happened just like that, in the course of normal operations. Surely Ames was betrayed. In that case, the blame lay squarely with us.

Counterintelligence services rarely expose agents. In my own experience, one of the few cases was that of Oleg Penkovsky, a celebrated spy for the CIA and British Secret Intelligence Service (SIS). A top aide on the Red Army General Staff, Colonel Penkovsky supplied secrets to the West from 1961 until his arrest in 1962, when he was tripped up by the incredibly sloppy way in which British and American intelligence ran him, setting up meetings in broad daylight in the center of Moscow.

Such mistakes were almost impossible now. I instantly ruled out a communications slipup. Our methods were too well developed for agents to make blunders during liaisons or by picking up information at special locations called dead drops. I kept coming back to the same conclusion: Someone must have exposed Ames from the inside. Was a mole in Russian intelligence responsible?

Now Ames would surely spend the rest of his life in prison. What a fate! Considering that the failure was ours and not his, my heart sank. I'd been instrumental in bringing Ames in and convincing him to give us the real goods instead of handing over the useless information he offered us initially. Now I tasted bitter helplessness, unable to do anything for him in return.

To Americans, the man dominating the headlines was of course a monster. But that was the nature of the game—so much of which turned out to be nonproductive, even damaging, to all its players, as I eventually realized. The U.S. officials now prosecuting Ames treated as heroes Russians who betrayed *their* country. Ames was a human being, and I felt much sympathy for him for that, even though I'd only dealt with him professionally and shared no personal ties.

I racked my brain. Perhaps there was something I could do, after all. Although Ames—and Rosario, his wife—were out of reach in prison, his five-year-old son wasn't. I resolved to help him. I'd propose bringing him here and raising him myself, in a caring family, in a way of which his father would approve.

Then I thought of how the arrest would affect me. Very few knew me as the man who had recruited the most damaging spy in CIA history. I had no idea how that fact would now play. I'd always hoped the story would forever remain unknown, except to a handful. Since retiring three years earlier, I'd had almost no contact with KGB headquarters. The retirement had been less than genial. I'd been blocked out and partially exiled, and Ames's arrest would probably cement that condition. The Russian Foreign Intelligence Service (SVR), the successor to the KGB's foreign intelligence wing, the First Chief Directorate (FCD)—had no use for a retired colonel, even one with my experience.

Or so I thought. Little did I know that in time my name would once again become associated with Ames's—but for a far different reason.

2

The phone rang on a cold, rainy November day in 1997. I was sitting in the offices of the new, swank Actyor Gallery business center on Tverskaya (formerly Gorky) Street, Moscow's brightly lit main drag and commercial showcase of the new capitalism. The office belonged to my Swiss partner, with whom I'd started working after leaving the bank to set up my own security company.

My friend Nikolai, or Kolya, was on the other end. He asked if I'd seen the latest issue of *Voprosy razvedkii i kontrarazvedkii* (Intelligence and Counterintelligence Issues).

"Did you see what Kirpichenko said about you?" Nikolai continued. Vadim Kirpichenko, a top adviser to the SVR, had been my superior when he was first deputy of the FCD. "*Bozhe* [God almighty]! Go—get a copy!"

I hadn't an inkling of what could be important enough for me to venture outside onto the rainy, muddy sidewalks. The ex-deputy intelligence chief was a longtime ally of Vladimir Kryuchkov, the former KGB chief who helped lead the 1991 coup d'état against Mikhail Gorbachev. What could Kirpichenko be saying about me now? I'd never worked with him directly. For that reason among others, he never really knew me.

"So what is it, Kolya?"

"You'd better see for yourself," Nikolai said, refusing to elaborate. His urging seemed odd. Everyone knew Kirpichenko spoke chiefly for himself and, despite his high rank, certainly didn't represent the views of the intelligence service. But the concern in Nikolai's voice prompted me to grab my coat. I ducked outside to a newspaper kiosk on Pushkin Square, site of the poet's statue as well as Russia's first McDonald's, where business still boomed, if not as wildly as during its first years.

I bought the paper and brought it upstairs. Nikolai hadn't been kidding. The dirt came in an article by Kirpichenko accusing my former friend Oleg Kalugin of betraying Ames to the Americans. The allegation would have been more shocking if Kirpichenko hadn't made a practice of accusing Kalugin—who had years before denounced the KGB and moved to the United States—of spying for the Americans. Aside from the new twist about Ames, there was little new.

Kalugin had graduated at the top of his class before zooming up to become the youngest KGB general ever, at forty-one, and head of the FCD counterintelligence department. Then rumors began to circulate that he was an American agent. Kryuchkov soon demoted Kalugin, which helped set my old friend on a path that would lead him, ten years later, to denounce the KGB. The decision brought the wrath of his former colleagues. Convicted of treason in absentia in June 2002, Kalugin was labeled a traitor by no less than that well-known ex-KGB officer, President Vladimir Putin. Kalugin then made his critics even more livid when he took U.S. citizenship the following year.

I read on about how Kalugin had obtained his information about Ames from a "friend." Not just any friend, but someone whose profile was extremely familiar, down to the very name "Victor," which happened to be mine (the surname was omitted) and the claim that he'd been secretly awarded for handling Ames. That accusation was stunning. In the highly compartmentalized world of intelligence, our commodity—information—was sacred. Only those who had to know were informed. To have spoken about Ames even to Kalugin—my former boss and friend—would have amounted to treason.

I reread the article to make certain. Yes, there it was. Leaving out only my family name, Kirpichenko accused me of betraying one of our most valuable spies ever, the man whom I'd handled myself with all the care and devotion I could muster.

So almost fifteen years after the dirty rumors about Kalugin first began, they were again playing into Kirpichenko's hands. The allegation was as hypocritical as it was disgusting. After all, it was another officer who ran FCD counterintelligence when the blows of the early 1980s were battering the KGB. He was supposed to lead the search for moles in our system—and failed to. How very convenient to pin those setbacks on someone else—Kalugin, no less—when in fact the blame belonged to people like Kirpichenko. Any real suspicions would have been thoroughly investigated—in secret. Instead, to publicly level general accusations without a shred of proof laid bare Kirpichenko's real intentions. It was not only highly unprofessional, it showed the greatest disrespect to his fellow KGB veterans.

As for my own reputation, this certainly wasn't the first attempt to damage it by linking me to Kalugin. Not that we *weren't* closely linked. Before Kalugin openly turned against the KGB, we'd often spoken candidly about its failures. That continued even after he came under suspicion and I, knowing our phones were bugged, risked running afoul of the leadership. But I didn't care. What could they do to me? Besides, everyone knew Kalugin and I went way back to when we were roommates in our elite KGB foreign-language institute. Then, in the late 1970s, I worked under him in Moscow, and it was he who sent me to Washington in 1979.

My Order of Lenin (I was among those awarded one in 1986, for my work with Ames) later helped prompt more rumors about Kalugin, suggesting he may have known I'd had something to do with our sudden successes. But to prevent the CIA from learning of our celebration, which would have sent them hunting for its cause, the ceremony had been kept secret. Even my closest friends didn't know about the highly prestigious honor. That upset Elena, who felt it unfair that we couldn't tell those we completely trusted—even though she didn't know exactly why I received the award. I could remember saying nothing to Kalugin that would have even hinted of my work with Ames.

That heated the resentment that now burned inside me—not a good feeling for a trained intelligence professional. I felt I had to do something, but what? I didn't want to go to court, which would have been even less seemly for an *ex*-intelligence officer. At the same time, I couldn't let the accusation stand. I snatched up the phone and dialed the number of Leonid Shebarshin, an old confidante and my former boss. Shebarshin—who was KGB number two for many years and rose to the top position for one day in 1991—always kept a level head and reached sound judgments.

He thought about my news for some seconds, then answered calmly and disappointingly in his deep smoker's baritone. "Don't do anything," he said.

"*Shto* [say again]?"

"Your surname's not mentioned."

"So? Everyone will surely know it's me."

"But what can anyone actually say? There's no proof Kirpichenko meant you. But if you start going around making loud
noises, everyone will indeed think it's you. So just ignore it."

I took his advice. Throughout my career, I tried to keep my
profile low. After retiring from the KGB, I avoided interviews—
except for a very few I granted to small newspapers as favors to
former colleagues. Following my professional instinct to stay out
of all limelights, I rejected lucrative offers to work as a consultant
to NTV television, then the country's top independent channel.
And the more I thought about my present urge to challenge the
slander, the more I realized nothing Kirpichenko said could affect
me very deeply, if only because of his own reputation. The lies
and insinuation of treason were outrageous, but I wouldn't rise to
the bait.

Then the ante was upped. Maybe it was only a matter of time.
Another journalist printed Kirpichenko's accusation and this
time included my full name. Now it was "Victor Cherkashin" the
traitor—when Victor Cherkashin had actually spent his entire career serving his Motherland as faithfully as he could and scoring
major victories against the Main Adversary. I could no longer stay
silent.

– 1 –

INSIDE THE LION'S DEN:
WASHINGTON STATION

1

I wasn't even supposed to be in Washington when it happened.

Elena and I were preparing to return to Moscow in early 1985. Officers' tours abroad usually lasted three to four years, and I'd been in Washington since 1979. It was painful to be separated from our young son, who had to remain in Moscow to attend school, and we were looking forward to being reunited with him. My replacement had already been picked but he was held up in Moscow, postponing our departure.

Not that I was in a rush to get back to "the Center"—KGB headquarters in the Yasenevo suburb southwest of Moscow, housed in a complex exemplifying the "soulless modern" architectural style. I knew my superiors, among them Vadim Kirpichenko, were hardly eager to see me. Kirpichenko saw me as an ally of Oleg Kalugin's, the man he'd helped remove as counterintelligence chief and my boss, six years earlier. I didn't want to suffer my friend's fate of being shunted out of counterintelligence.

So we remained in Washington. It was like no other posting. It's not easy getting used to the feeling of *always* having to be on guard. That was especially true for Elena, who by then had worked many years for Soviet intelligence. She'd never felt as tense during any of my other tours abroad. In Washington, she rarely went out by herself. Wary of being set up even for a shoplifting scandal, she kept track of every item in her shopping carts and made sure to check her pockets.

That was as much a result of the Center's foolish policies as anything else. The KGB's constant suspicion of its own officers and agents encouraged the Americans to put us in compromising situations. That was brought home after the arrest of an officer of the *rezidentura*—as KGB stations, usually housed inside Soviet embassies, were called. He was apprehended, ostensibly for shoplifting, during my tenure in what seemed an obvious provocation, what we called a harassing act or procedure to flush out surveillance or compromise agents or officers. He immediately returned to the embassy and reported the whole thing, insisting that security guards had planted the allegedly stolen goods. The incident was probably captured by closed-circuit video, but the Americans refused to show us the footage. Why didn't we believe one of our own? Because the Center didn't. He would have been sent back in disgrace if I hadn't convinced Moscow to let him off.

The rescue was unusual. The KGB wasn't unique in returning intelligence officers targeted in recruitment attempts by the other side. It meant, first of all, that they were known to the adversary. There was also the possibility that they'd accepted an offer, no matter how convincingly they denied it. Even in cases where they clearly turned "pitches" down, they nonetheless remained tainted. But all that went double for the KGB.

The level of mistrust in Yasenevo's corridors was so high that the first whiff of anything out of the ordinary could mean the end of a career. Such suspicion only made it easier for the CIA to recruit our men. Fear of losing their jobs inevitably led some to work for U.S. intelligence. A political intelligence officer named Sergei Motorin, who was caught trying to sell a case of vodka, didn't want that negligible misdeed made known to his bosses. The incident eventually helped convince him to spy for the FBI—until his exposure to us and his subsequent execution, thanks to Aldrich Ames.

Careful of the company we kept, Elena and I had few friends in the embassy. She never lacked the discipline required for semi-solitude. I sensed that right from the start, after we saw each other for the first time at far ends of a hallway in Lubyanka, the KGB's forbidding Moscow headquarters. As she later revealed, she told herself right then and there I was the man she'd marry. Such dedication, together with my position as head of the department that searched for traitors, kept us in virtual isolation—which, however, also reflected the suspicion that suffused our embassy in the Main Adversary's backyard.

By 1985, Elena and I were old Washington hands, otherwise comfortable in the city and relatively inured to the embassy's tics. Our precocious daughter, Alyona, was happy in her nursery school and we were proud she was growing up speaking English. We genuinely liked Americans, with their big-hearted hospitality and easygoing manner. And we loved the broad expanses of untouched wilderness. The United States was a good place to be.

It was a quiet time for the *rezidentura* itself, although that didn't mean work was easy. The Center sent a constant stream of questions about security, to which we strove to respond quickly. In the wake of our 1979 invasion of Afghanistan and the U.S. decision to boycott the Moscow Olympic Games the following year, relations between Washington and Moscow remained rancorous. The division was sharpened by Ronald Reagan's proclamations of the Soviet Union as the "Evil Empire" and his proposed Star Wars space missile defense system, with which we couldn't possibly compete.

Meanwhile, the Soviet Union's internal uncertainties loomed over us. It was still unclear who would succeed Leonid Brezhnev as Communist Party general secretary after his death in 1982, and the uncertainty grew as one leader replaced another in quick succession. Deeply concerned about possible abrupt changes to domestic and foreign policy, we put all operations on hold. Reducing communication with the Center to a bare minimum, we prepared ourselves to be ready for anything, even war with the United States.

When former KGB chief Yuri Andropov assumed the Soviet leadership after Brezhnev, we felt relieved and hoped for improved domestic conditions. But our expectations were deflated when Andropov died in 1984 and was replaced by Brezhnev's crony Konstantin Chernenko. He was so ineffectual that by the time he died the following year, we'd stopped worrying that the change would affect our work in any substantial way. Then came Mikhail Gorbachev's appointment in March—which we applauded. It would take years to suspect that Gorbachev would bring everything we knew crashing down around us.

By April 1985, the Washington station's routine had been more or less reestablished. My chief concern was a change in FBI surveillance practices. Instead of trailing almost every member of the staff, agents were letting most of our people go about their business and focusing solely on KGB officers. Stark evidence of the change had come in February 1984, when *rezidentura* technicians found twenty-five radio-transmitting beacons in the cars of embassy employees during a routine check. Twenty-four were in the cars of intelligence officers. The twenty-fifth was found in the car of a consular officer who was a friend of several KGB officers. That caught us off guard. I ordered the unit assigned to monitor and decode FBI radio conversations and other indications of their surveillance of our activity to analyze the data we'd collected over the previous years. The group used radio scanners and other devices to intercept communications "chatter" between FBI agents assigned to follow Soviet staff. The results were clear. The FBI had trailed all Soviet personnel—from our Foreign Ministry, the KGB, GRU military intelligence and trade representatives—until October 1982, when the surveillance suddenly became much more efficient.

How could they know? Certain officers, including myself, were of course recognized by the FBI. But how did they single out which cars leaving the embassy mansion were driven by KGB personnel, even newly posted ones? That could only mean that an agent somewhere in our system was passing along the information.

That worried me deeply as I approached our embassy on 16th Street on a beautiful spring day during cherry blossom season. Returning from several meetings in town and girding myself to write a routine report to the Center, I passed the guard and duty officer who observed all comings and goings, then entered the stately Parisian-style building that had once belonged to the widow of railroad car magnate George Pullman.

The diplomatic quarters were on the first floor. An elevator took me up past the ambassador's quarters to the fourth floor under the building's mansard roof, where a coded digital lock opened a thick steel door leading to our crammed *rezidentura*, constructed by KGB technicians to foil FBI eavesdropping. The space was so small that if everyone who worked there showed up at the same time, there would have been too few chairs to seat them.

Before I reached my office, the duty guard told me to see the *rezident*—as the head of station was called—immediately. Ducking around the corner, I knocked on Stanislav Androsov's door and entered his office.

"Hello, *tovarish*," I said, using the word for "comrade" half ironically. He didn't ask me to take a seat. In fact, he didn't say a thing, indicating a high level of concern on his part. His balding crown and straight, mild-looking features gave him an academic air. Maintaining his grave silence, he handed me an envelope with his name handwritten on the front. I opened it and removed a typed letter.

It was an extraordinary read. The author claimed to be an American intelligence employee. He was writing to offer us information on CIA operations against the USSR in return for $50,000. He said he was ready to meet with a representative of Soviet intelligence to discuss the conditions for a deal. To convince us of his sincerity, he enclosed copies of several documents. I shuffled through the small sheaf, which mostly concerned U.S. intelligence on Soviet naval forces deployed in the Middle East. Although the documents looked real, it was impossible to say whether they came from the CIA. The State Department or a private think tank, even a journalist might have produced the same analysis. The supposed proof was too general to be useful either as evidence of the writer's bona fides or as intelligence.

I glanced up at an intense-looking Androsov. "Where did you get it?" I asked.

"Chuvakhin brought it in." Sergei Chuvakhin, one of our arms control experts, was a diplomat, not a KGB officer. "It's from his contact Wells," Androsov added. "Chuvakhin himself didn't read it."

Wells. Of course I remembered Rick Wells. He'd recently contacted the Soviet embassy press attaché, Sergei Devilkovsky, claiming to be a political scientist connected to the State Department. He wouldn't be more specific. He wanted to discuss U.S.–Soviet relations, he said. Devilkovsky had informed the resident, and we'd deliberated over how to handle the fishy approach.

Naturally, we suspected that Wells was a CIA operative trying to recruit agents in the Soviet embassy. We later learned the CIA was in the thick of Operation COURTSHIP, a program to step up recruitment efforts among our personnel. But knowledge of COURTSHIP wasn't needed to suspect Wells's motives. Nevertheless, we decided to approve a meeting. We'd play along to see what we might get out of him. Contact was a necessary variable in the double-sided game we played, and if there was a possibility of recruiting someone trying to sign up one of our men, we had to explore it.

Devilkovsky himself didn't know we suspected Wells. That was how the system worked. Intelligence information was so compartmentalized that we didn't tell even people who were involved unless there was a need for them to know. Moreover, Devilkovsky was a "clean" diplomat—there was no need to include him knowingly in KGB work if it wasn't necessary.

Devilkovsky met Wells several times to talk about U.S.-Soviet relations and began to have his own doubts that the American was interested in him exclusively for the exchange of official information. In any case, before he was routinely rotated back to Moscow, Devilkovsky suggested to Wells that he contact Chuvakhin, the arms control expert.

Chuvakhin was an ideal point man. A disciplined attaché whom the CIA stood little chance of recruiting, he spent much of his free time building telescopes from scratch and grinding the lenses himself. He also wasn't informed that Wells was a possible CIA officer. Since Chuvakhin was clean, using him as a knowing participant in the Wells affair would have been problematic for the embassy. Moreover, the headstrong diplomat likely wouldn't have agreed to serve as a go-between if we'd asked him.

We also wanted to keep those who knew of our intentions to a minimum because Wells didn't look like a promising candidate for our own recruiting efforts: his behavior was inconsistent; he refused to disclose where he worked; he took pains to conduct his meetings in public places in the city instead of in the embassy or in his own office; and his explanation of his interest in Soviet diplomats was unconvincing. Besides, the strict FBI observation of Soviet embassy employees made it unlikely that a genuine State Department official would be allowed to approach one of our diplomats. All those factors discouraged us from trying to "develop" Wells; instead, our top priority was protecting Chuvakhin from possible U.S. recruitment.

During several meetings in Washington restaurants, a down-to-earth Wells showed no particular interest in Chuvakhin, asking only about his opinion of U.S.-Soviet relations. But he did share his own views on U.S. policy, and eagerly. In Chuvakhin's reports, they seemed moderate and balanced.

Only later did we learn that Wells's motives differed from those we ascribed to him. He was indeed a CIA officer assigned to recruit a Soviet agent, but he was actually trying to do the opposite: searching for a contact with Soviet intelligence. For that, he needed someone who'd be hard to corrupt, giving him a pretext to continue meeting while reporting little progress with the bogus recruitment effort. Devilkovsky had been too pliable for that purpose, and Wells needed someone who would balk at collaborating with U.S. intelligence. That would give him time—enough to achieve his real goal.

As far as we knew, Chuvakhin's meetings with Wells were fairly routine—until that April day when Androsov handed me his letter. Chuvakhin had agreed to meet Wells for lunch at the staid, colonnaded Mayflower Hotel on Connecticut Avenue near the Soviet embassy. Wells showed up, not knowing that the diplomat had no intention of keeping the date. Chuvakhin had grown weary of the meetings, feeling that he'd gleaned all the information he was likely to get. He decided to use the chance to brush Wells off without a confrontation.

Alone in the dark, wood-paneled lobby bar with its business lunch crowd chatting on leather sofas and chairs, Wells ordered a vodka, deciding how long to wait. After some minutes, he chose to take the initiative himself. He walked out through a side door and headed toward the Soviet embassy one block away. He knew the FBI would track his movements. But since he was authorized to contact Soviet personnel, he had an excuse to do so. He approached the embassy and entered through the main door, walked up to the security guard on duty and asked him to see Chuvakhin. He waited until Chuvakhin came down, surprised to see the man he'd just stood up. Chuvakhin apologized, saying he was busy and couldn't meet, whereupon Wells handed him the envelope addressed to Androsov and walked out.

"What do you think?" Androsov now asked, staring up at me.

"I don't think we can say anything for sure right now," I replied, stating the obvious.

My first thought about an offer to spy for us always went to the real motives. Most propositions were either provocations or solicitations from people who didn't have access to information valuable enough to justify the effort and risk required to obtain it. Was Wells's offer part of a CIA attempt to produce evidence of the KGB's anti-American plans? The CIA and FBI used the same tactics against Soviet organizations inside the USSR. Wells's letter had no convincing proof of his intentions. On the contrary, our belief that he'd probably been ordered to recruit Devilkovsky and Chuvakhin meant we had to be very careful. Moscow usually supported us when we decided not to accept such offers. If we turned down Wells, the Center would almost certainly back our reasoning and decision.

But that was only my initial reaction. I had spent much of my career in counterintelligence trying to recruit agents. When one *offered* himself to us, my instincts almost always told me to risk it—otherwise what was the point of our work? Besides, Wells's letter was intriguing. His documents may have been less than convincing, but maybe he wasn't trying to impress us with them. After all, if the CIA was really trying to trap us in something, it could easily have provided truly tempting documents. If the U.S. government wanted to stage an event to discredit us—exposing our efforts to recruit CIA officers, for example—it would easily find another pretext. And if this person who'd sought us out was sincere, the information he might be able to provide on CIA activities against the USSR would be worth the risk.

"If he actually had some good information," I said after a pause, "it might be interesting for us."

"So you think we should answer?"

"*Da*. Actually, we don't have that much to lose, do we?"

My guarded yes seemed to encourage Androsov. "All right. How should we set up a meeting? And where should it be? Right in the city?"

"I don't know. How and when, I don't know. What I do feel is that we *should* meet him. What if he can really deliver something?!"

"Whom should we send?"

I thought for a moment. The most logical answer was—me. Androsov was worried about a provocation, but I believed that if Wells's request for a meeting really were a CIA ploy, I was best equipped to cushion the blow. Besides, what if he turned out to be an interesting guy, this Wells? It was hard to turn down such a challenge.

"All right, it may well be a provocation—but so what!?" I said. "The worst-case scenario is that I'd have to leave for Moscow. My tour's almost up anyway. What real difference would it make?

What can they do? They can't arrest me. I'm not going to take anything from him. They know who I am. I'm ready to meet."

"Okay, then where?"

"He came here to drop off his letter, right? Well, then, let's suggest meeting here. If he doesn't go for it, we'll offer somewhere else."

Androsov agreed. During the following days we started making preparations for a possible meeting in the embassy.

There were a slew of issues to deal with. FBI officers monitored the embassy from an office out in front. If they'd seen Wells when he delivered his letter, there was a good chance they'd want to outfit him with a hidden microphone for a possible second visit. Or if he'd been on assignment to begin with (which didn't eliminate the possibility of his being sincere about wanting to work for us), the CIA might plant a bug. Either way, we'd have to remember he would be even more than ordinarily careful about what he said.

At the same time, it was essential to structure the conversation so that Wells would be convinced of our seriousness and willingness to take effective measures to protect him. To the Center, I suggested demonstrating our trust by not insisting he deliver more information. Instead we'd ask for his suggestions for the best way to establish communication with us.

Chuvakhin's involvement was another sensitive issue. We wanted to both continue using him as a contact for Wells and keep him clean. He therefore had to be told why he'd now meet Wells in the very embassy the American had previously refused to enter. We made up a good story, telling him the U.S. authorities had approached the *resident* with a proposal to establish a back-channel contact to exchange information on delicate issues with the Soviet leadership. If it worked, Chuvakhin would believe he was serving as a liaison between the U.S. and Soviet governments—not a courier transferring money and documents to and from a spy—during his continued meetings with Wells.

We kept our plan top secret. Even Anatoly Dobrynin, the influential longtime ambassador to Washington, was kept in the dark. Vladimir Kryuchkov, head of the First Chief Directorate, cabled the ambassador informing him of the bogus back channel between Chuvakhin and Wells—and asking that any information or documents received should be handed directly to me.

Adrenaline pumped as the scheme came together, inevitably increasing the number of variables to iron out. Every possibility, every moment had to be meticulously imagined and planned. We devised conversation topics that would help us understand Wells's motivations and competence. Our models for responses and future actions covered all the scenarios we could conceive, including the possibility Wells would make an offer but avoid further negotiations if we didn't agree to his conditions. Underlying everything was the larger possibility that he might be meeting us under CIA orders while simultaneously seeking to establish secret contact with us.

Deciding to communicate on paper to avoid the risk of wiretaps, we drafted a letter to hand to Wells. "Do you have any recording equipment on you?" it asked. "Are you ready to talk openly?" I fired off a cable to Moscow detailing all the arguments and proposing my candidacy for the job. I assured the Center we'd hold the meeting in a secure place in the embassy, where we could prevent Wells from recording our conversation.

A brief reply came almost immediately. It approved our plan and authorized us to proceed with it. Chuvakhin called Wells and scheduled a meeting for May 17.

When Wells appeared at the embassy, Chuvakhin met him at the entrance and escorted him past the security guard and the duty officer. We learned later how lucky we were at that moment.

Wells knew there was a mole in the embassy reporting on our activities to Langley. Not ready to tell us that, he nevertheless realized he was taking a big risk. If that spy or some other American agent in the embassy had been on guard that day—a duty rotated daily among most diplomats, including KGB officers—he'd likely have reported Wells's presence to the CIA, exposing our activity before it got properly started.

Chuvakhin led Wells into a specially outfitted room to check for recording devices. The next stop was an isolated secure room on the fourth-floor *rezidentura*. Chuvakhin left and I entered. Saying nothing as I sat down at a table opposite Wells, I handed the mousy, bespectacled volunteer the letter we'd prepared. He read it, indicating he was neither wired for sound nor being run by the FBI. Then we began talking more or less normally in English, except for the tenseness of our dialogue. If I felt very cautious, Wells was visibly anxious.

I told him my name. "I know who you are," he shot back. "You're the deputy head of the *rezidentura*." I said we would pay the $50,000 he'd requested, that we were ready to work with him and that we should communicate via Chuvakhin—who wouldn't be aware of his liaison role. We limited our conversation to thirty minutes because a lengthy visit by Wells would arouse the suspicions of the FBI officers watching the embassy. Wells agreed to our acceptance of his terms, and everything went like clockwork.

Then Chuvakhin took our visitor out to lunch.

2

Moscow. I sat in the office of a colleague in the American department of foreign counterintelligence at KGB headquarters in Yasenevo. The complex was no Langley in size, but it was fairly new and functional, with a sports center and other facilities that made us feel we were adequately taken care of. It was August 1985, just a few months after my first meeting with Wells, but I was living in another world. So much had happened in that time—and I had to keep it all to myself. As far as everyone, or almost everyone, in Yasenevo was concerned, I was on a long-overdue vacation, running some errands and taking care of odds and ends.

I thought back to my third meeting with Wells, the moment we hit the mother lode, the moment the tables turned on the CIA, the moment I felt—more than anything else—lucky. Fate, I thought, had rewarded me for the days and nights of hard work I'd put in over the previous three decades. But gamblers know how fickle fate is. I should have known how few endings are entirely happy.

That third meeting on June 13 may have done more harm to U.S. intelligence than any other single incident. The CIA didn't recognize what hit it, and still doesn't. To this day what really took place in Chadwicks restaurant on Washington's riverfront K Street is known only to the three principals.

The balmy weather matched my mood. At lunchtime, I drove to the restaurant by myself. My goal that afternoon was to display to the FBI that we were doing our job by monitoring Chuvakhin's meetings with Wells—and that we were taking protective measures against any attempts to recruit him. That would help Wells preserve his cover of working to recruit Chuvakhin. We'd had a brief, similar meeting earlier in May.

I would also help Wells maintain his reputation as a conscientious CIA officer, since his report of my presence would demonstrate his vigilance. Furthermore, my visit would help us prepare him to pass lie detector tests. If asked whether he knew any KGB officers, he'd be able to say he did without causing suspicion. After all, the FBI would have seen him together with me, a known KGB officer.

So far, the documents Wells had given us following the first April meeting in the embassy had been of marginal use—apart from providing circumstantial evidence that helped us identify two CIA and FBI spies in our *rezidentura*. One was Valery Martynov, an officer in Line X, the KGB division responsible for scientific and technological intelligence. The other was Sergei Motorin, of Line PR—military, economic and political intelligence—who had recently returned to Moscow. Important as that information was, it didn't necessarily promise more to come. Wells was saving his own skin by betraying Motorin and Martynov. If either learned of his activities, the CIA would know about them in short order. Wells also exposed several Soviets who had approached the CIA with offers to spy for the agency—but were suspected of being double agents run by us. Since those men, known as dangles, were KGB agents, he felt his reports about them weren't hurting American national security. Clearly he was trying to dupe us by playing a game to benefit himself at our expense.

But much of my work went toward encouraging agents to become more forthcoming. That rarely happened at the start. If it happened at all, it was usually on a foundation of rapport and trust. Both had to be built. I had to demonstrate my concern for an agent's well-being. I had to show we understood his motives and shared at least some ideological and political ground. Above all, I had to remove all pressure from the agent, giving him as great a sense of security as I could.

Chadwicks, a small local happy-hour place, was almost empty. Wells and Chuvakhin were sitting at a round table in front of a window when I entered—the American looking calm as well as smart in a dark suit. He showed no sign of the nervousness of our first meeting in the *rezidentura*. More than that, he seemed pleased to be meeting us, which I read as the necessary trust.

Soon after our April recruitment of Wells—or vice versa, considering the initiative was all his—I'd flown to Moscow on another case, that one concerning the KGB London *resident*, Oleg Gordievsky. A Washington-based British journalist who occasionally

provided us with information had tipped me off that Gordievsky
was spying for the British Secret Intelligence Service (SIS), and I
had to report about that personally. I did so to Vladimir Kryuchkov, head of the First Chief Directorate (FCD), the agency's pride
and joy in charge of foreign intelligence. When we'd finished
about Gordievsky, Kryuchkov inquired about problems and prospects in the United States. My mention of Wells interested him,
but there was little to report about the potentially positive development to prompt any great enthusiasm. At another meeting
before I returned to Washington, however, Kryuchkov gave instructions for running Wells. One of my tasks would be to discover
his real identity.

It took me several weeks to puzzle it out. Painstaking study of
a directory of CIA officers helped narrow the list of operatives
to one "improbable probability," and when I reported my conclusions to the Center, Kirpichenko flatly declared me wrong. Despite my confidence in my detective work, his reaction was
understandable. Even at Chadwicks, it was hard to imagine that
the person sitting with Chuvakhin could be the man leading the
effort to foil us—the CIA's chief of Soviet counterintelligence!

"Sergei, would you give us a couple of minutes, please?" I asked
Chuvakhin, who immediately got up and left for a short walk.
Then I began to work on Wells.

"We have good relations with you," I said, trying to be as warm
as I could. "We trust you. But our relationship seems one-way." I
brought up one of the two FBI agents in the Soviet embassy
Wells had already helped expose. "It's not enough for you to say
simply that agent number 1114 met a CIA officer. We need more
information."

Wells was quick in replying. "I understand whom I'm working
with," he said. "But at the same time please realize that I've put
myself in a very difficult situation by meeting with you."

Over the years, I had found that when a level of trust has been reached, direct questions sometimes work best. I began with the simplest one. "I know you aren't Rick Wells. Are you Aldrich Ames?"

He maintained a poker face. The trust evidently wasn't there. *Chiort* [damn]! I thought. From the moment he'd handed over his letter to Chuvakhin, I had kept all pressure off Wells. I'd asked nothing of him and expressed only profuse gratitude for the largely uninteresting material he'd been giving us.

"Look," I continued, exaggerating, but not really dissembling, "our main concern—our one concern—is your security. I want you to know that for certain. Everything else is secondary. You tell me what you want us to do and we'll do it—we'll play by any rules you give us."

I sensed Wells relaxing. He sat back in his chair. I pressed on. "But for us to be able to protect you, we need to know as much as we can about you. If your name is Ames, but you tell us it's Wells, how can we watch out for you? We'll be doing our best to watch for FBI communications about Wells. Something about Ames would slip right by."

Wells thought for a moment. "Okay," he sighed. "You're right. I'm Ames."

Of course I was pleased—but there was much more to find out. When it comes to volunteer agents—and often even those coerced into spying—someone who doesn't actually want to engage in espionage rarely becomes a spy. Intelligence officers might think they're chiefly responsible for recruiting agents, but most of the work really consists of finding people who *want* to be recruited. I pressed Ames about why he decided to spy for us.

To undertake the risk and expenses required to run an agent, you have to trust him to a certain extent. A large part of that trust comes from knowing his motives—his real ones. The standard

answers are hardly ever the real ones. Say someone needs $50,000—
he spent money on a lover or gambling or something else and he
needs to cover it up so his wife won't find out. He's never going to
tell that to the KGB. He'll say, "Well, you know, I want world
peace." Or "I'm for mutual understanding between the United
States and the Soviet Union." Agents always say that—always.

I put the question to Ames. "You know the situation, the danger you're in. You said it yourself. You know the FBI monitors
everything we do—yet you still decided to give us information."

Ames laid out his rationale. "I have financial problems, as
you know," he said, sighing. "But that's not the most important
thing. It's that I work for an agency that's deliberately overestimating Soviet capabilities to wrangle more money for its own
operations."

Ames directed his criticism at the CIA leadership. Some of his
dislike for the agency's top brass had come from his father, a less-
than-successful CIA officer in Burma in the early 1950s. Ames
said he began to object to the leadership when he started to realize it was pulling one over on Congress and the American people.
He thought the Soviet Union was less powerful than the agency
made out—that the USSR didn't have the economic or military
potential to back up its public threats. The CIA knew that but
said the opposite, which he felt constituted lying. He was certainly right in that respect.

Ames also made it clear that he was against communism, that
he felt patriotic about the United States—but that he respected
the Soviet Union too. His explanation was businesslike but
friendly. He appeared sincere and decisive. It seemed he'd made a
crucial decision in his life and was now living with the consequences. Impressed by his courtesy, I responded in kind. Most important for me was his apparent acceptance of my suggestions—a
crucial factor for working productively together.

I steered the conversation back to Ames's security. "It's in your interest to tell us as much as you can about any of your agents inside the KGB," I said.

"I know we have agents there," Ames replied. "But what I don't know is how you would apply the information if I gave it to you. I don't know who else knows about our meetings. The difficult situation I'm in is making me tell you we have a lot of agents—but that makes my situation even worse."

"How many agents?"

"There's a very big network."

"How can we protect you if we don't know who's in a position to inform the CIA about you? If you're concerned about your security, it's up to you *and* us to minimize the danger for you. We need to know whom to protect you from."

Then began the second chapter of Ames's spy career. He hesitated, then took out a notepad and paper and began writing down a list of names. He tore out the page and handed it to me. I was shocked. That piece of paper contained more information about CIA espionage than had ever before been presented in a single communication. It was a catalog of virtually every CIA asset within the Soviet Union. Ames said nothing about whether the men he'd listed should be arrested or removed. "Just make sure these people don't find anything out about me," he said.

The conversation had lasted over half an hour. When Chuvakhin sauntered back into Chadwicks, I got up, leaving Ames and Chuvakhin to discuss U.S.–Soviet relations. My mind was racing and reeling. I was going back to the embassy and offered to take a plastic bag Ames had brought with him for his meeting with Chuvakhin. Back in my office, I saw that it contained intelligence reports disclosing even more about CIA operations.

I sat down to write a cable to Kryuchkov to be sent on my private channel to him. It was his turn to be shocked.

It was a stunning coup. In all my years in counterintelligence, I'd never hoped for anything so rich. That was only natural, since no counterintelligence officer can set concrete goals for recruiting agents and uncovering secrets. Yes, a handful of the talented and skilled had managed to secure access to valuable secrets needed at a given time. But—except in rare exceptions, such as the scientists and others who stole A-bomb secrets from the United States during the war—those officers hadn't been instructed to obtain that data. They merely turned over what happened to come their way.

Some information comes easily. Plans for the U.S. space shuttle cost the charge for photocopying them in the Library of Congress: five dollars. But we could hardly have set ourselves the goal of identifying the CIA agents inside the KGB. With huge patience and effort, limited information about particular agents could perhaps be acquired. But establishing contact with CIA officers, let alone any who might be remotely recruitable, was always difficult. It required finding a likely candidate, getting to know him personally, ascertaining his interests, uncovering his vices and possible Achilles' heel. If and when all that was accomplished, the "find" would still be unlikely to collaborate with us. Even the worst bastard, wife beater and cheat doesn't necessarily betray his country.

June 13, 1985, was one chance in a million. That's how rare it was to find someone who had sensitive information and a willingness to provide it to Soviet intelligence—and, no less important, the opportunity to establish contact and communicate with us. Considering the importance of Ames's information, maybe one in a million is an understatement. It was unimaginable but true. One brief meeting had dramatically altered the landscape of U.S.–Soviet espionage.

I was living in a new reality. So why wasn't I ecstatic? What kept me from being at least contented as I relived the events two months later in Yasenevo? Maybe I was wondering whether my massive contribution to the KGB would earn me a major promotion. But what I actually felt was a major burden. The information Ames provided was almost too upsetting to digest. It showed that our intelligence community was rotten through and through.

I knew many of the people on Ames's list. I'd talked to them, worked with them. Some would now be taken to an execution room and made to kneel for the delivery of a bullet to the back of the head. I was as responsible as anyone else for what was inevitably going to happen. Later I myself put one of the men on a plane back to Moscow. I was only doing my job, but the moral dilemma weighed heavily. As far as I was concerned, officers who turned traitor should be fired and deprived of their pensions. That's enough. There's no need for execution.

The telephone on my desk rang. Cutting off my thoughts, it brought me back to the small office in Yasenevo. "Kryuchkov wants to see you now."

The appointment had been scheduled to discuss operations in the Washington *rezidentura*. To keep Ames's recruitment as secret as possible—especially after learning the extent to which the CIA had penetrated our operations—no one in the Center was to be given the slightest hint that anything had happened. I would not be linked in any way to the forthcoming spate of arrests of KGB and military intelligence (GRU) officers.

My attempt to hide my depression evidently didn't pass muster. Bald, bespectacled Kryuchkov seemed pleased when I entered his office, but his usually stern eyes went quizzically narrow as I sat down.

"What's wrong?"

I had to be careful about what I said to the foreign intelligence chief. The fate of others—chiefly Kalugin—was an object lesson in the importance of appearances in Yasenevo. My association with the departed Kalugin hardly recommended me to Kryuch-kov. Susceptible to rumors fanned by his own associates, he formed opinions about people quickly and seemed unable to change them—which explained why deputies like Kirpichenko had so easily influenced him. My every word would be important.

As head of foreign intelligence, Kryuchkov reaped the greatest praise for obtaining Ames's intelligence, and that praise further whet his appetite for reaching the top of the heap—the KGB chairmanship. The reverse implication—that the KGB's penetration by so many American agents reflected badly on the leadership of foreign intelligence—was obviously less good. But the many arrests immediately following Ames's exposures enabled the leadership to applaud its new determination to eliminate the moles.

As for me, I knew my dark thoughts weren't appropriate. But in the end, Kryuchkov was a fellow officer. Surely he'd understand. "What's there to be happy about," I replied, "when there's so much rot around us?"

Kryuchkov lowered his eyes, then looked away. Evidently the thought of so many KGB officers busily aiding the Americans until a walk-in identified them for us did disturb him. In any case, he frowned. "Eh! What can you say about it?"

But that was all he managed to pronounce about our colossal failures. Waving his hand in dismissal, he changed the subject.

Had I learned nothing? *Hide your feelings! Never let the foreign intelligence chief, of all people, see you depressed!* Why didn't I tell myself to go into Kryuchkov's office gleefully boasting of my great success? Remember never to show my cards, never give a true opinion—positive or negative—about the state of KGB affairs. But I *was* depressed, and that rare condition for me surely did me no good. Anyway, the importance of the *should haves* would make itself clear only later.

Kryuchkov and I moved on to discuss Washington operations and my further handling of Ames, which he personally headed at

Yasenevo but left largely to my discretion in Washington. "Just continue working as you have," he said. "Make sure there are no slipups."

Of course that was the trick. On my way back from Moscow, I tried to put its politics behind me and concentrate on my operations. As far as Ames was concerned, the most difficult tasks—finding an agent, establishing means of communication and building up a personal relationship and feelings of mutual trust—had been accomplished. But in my trade, eternal vigilance was no empty slogan. A single mistake can cost many years of work and many millions of dollars. I'd spent an entire career learning that.

$-2-$

THE TRAINING OF A KGB HANDLER

1

The sound began as a faint drone, growing louder until it became a thunderous roar and I could see the planes flying low in formation above the dark firs and tall birches. They flew as if in slow motion through the bright, cloudless summer sky, making their way steadily toward me from the northwest. I was nine years old, school was out and I was playing soldier with my friends, darting along dusty lanes and among the trees and bushes surrounding the wooden houses in which we lived. It was a typical Sunday in the tiny Ukrainian town of Kotovsk, north of Odessa on the Black Sea and just east of the border with Moldova, then part of Bessarabia. My family—mother, father, two brothers and sister—lived in one of the small, one-story houses near the railroad tracks that cut through town.

My father was Ivan Yakovlevich Cherkashin, a stout, broad-shouldered officer of the great People's Commissariat for Internal Affairs (NKVD), as the secret police was then named. He was away for several days, fighting counterrevolutionaries somewhere. My mother and some friends sat on benches gossiping. I clambered up a tree to get a better shot at the enemy. Looking up at the planes, I thought how fortunate it was for our game that they'd joined us. My fellow soldiers raised their stick guns in the air as the aircraft approached.

With no warning, a deafening explosion rang out. Then another, and a shock wave threw me from the tree. I lay on the ground, looking up to see my mother running toward me. She grabbed my arm and dragged me to our nearby yard, depositing me in a ditch. My ears were ringing. She threw a coat over me. "Vitya! Keep your head down! For God's sake!" she screamed.

It was June 22, 1941, the first day of Hitler's Operation BARBAROSSA, the German invasion of the Soviet Union. That was how the war began for us, hours after it started in general. The planes bombing the railway line were part of a massive Nazi force staging air strikes and blitzkrieg attacks along the Soviet western border. In time, I'd live through countless other bombardments. I'd see planes unloading their cargo, the bombs falling and spinning, slowly at first, then faster and faster until I couldn't see them anymore, just waited for the impact and the din.

My family had arrived in Kotovsk two years earlier. I was born in 1932 in the village of Krasnoe, meaning Red, in the fertile Kursk region south of Moscow. Half the village consisted of Cherkashins of one stripe or another. Like most other families of peasant stock, mine led a hardscrabble existence, and I remember feeling cold and hungry during that time. My father, a rebellious miller's son, had fought for the Bolsheviks in the bloody civil war that followed Russia's 1917 Revolution. As one of Krasnoe's few literate inhabitants (having attended the village's two-class church school), he was appointed to oversee the organization of a collective farm. He joined the NKVD in 1935 and was assigned to the Siberian town of Achinsk in the distant Krasnoyarsk region in 1937. Then, in 1939, he was sent to Kotovsk. (The secret police kept its officers moving around so they wouldn't put down roots in any one area.)

I adored both my parents but especially my mother, whom I always felt, inexplicably, to be old, frail and near death. Father, whose talents included playing the piano and balalaika, was almost always at work. He started at ten in the morning and stayed until five in the afternoon. After a break until eight, he'd return until two in the morning. I never asked him, and he never told me, of what his work actually consisted. Meanwhile, much as I tried to please my hardworking parents, my constant transgressions—clambering on roofs and trees and joining any fight I happened to be near—earned me hooligan status. One teacher begged my mother to withdraw me from school.

My acquaintance with the means for war, if not war itself, began when military trains started passing through Kotovsk following the August 1939 agreement with Germany, the Molotov-Ribbentrop Pact. The trains ferried soldiers into Bessarabia, ceded to the Soviet Union by Romania in the deal. Some of the men bivouacked in town, prompting the inhabitants to complain glumly of the town's likely destruction if war actually broke out. But it was a grand time for me. It was a stiflingly hot summer, and soldiers would often shout to me to run and fetch them water from one of the wells. I did that happily. I found it all fascinating—the tents, the rifles, the troops. War was very impressive and exciting—a lot of men talking, playing cards and hanging about.

The real thing came two years later—with Hitler's main southern flank, Army Group South, moving over the border north of us toward Kiev; orders were given to evacuate immediately. My father's status as an NKVD officer ensured priority for my family, and we were among the first to be moved out. Assured we'd only be gone for a week or so, we took almost nothing with us. With my father still absent on assignment, my mother packed up my seven-year-old brother Petya, twelve-year-old sister Masha and me and hustled us to the boxcars of a waiting freight train. My elder brother Vasya was sick in a hospital in Crimea at the time. Climbing on the train with the other evacuees, we set off back to Krasnoe in Kursk, where I'd been born and our relatives still lived. We never returned to Kotovsk.

Krasnoe lay seven kilometers from the site of the famous Prokhorovka battle—better known to the world as the Battle of Kursk—that took place in July 1943. That battle, one of the largest tank engagements ever, was a major turning point in the war. Wiping out fifty German divisions, the Red Army put a final halt to Hitler's eastern offensive. Only two hundred of our village's roughly seven hundred houses were standing when it ended.

Long before that crucial battle, however, the German advance forced my family to flee again, only three months after our return to Krasnoe. This time, we were allotted a horse, a cart and a driver who was ordered to leave his own family behind. His dilemma left my mother at a loss until, on the day before our departure, my father surprised us. Happily but briefly reunited—he was given leave only to accompany us on the trip—we joined a column of civilians fleeing the fighting on foot, in horse-drawn carts and cars.

We headed due east toward Voronezh, around two hundred miles away. I wouldn't wish that trip on anyone. Some workers from collective farms brought along flocks of sheep and cows. Not milked for days, they bellowed piteously as the ragtag stream of people and livestock inched eastward. Horses and cattle dropped dead by the wayside—and began to stink. We avoided open roads to escape bombardment, passing through fields and woods instead. The slog took eighteen days. German planes flew overhead, dropping anti-Soviet leaflets, while lines of gloomy soldiers passed us heading in the opposite direction.

When we finally arrived, exhausted, in Voronezh, my father deposited us on a train heading south to Kazakhstan. That journey too was painfully slow, with stops at almost every station as we yielded to numerous military trains heading toward the front. Our destination was an industrial city called Kyzylorda, just above the Syr Darya River in the dusty desert land of southern Kazakhstan. We were put up in a shed belonging to a family whose two-room house was already sheltering another evacuee family of five. The first days we were cold and desperately hungry. We built a makeshift bed, where all four of us slept together for warmth—even after Masha and Petya contracted typhus.

My mother spent weeks obtaining the documents necessary to prove our evacuee status and obtain some rationed food. To supplement that meager intake, she joined other evacuees walking through outlying suburban villages, begging for vegetables. For my part, I trailed behind carts trucking produce from local gardens to market—carrots, potatoes, beets—and dashed to snatch up any that fell out. As spring turned to summer, I'd often watch Kazakh children playing a game similar to marbles, using small pieces of meat bones. I couldn't take part because it was a betting game and I had no money. But after I explained that to a well-dressed Kazakh boy, he reached into his pocket to give me a couple of precious kopeks. I was flabbergasted, but his kindness reflected the generally good treatment Kazakhs showed us evacuees.

As fall approached, there was no question of my going to school, even if we could have spared money for books and clothes. Meanwhile, the misery of the cold was made worse by our outdoor toilet, which I dreaded having to use at night. But we survived the winter. As spring approached and the Germans pulled back slightly, we received news that my father was still alive. He was stationed near Stalingrad, between the Volga and Don Rivers. My mother decided to take us there.

We succeeded in finding my father and spent three months in the town of Kotelnikovo—about a hundred miles southwest of Stalingrad and just east of the Don River. Then the Nazis started their 1942 offensive and we had to evacuate yet again. This time we fled to Kyrgyzstan, leaving my father behind to take part in the Battle of Stalingrad. Crossing the Volga, we had to wait a week for a ferry that only ran at night to minimize damage from German bombing. Famished, we ate algae-laden clay from the riverbank. It made us sick.

The fighting in Stalingrad ended in February 1943. We returned to the ruined city the following month. It was still very cold. Whole blocks of ghostly gutted buildings stood amid ruins covered in snow. Footpaths cut through the city's mine-infested expanse. Frozen corpses lay scattered in the streets alongside ruined machinery, weapons and other debris. Many who survived the battle were still dying of famine, but my family's dire food situation improved because we managed to obtain ration cards for bread, grain, salt and sugar. My father's wages bought us vegetables and meat at the market, and I helped by taking cigarettes allotted to us by ration coupons to the railroad station and selling them. My parents turned a blind eye to the illegal private enterprise.

Later that year, trains passed through the city carrying evacuees from the Leningrad siege, mostly children. Guards at the train stations stopped locals from handing food to the survivors, who were so emaciated they would have died from eating too much too quickly. Many died anyway, and their corpses were piled on trains for burial in mass graves. Still, Stalingrad was a relatively happy place for me. I joined other boys clambering over junk heaps looking for shells to defuse, pouring out their gunpowder to make their own bombs. Shells with delicate silk bags holding gunpowder inside were especially prized. We opened them by hitting the casings at an angle with other metal objects. Some of my fellow scavengers were blown up in front of my eyes.

By 1944, the war was going decisively in our favor. My father was reassigned to Belorussia, to help secure the Red Army's rear as Soviet forces pushed the retreating Wehrmacht west into Poland and on toward Berlin. We settled in Pinsk, a village one hundred miles east of the border city of Brest. My elder brother Vasya, who had been separated from us in Crimea, joined us there. Victory Day—May 8, 1945—was unforgettable. Villagers laughed, wept and hugged each other as soldiers fired rifles into the air. At thirteen, I returned to school in the fifth grade. As part of the celebrations, teenagers were encouraged to join the Komsomol, the Communist youth league. All my friends joined, so I signed up too, despite the fourteen-year-old minimum age. Even with my new credentials, however, I remained a troublemaker. My teachers finally persuaded me to quit school at the end of seventh grade, the legal minimum. Handed a graduation certificate, I left for nearby Brest to look for an institute that would accept me.

Impressively large Brest had a textile institute, a medical college and a railway engineering school. Since I'd always lived near railroads, I decided to try for the latter. Passing my entrance exams, I joined the department of railway construction and maintenance and did well in my studies. The following year, I found myself elected to one of four positions as Komsomol department secretary. (All four of us later ended up in the intelligence service.) Meanwhile, despite the misery of the war—or perhaps because of it—Brest was full of optimism. Locals felt they deserved better after their wartime sacrifices. I did too. I took up boxing, gymnastics, soccer and volleyball. On weekends, I went dancing and attended the theater. I also made friends with some of the many Poles in Brest—who had been displaced by the war—and learned to speak Polish.

After graduating in 1952, I was posted to the Arkhangelsk region in the far north to work as a railway engineer. But just before

I was to depart, the local office of the Ministry of State Security (MGB, as the NKVD had been renamed) summoned me. There I was solemnly informed I'd been recommended as a candidate to join the service. Although I'd been looking forward to working as an engineer, I answered without hesitation. I'd never asked my father what his work entailed—aside from fighting enemies of the people—but I was certain he was a decent person in all respects and that whatever he did was honorable. I respected the NKVD. Its work carrying out Stalin's policies seemed highly important. I accepted the job on the spot.

I was selected for the secret service because of my exemplary record as Komsomol department secretary, but of course my father's record helped. I'd be joining the local Brest directorate after two years of training at an MGB institute in the small industrial city of Mogilëv, east of the Belorussian capital, Minsk. I arrived at the end of the summer, only to be told to pack my bags again.

Miffed because I'd just unpacked, I complained to the administrator in his office. "You've been chosen to study foreign languages in Leningrad," he told me. "You'll be working with foreigners."

That made me extremely skeptical. I'd studied German and English in school and did poorly in both. "I can't speak any foreign languages," I insisted.

"*Nu koneshno* [of course]. That's the point, isn't it? They'll teach you up there."

My further protest was equally in vain. Three other young hopefuls and I boarded a train that same day. We headed for the old imperial capital.

2

The new MGB Institute of Foreign Languages stood on Vasilievsky Island, across the broad Neva River from the Winter Palace.

Close to the island's main street, Bolshoi Prospekt, the institute also conducted a training program for SMERSH, the infamous—in the West—wartime counterintelligence service (derived from *smert shpionam*, or "death to spies"). The short-lived SMERSH, a feared military intelligence agency under Stalin's direct control, was detached from the NKVD in 1943 to step up the hunt for Nazi collaborators and traitors, then reattached three years later. Former officers from the division were still studying German at the institute when I arrived.

Much of the great, ornately baroque former capital was under reconstruction after the siege of Leningrad, and life for its shell-shocked residents was slowly improving. I found it all glorious. After checking into a two-story military barracks, I was scheduled to take an entrance exam I felt certain to fail. Still disoriented from my trip, I was asked whether I wanted to study English or German. Which was easier, I inquired. English was suggested. In the exam hall, a middle-aged woman watched as I translated five lines of text. I looked up each word in a dictionary but still failed to grasp the meaning of the phrases. Glancing over my paper, the examiner laughed and commanded me to start over. I looked up each word again and came no closer to the meaning. Dejectedly leaving the exam room, I saw myself on the next train back to Belorussia. But no order to pack up and leave came that day. When the names of those who'd passed their exams were posted several days later, I found mine among those assigned to the English study group. My surprise could hardly have been greater.

The institute's language instructors were top-notch and I quickly lost my apprehension about studying foreign languages. I learned German as well as English. I also took courses in counterintelligence methods, learning about agent networks and surveillance and communications techniques. I studied the types of people and organizations we'd be working against, including anti-Soviet networks, émigrés and clergy. General subjects such as jurisprudence were in our curriculum too. Meanwhile, I was again elected department Komsomol secretary.

Aside from the older students—including intelligence personnel sent back for more study and others like me, who had quickly matured during the war—most of my classmates enrolled straight out of tenth grade. I soon fell in with a group of friends who would go out dancing and attend the theater—anything, anywhere to meet girls. Among my classmates was Yuri Gulin, son of a Siberian doctor and a huge music fan, an ex-sailor named Vladimir Korovin who found learning English exceedingly hard, and a Ukrainian called Boris Gechel, a devoted communist who was utterly earnest and remarkably decent. I met another student—one of the relatively sheltered boys—soon after my arrival in September. His name was Oleg Kalugin. An only child, Kalugin astounded me with his perfect English, an almost impossible achievement at the time. Later when Kalugin won a competition for best translation, I came in second. Kalugin was very sociable, and we became friends quickly. He married a local girl called Lyudmilla, and it seemed perfectly logical that after graduation, the gifted Kalugin would be assigned a job in the FCD, the KGB's flagship department that ran foreign intelligence.

Stalin died during my second year of study, in March 1953. The announcement, made at an all-school meeting, was a deep shock. The certainties I'd grown up with—that society was on a path to postwar improvement, that we were indeed building communism—now seemed less certain. By smashing the Nazi war machine, the Soviet Union had become a great power with which the Western countries had to reckon. Stalin had led us to that victory. In the years that followed, he oversaw the rebuilding of the state, its infrastructure and industry. Food rationing ended in 1947. Inflation diminished. A general sense of dynamism reigned, and we owed it all to Stalin. I was far from the only one in the hall to shed tears that day.

Graduating three years later, in 1956, I resolved to prove myself by serving the Party and helping implement its policies. Under a new chairman, Ivan Serov, the MGB had recently been renamed the Committee for State Security (KGB). I was assigned to serve in its Second Chief Directorate (SCD), which was responsible for internal security and counterintelligence. I'd be working in the Second, or English, department, going head to head with British intelligence on Soviet soil. (The American department was the First and the German, the Third.) The Second department kept a close watch on all British citizens and, among other objectives, sought to recruit them as agents. I was assigned to help control the British embassy in Moscow. I couldn't believe my luck. A fresh graduate could not expect such a plum job.

Early one morning two months later, I arrived at the capital's ornately neo-Slavic Belorussky train station, from which many troops had departed to fight the Germans at the front. By now a well-disciplined young man, I followed orders by finding a public telephone first thing and dialing the number of the KGB personnel office. There was no answer. "Maybe work here starts later than usual," I thought. I didn't know a soul in the city. I had nowhere to go, and very little money. I'd been told only to phone immediately on my arrival to receive instructions—and that's what I'd do.

I sat down on my suitcase and waited half an hour, then tried again. Still no answer. Nor two hours later.

I was still at the train station at five o'clock. At eleven, I started to think about where to sleep. Even if I had the money, it would be impossible to simply show up at a hotel without a reservation and authorization of some kind. I curled up on a bench.

I tried again in the morning. Still no answer. By noon, I was seriously worried. Approaching a policeman, I sheepishly asked the location of KGB headquarters. He eyed me suspiciously before re-plying curtly, "Dzerzhinsky Square, *koneshno* [of course]!"

"Uhh, would you please tell me how to get there?"

The officer took another long look at me. "You'd better go by metro!" he yelled as I started off toward Gorky Street, Moscow's main avenue. Following his directions, I arrived opposite Lub-yanka, an imposing, yellow neoclassical hulk of a building that housed KGB headquarters. It overlooked a large traffic circle called Dzerzhinsky Square, in the middle of which stood a tall, solemn-looking statue of Felix Dzerzhinsky. "Iron Felix" founded the Cheka, the KGB's predecessor, in 1917. The impressive scene put me at a greater loss. One didn't just blithely walk up and en-ter the main entrance of the central KGB building.

In any case, the massive doors were shut fast. A guard posted outside directed me to an information office a few blocks away on an old street called Kuznetsky Most (Kuznetsky Bridge). I found it and told my story to a clerk. Flipping through the directory he gave me, I saw the number for the personnel office had changed. I held my breath and dialed the new one.

The personnel director chuckled at my predicament. "You weren't given the new number? Well, they were all changed last year. What else is new?" Several phone calls later, I found myself billeted in the posh, new Peking Hotel on Triumphalnaya Square, near a large statue of poet Vladimir Mayakovsky. I'd live there a month before being assigned to a KGB hostel. I was to report to work the following morning at ten.

Moscow was like nothing I'd experienced. Stalin had trans-formed the teeming city into a showcase of Soviet might, from its lavish metros to the seven wedding-cake skyscrapers. Grand boulevards lined with monumental hulks of buildings cut swaths through the prerevolutionary jumbles of narrow streets.

But I had little time for sightseeing. As I'd soon learn, the great-est KGB successes against British intelligence were already history.

Two of the famous "Cambridge Five" spies—Guy Burgess and Donald Maclean—had recently defected to Russia. Meanwhile, our most important agent, Kim Philby, had been recalled from his post as the Secret Intelligence Service (SIS) station commander in Washington, ending the hope he'd rise to the top of British intelligence. Foreign spies were becoming increasingly active, I was told. I had to begin operative work as soon as possible.

3

I was assigned a desk in a small, four-man office in Lubyanka. The huge building, with its long corridors lined by a strip of red carpeting, resembled a typical Soviet administrative office. I'd be in charge of three other men, who ran our agents monitoring the British embassy's cipher officers, security guards and consular and administrative sections. Department head Ivan Markelov—to whom I took an immediate liking—briefed me on counterintelligence work against the embassy and introduced me to the agents I'd be controlling. Some were British embassy employees, such as drivers and secretaries. There were also writers, musicians and others who had personal contacts with the diplomats.

Britain, it bears repeating, had been deemed the Main Adversary of Soviet intelligence until after the war, when the distinction passed to the United States. The venerable British intelligence service, the world's most experienced, was especially active in Russia in the late 1940s and early 1950s. That forced the Second Chief Directorate's English department to work hard to devise countermeasures. One major operation involved feeding double agents to the SIS in the Baltics, where the British service had been especially successful in developing a network of agents after the war. By the time I joined the department, the British had realized they were being had, and their operation was winding down.

The British embassy was housed in an opulent mansion that once belonged to prominent nineteenth-century merchant Pavel Kharitonenko. The building stood on an embankment of the Moscow River directly opposite the Kremlin. Infiltrating the embassy's sections—administrative, communications, political, cultural, press, security and so on—required different approaches for each. We monitored diplomats' activities, trying to establish the identities of their local contacts by using agents, surveillance and eavesdropping equipment. The department's main task was to determine whether meetings between British personnel and Soviets were above board or indicated the SIS was trying to set up contacts. For instance, it was known that their press attachés met with Soviet editors, journalists and publishers. We knew part of their work consisted of asking their Soviet contacts why, for example, certain articles on Soviet–British relations had been written. But if they began inquiring about people or affairs outside the scope of their professional activities (e.g., about contacts in the defense or foreign affairs ministries), they would immediately raise suspicions and become targets of our "active measures."

If a diplomat came under suspicion, we'd first debrief his (it was almost always a man) contact to collect more information. We'd also use Soviet contacts to pass along disinformation to the other side. Then we'd step up monitoring the target, installing eavesdropping equipment where he lived or worked to find out whether the target was in the SIS or simply had displayed imprudent curiosity.

The next task was damage control: cutting off the target from all possible access to classified or otherwise sensitive information. If we suspected the diplomat of being an intelligence officer, we'd also watch for recruitment attempts on his part. But we wouldn't close in. First, we'd try to control the target's intelligence activities. If it turned out that he was making a recruitment pitch or already handling one or more agents, we'd play an operational game. We'd study the target while continuing to feed him false information and fake agents. However, while reports of suspicious behavior by British embassy staff came in regularly, large-scale operations were rare.

The next stage was to turn intelligence officers into assets for our side. That involved ascertaining their likes and dislikes, political leanings and backgrounds. It also included studying their activities to find weaknesses—prostitutes, say, or gambling—and the best ways of taking advantage of them. If a target seemed recruitable, we'd usually try to goad him into working for us by means of money and sex. A common form of blackmail involved setting up targets for "hard currency speculation"—illegally exchanging foreign currency for rubles.

The most successful cases involved "swallows," male or female agents sent to seduce targets. A foreigner who became sexually involved with a swallow could be confronted with secret photographs or recordings. He could also be subjected to scandal. A swallow would claim pregnancy and demand an abortion, or fictitious outraged family members would surface to threaten action. Then a marginally involved benevolent figure—I or another counterintelligence officer—would offer to intervene and provide rescue, only to ask for certain favors later in return. Those favors, of course, involved obtaining information about the British embassy or SIS. The trick was to develop targets into agents through progressive involvement in the spying game.

We didn't have to look far for blackmail scenarios. One British diplomat had sex with prostitutes in a car. (Given the difficulty of booking hotel rooms, he wasn't the only one. Taxi drivers even had pimping networks.) We investigated him and found he was married, then took photographs and confronted him with the evidence. In that case, however, the ploy didn't work. The target refused to collaborate, reported our attempt to the ambassador and was sent back to England. Many of our efforts ended similarly.

One of my agents, whom I'll call Larissa, was an attractive, twenty-five-year-old, English-speaking blonde who worked for UpDK—the state agency that provided housing, furniture, food and most other services to Moscow's foreign embassies. Larissa met foreign diplomats and staff in several embassies, including the British. A committed, professional agent, she could turn on her considerable charm at will. As with most of my agents, I regularly debriefed her in apartment safe houses, the kind rented by the KGB all over the city. (I couldn't meet with agents in public, nor could they be seen entering KGB buildings.) During one such meeting, Larissa reported that an employee of the British embassy's administrative section had shown an interest in her. Back at Lubyanka, I looked up our files on the man. A forty-year-old married diplomat, he'd been serving in Moscow for two years. I'll call him Edward Johnson. We'd had nothing unusual on him; his interest in Larissa was the first crack.

As a matter of course, I asked Larissa to write a detailed report on Johnson for our files. I also instructed her to respond to his flirtation to find out whether he was really keen on her or simply joking around. We monitored the several dates she organized. I didn't know whether I had enough incriminating evidence to try to take advantage of him or whether he had access to information of any importance. But when Larissa reported that he'd become infatuated with her, I decided to try to entrap him. It was worth a try, Larissa agreed.

When Johnson began to press Larissa to have sex, we procured a suitable apartment and stuffed it with eavesdropping bugs and hidden cameras. When she took him there for a night of love-making, she told him the flat belonged to a friend. The following day, I thought we had enough material on the diplomat to make an approach, but English department chief Markelov disagreed, saying it would be better to compromise Johnson doing something actually illegal. So it was back to the drawing board while Larissa and Johnson continued their meetings. Several days later, I instructed her to tell him that a friend of hers was traveling abroad and wanted to buy hard currency. Johnson agreed to sell some pounds.

I showed up as the friend. Dark-haired Johnson was tall, slim and strikingly good-looking in his well-tailored suit. I could understand Larissa's willingness to take part in the operation. His aristocratic bearing made me wonder why he agreed to take risks. Was his life too boring? Did he dislike his wife? Or did naïveté about how our system worked give him a false sense of security? From Larissa, I knew Johnson took socializing seriously. He was visibly relaxed. He met Russians regularly and told some jokes to break the ice with me. I decided to help in that too. Finding a bottle of vodka in the kitchen, I poured a couple of shots. We toasted and got down to business. Hidden cameras snapped away as we exchanged money. We drank more vodka. Then I thanked him and left the couple to get on with their more exciting business—which was also photographed.

A month later, Markelov ordered me into action. Larissa informed Johnson that I'd returned from my trip abroad and wanted to thank him and return a favor if I could. He agreed to see me, and we three met at the apartment again.

"Thanks so much for helping me, Edward," I said. "It would have been difficult for me to buy anything because we're only allowed a pinch of foreign currency, even abroad." For good measure, I added some self-pity. "We're always being watched, you know." Johnson was completely taken in. I almost felt sorry for him.

A loud knock sounded at the door. Larissa got up to open it. Two men in gray suits entered. Johnson turned ashen. One of the men introduced himself in Russian while the other translated. "I'm an officer of the state security committee! We have information that you have engaged in an illegal activity in the Soviet Union, involving the sale of hard currency!"

Johnson looked back at me with questioning eyes, but it was clear he still had no inkling I was involved. The officer addressed Larissa and me: "Will both of you please leave the room now while I speak to Mr. Johnson?" We quickly got up. My colleagues then sat down and outlined their proof to the incredulous Johnson, showing the photos of him together with me. To strengthen their argument, they announced their knowledge of a "moral" lapse on his part—and handed over pictures of him and Larissa cavorting in bed.

The operation proved to be a failure. Johnson never informed his embassy about what had happened, but he cut off Larissa and soon returned to England. His case was typical of the kind of operation the SCD conducted at the time. I often found the work dull, but I knew it was a necessary part of protecting the Motherland—and I felt privileged to be serving the KGB.

4

Political events moved quickly after Stalin's death. Lavrenty Beria was arrested and executed by Stalin's deputies, who feared the secret service chief would unleash his terror on them. Then came talk of Stalin's deplorable extremes and the need for change. Hindsight often makes past events appear obvious, but at the time, the country's future was unclear. I perceived Stalin as he was presented to the public by the Soviet propaganda machine: the one person who could give us a better life. Countless newspaper articles, television programs and billboards told us that with the onset of the Cold War, only he could protect us from our enemies in the West.

But the Soviet Union was moving on. By the late 1950s, Khrushchev's policy of de-Stalinization was in full swing. It began with his famous "secret speech" at the Twentieth Communist Party Congress in February 1956, when he first publicly denounced Stalin and attacked his cult of personality. Khrushchev had to fend off an attempt to unseat him in 1957, but by 1959 he was consolidating his rule, based on his policy of reforming the Party.

One of Khrushchev's moves was to pardon thousands of Gulag inmates, who left Stalin's camps and streamed home. Another was to transform Soviet intelligence. Departments and counterintelligence operations such as SMERSH had been empowered to interrogate and kill traitors on the spot. By the time I began working at the KGB, however, the service was a different organization. To erase evidence of its excesses under the Lenin and Stalin regimes, the Communist Party's Central Committee in 1959 ordered the security service to burn archived files on those arrested and later rehabilitated or otherwise deemed innocent. Officers in each section, including me, were ordered to destroy files with no operational or historical value. Among the documents I culled were multivolume files from the 1950s on Vladimir Schneiderov, a well-known film director. They included KGB reports alleging he had made anticommunist statements. The evidence was obviously false. No real information discredited the eminent director.

In another typical example, a file from the 1930s contained a death certificate stating that a peasant named Ivanov had been arrested, sentenced to death and executed for counterrevolutionary activities. Several pages along, I found another certificate, stating that the wrong Ivanov had been accused, but that the matter was closed because the right one had also been arrested and shot. I wondered how it had been possible for human life to have been treated in that cavalier way. (Much later, I came to believe it was a great mistake to execute the spies I myself helped expose. Most never provided information in any way damaging to our national security, just names and information the CIA or SIS likely already knew something about—yet they were shot!) Of course it's easy to condemn Soviet excesses in retrospect. Although I found many mistakes of the 1930s deplorable, I also felt they were unavoidable in building the foundation of the Soviet state. The harsh measures reflected the rough conditions of the time. Russia was an uneducated country, most of it run by peasants. There was little chance the state's problems would be solved in a civilized way.

My work in the archives didn't last long, for I was soon picked for my first trip abroad. The SCD was tasked with monitoring Soviet delegations abroad, and I was assigned to accompany a group of exchange students who would spend a month in England on a summer program run jointly by the British Council and the Soviet Education Ministry. The language students would be dispersed to various parts of the country, each living with a local family. Since few SCD officers went overseas, I took the assignment as a reward for my hard work. Elated about the trip, I was also under great pressure since I had to provide "security" for all thirty students. It would be up to me to foil any attempts by British intelligence to recruit them.

Knowing the Soviet media presented life in the West in the worst possible light, I was keen to see what it was really like. As far as operative matters, my task proved impossible. Since the students were sent to different places, two students per family, there was no way to keep track of them. Luckily, nothing unusual took place and everyone returned safely to Moscow. I found London fascinating and the British well-dressed, intelligent and polite. Their standard of living was significantly higher than ours, but I didn't let that bother me. I was carrying out an important job for my country, and I felt proud to do it.

5

Back in Moscow, I occupied my scant free time by going to the theater and visiting museums. In 1958, I met a dark-haired young woman called Elena. She was walking down a corridor in Lubyanka toward a typing office to work on that day's cable translations. She was twenty years old and beautiful.

Elena's path to the KGB started in junior high school, where a teacher advised her to apply to a foreign language institute. With no intention of becoming a teacher, Elena applied to study at the prestigious Vneshtorg, the Soviet foreign trade organization. A course director praised her for scoring well on her entrance exam. "Certain people," she said, were interested in her. Two years later, Elena was working in Lubyanka.

I saw her again at a party. To arouse her interest, I asked another woman to dance. When I next spotted Elena, she was heading toward the door with an older officer on her arm. She later told me that he took her out to a restaurant—a rare treat in those days. I knew he had his own apartment, as well as a dacha in the country—almost unheard-of luxuries.

Realizing my mistake, I was too nervous to approach Elena. Then I fell ill with the flu—luckily, because she visited me and we became friendly. When I recovered sufficiently, I took her out to a restaurant. As we were sitting down, someone gruffly called my name. I turned around to face the man with whom Elena had left the party where I'd danced with someone else. The man glared at me, addressing me with thick sarcasm. "I thought you were sick." I knew he could make things unpleasant for me at Lubyanka.

"Oh . . . uh, I am. But I just recovered." I found my footing quickly. "I'll be at work tomorrow."

"What are you doing here, sick boy?" he shot back, his voice edged with menace.

"I'm just having a drink. I don't think there are any laws against that."

"Maybe not." The angry man stared at us before returning to his boisterous friends.

Later that night, I proposed. Elena's acceptance made me happier than I had ever been in my life. We married on May 31, 1958, and moved into a room in a communal apartment. Elena's mother came to live with us, and Elena soon became pregnant with our first child, a son we named Alyosha.

6

Without Oleg Penkovsky, we might have been nuked. The reason he's been called the spy who saved the world is that we knew we could delay [invading Cuba during the Cuban missile crisis]. There was great pressure on [U.S. President John] Kennedy to mount a preemptive attack on Cuba to take out the missiles. Information from Penkovsky helped lead the intelligence community to ascertain that the Cubans were armed with tactical nuclear warheads—and that the generals on the ground had the authority to launch them. Without Penkovsky, we would have invaded. For that they would have nuked us and we would have nuked them back.

—David Major, retired FBI supervisory special agent and former
director of counterintelligence at the National Security Council

I went through [CIA training at] the Farm and can only say what we young officers were told about Penkovsky. And that was that he was a great patriot and he did what he did because he hated the Soviet Union and did it for Russia.

—Milton Bearden, former director of CIA's
Soviet and East European Division

It would be stupid to ignore the damage Penkovsky caused to our
country. But to call him the "spy who saved the world" . . . is simply
absurd.

　　　—Rem Krassilnikov, former head of the Second Chief Directorate
　　　　　American department (KGB protif MI–6, Okhotniki za
　　　　　shpionam [Moscow: Sentrpoligraf, 2000], p. 211)

————————

Moscow's short, often hot summers end abruptly in late August. By
December, the city is blanketed with snow and ice. The one re-
prieve in the middle of the endless-seeming cold season is the New
Year's celebration, the Soviet equivalent of Christmas in the West.
Preparations start in early December and the heavily lubricated fes-
tivities continue for many days.

In 1961, I routinely reviewed some of my cases on December
30, the day before the reveling began. An internal Lubyanka telephone line rang. One of my subordinates, Mikhail Fyodorov, was
on the other end. Misha was tracking Roderick Chisholm, a second secretary in the British embassy's consular section. That was
his operating cover; information from George Blake in West
Berlin had alerted us that Chisholm, who'd also served in Berlin,
was actually the MI6 Moscow station chief. Conveying that the
KGB Seventh Directorate, which conducted local surveillance,
had reported something unusual, Fyodorov asked what to do.

Some fifty Seventh Directorate officers cased the British embassy. They knew all about its employees, including where they
lived and what cars they drove. Chisholm wasn't followed all the
time, but in twenty-four-hour shifts. When he left the embassy
grounds, up to three cars kept track of his movements. His wife
was watched too. She was often seen taking her two small children
to a park near her apartment in northern Moscow. This time, several of our men followed her as she left her building for a walk. She
was soon seen entering a nondescript residential building nearby.

She remained inside for a few minutes, straightening her skirt when she came out as if she'd ducked into the entrance to adjust her underwear.

As the Seventh Directorate officers prepared to follow, one spotted a man hastily leaving the same building. He wouldn't have attracted attention but for one thing—he'd entered right after Chisholm. For all the officer knew, the man lived there. But the coincidence of his departure seemed a little odd. The officer hastily described what he'd seen to a colleague, and as the two debated their course of action, they lost track of the unknown man.

Listening to Fyodorov on the phone now, I didn't think the incident meant much, and neither did Fyodorov. But we agreed to inform department head Markelov, who thought differently. He ordered reprimands issued to the Seventh Directorate for letting the man slip out of sight. My entire department was also alerted. Everyone was to be on the lookout for the mysterious figure who'd spent a few minutes in the same building as Janet Chisholm.

If the surveillance team had followed the man, the matter wouldn't likely have drawn the SCD's attention. But the mistake and the dressing down for it put him prominently on our radar screens. Nevertheless, I expected the incident to fade away. It didn't. The very next day—on New Year's Eve, when we were still in pursuit—Fyodorov called again. "He's been spotted!"

It was incredible but true. The very same surveillance officer who'd lost sight of the man the day before happened to be in a group watching a military scientific institute on the Moscow River's Ovchinnikovskaya embankment. Out walked the unknown man, this time wearing the uniform of a Red Army colonel. What a coincidence! The department's dour atmosphere lifted. Now the surveillance officers didn't let the colonel out of their sights. They photographed him and brought back the film to identify the handsome mystery man of medium height and slightly graying red hair. It didn't take the Seventh Directorate long. His name was Oleg Penkovsky.

Together with others in the SCD English department, I was drafted to compile everything known about Penkovsky and write reports for the top brass. During the next several days, we discovered he wasn't just any army colonel but an intelligence officer, a member of the Chief Intelligence Directorate (GRU) of the General Staff. His cover was deputy chief of the Scientific Research Commission's foreign section, which oversaw delegations, missions and technical intelligence work with foreign countries. Penkovsky frequently traveled abroad. He'd visited London and Paris three times recently. As soon as we knew he was a GRU officer, SCD chief General Oleg Gribanov took personal command of our counterintelligence operation.

I still couldn't believe that spotting a man with Penkovsky's credentials in a building with the wife of an MI6 officer meant he was spying. And the more we learned during the following days, the more unlikely that seemed. Penkovsky had an outstanding Party record. He'd been a military attaché in Turkey, a regimental artillery commander and a general's aide. He also had a distinguished war record and was highly decorated. He was incredibly well connected and circulated in the highest circles of the military and political elite. His wife was the daughter of an important military man, artillery General Sergei Varentsov. He was also close to General Ivan Serov, who had become head of the GRU in 1958. But we also discovered a black spot on Penkovsky's record: His family came from the upper ranks of the tsarist civil service. His father, a White Army officer, was killed fighting Bolsheviks outside Rostov—making him a bona fide counterrevolutionary.

As soon as we were sure of our information, the SCD directors informed the GRU and the KGB Third Directorate, which handled military counterintelligence. Markelov asked me to write a report stating our suspicions that Penkovsky was a spy. "But we still have no factual basis for such assumptions," I protested. "Just do it!" Markelov snapped angrily. I had little choice. The case was then transferred to the special section of the English department in charge of planning operations, although my office continued to assist in planning the investigation.

Penkovsky wasn't your average suspect—*if* he was actually collaborating with the British. So before taking any move against him, we would have to have incontrovertible proof. I wrote recommendations to Markelov about how to proceed with observing Penkovsky, including advice on setting up eavesdropping bugs and secret cameras in his apartment. We monitored all of his contacts, which led us to one in particular: British businessman Greville Wynne, whose every movement in the Soviet Union and abroad was followed.

Penkovsky was trailed around the clock, and we soon had the incontrovertible proof. In January, he and Janet Chisholm were filmed as they routinely entered and left the building in which they met, as our surveillance report read, "with inevitable regularity." Eavesdropping equipment was installed in Penkovsky's apartment when he was out one day. We soon knew the agent the British code-named ALEX was passing secrets not only to them but also, as he himself would later learn, to the Americans as well. The process took many months because we had to make absolutely certain of our evidence. Janet Chisholm left Moscow in June, but Penkovsky continued meeting with other British handlers.[1]

We then had to decide what do with him. We knew Penkovsky was continuing to pass documents to the West even after his membership at the GRU library, from which he got much of the information he passed along, had been canceled. We also knew he had plans to defect. But we had to make sure not to tip him off in any way, enabling him to notify the CIA or SIS that we were on to him or even to escape. Finally, on October 22, KGB special forces swooped in to arrest him. His contact Wynne, detained while on a trip to Hungary, was brought to Moscow to face trial.

Penkovsky confessed to everything. He described first trying to make contact with U.S. authorities in Moscow in 1960. Approaching American students in Moscow, he asked them to take a letter to the CIA. They took it to the U.S. embassy. The letter described Penkovsky and proffered his services spying for the United States. But the understaffed Americans stalled, and he made three more approaches before establishing ties with the British through Greville Wynne. Penkovsky soon began spying for British intelligence, and the SIS eventually asked the CIA to help run him jointly. Penkovsky used three miniature Minox cameras, the espionage industry standard that could take up to fifty pictures without reloading. At his trial, prosecutors accused him of handing over five thousand separate photographed items of military, political and economic intelligence to the two agencies.[2]

Penkovsky's arrest came at a particularly tense time for international relations. In the weeks and months leading up to it, ties between the Khrushchev regime and the administration of the new U.S. president, John F. Kennedy, had become especially frayed. The exposure of American U-2 spy plane flights over the Soviet Union in 1960 had already quashed hopes of a détente between Khrushchev and Kennedy's predecessor, General Dwight Eisenhower. When Kennedy came to office, Khrushchev tried to take advantage of a young leader he saw as weak and inexperienced. Relations went from bad to worse. In 1961, the United States became mired in the Bay of Pigs fiasco that outraged the Soviet Bloc. In June of that year, Khrushchev tried to humiliate Kennedy by haranguing him during a summit in Vienna.

The Berlin Wall went up some two months later. Then something far more serious hit both sides. The day before Penkovsky's arrest, Kennedy appeared on national U.S. television to announce that Moscow had placed nuclear-tipped ballistic missiles in Cuba.

Penkovsky spied from April 1961 to late August 1962 under various cryptonyms, including HERO (CIA) and YOGA (SIS). The true value of his intelligence is still hotly debated. Many in the West say his information helped Kennedy decide to force Khrushchev to back off from his insistence on a 1961 treaty for a "solution" to the division of Berlin. More important, Penkovsky is credited with giving Kennedy the information necessary to take his stand during the Cuban missile crisis, making Khrushchev back down by removing the missiles and defusing a potential nuclear war.

But that's stating the case too strongly. For the West, Penkovsky was a gold mine, providing highly sensitive information, including missile specifications and Soviet military strategic plans. He even gave the CIA the manuals for the missiles we had on Cuba—which revealed, among other technical information, how long it would take the projectiles to travel to the American mainland. Still, it's improbable the information played the key role credited to it by CIA officers and others. Washington figured out by itself that something was brewing. For one thing, it was clear that Moscow had stepped up shipments to Cuba over the summer and had increased military activity on the island. Some in Kennedy's cabinet correctly surmised that the activity was meant to facilitate and conceal the true nature of our work—the installation of medium-range ballistic missiles. The United States took U–2 spy plane pictures of the Cuban bases. A batch taken on October 14 allowed expert CIA analysts to identify the missile installations.

The extent to which the CIA and SIS actually trusted Penkovsky also remains disputed. Without proof, it's impossible to say how much foreign governments base their decisions on intelligence. Despite their admiration for the man, even Penkovsky's handlers admitted he had a paranoid streak. Certain that Khrushchev was bent on waging nuclear war, he demanded a private audience with the British queen to warn her. He even offered to plant portable nuclear devices in Moscow.[3]

Penkovsky was arrested during the tensest moments of the crisis, a day after Kennedy announced his intention to blockade Cuba. Knowing the missiles on the island were on standby, Washington put its own nukes on alert. Nuclear war was a razor's edge away. During his arrest, Penkovsky managed to signal to his handlers that the Soviet Union was preparing a nuclear attack on the United States. The crucial fact is that U.S. intelligence treated Penkovsky's message skeptically. His handlers knew he was determined to paint the scenario in the starkest possible terms—and it was actually U.S. intelligence officers who, perhaps more than anyone else, saved the world from nuclear war. Penkovsky's threat of a nuclear strike wasn't conveyed to Kennedy, relieving him of the pressure to react. Four days later, after Khrushchev announced he might be willing to withdraw the missiles if the United States would dismantle its nuclear arms in Turkey, the crisis began to subside.

Another misconception about Penkovsky is even more misleading. It concerns the man, his motivation and his role in the history of Cold War espionage. The colonel worked hard to penetrate the top echelons of Soviet society. Cunning and able, he deserved his rewards—so why would he want to risk them for espionage? In fact, ideology very rarely, if ever, motivates treason. Personal reasons usually prevail, and ideological justifications often come after a decision to commit treason has been made for those much more private and immediate motivations.

Penkovsky's position in the Scientific Research Commission didn't satisfy his ambition. He'd suffered some setbacks in his career; for example, during his stint as attaché in Turkey he crossed swords with the GRU chief. After his superior made a series of inexcusable blunders, Penkovsky rightly accused him of mismanagement. But he did that by going over his head, sending a cable to the KGB *rezidentura* in Ankara, with which the GRU had a traditional rivalry. The move backfired. The incident reached Khrushchev's desk, after which Penkovsky was recalled and dressed down for insubordination. (Despite the official censure, Penkovsky was still considered in the right, and the GRU Ankara *rezident* was eventually dismissed from service.)

For that and other reasons, Penkovsky hadn't achieved his ambitions by the early 1960s. Sitting on recommendation committees for general staff medals, he put his own name down more than once. When it came to making the decision to spy for the Americans, his frustrations crossed into delusions of grandeur. Contacting the CIA, he made a bid to help decide the fate of the entire state, even of the Cold War itself. He saw himself taking a major part in international relations by playing one side off against the other. Hence the screeching warnings about nuclear war. He wanted the British and Americans to be afraid—and to listen to his advice.

After his arrest, Penkovsky made no effort to hide his espionage but didn't admit to treason. What's more, he tried to convince his interrogators to use him as a triple agent against the British and Americans, even suggesting ways to go about doing it—by entrapping a CIA officer recently sent to Moscow to help run him. Was that the pleading of a condemned man? Certainly—and of a naive one too. But his actions helped shed light on the man and the game he wanted to play. In any case, Penkovsky's interrogators—while never actually saying he'd be reprieved from the "ultimate measure," as we termed the death penalty—let him know his help was appreciated and held out hope that he could receive a lesser sentence for cooperating.

Meanwhile, we developed Penkovsky's idea of entrapping his CIA handler. In November, the SCD—almost certain the Americans didn't yet know Penkovsky had been exposed—ordered the spy to signal the CIA that he'd loaded a dead drop, a prearranged hidden location used to exchange packages, messages and payments. I was assigned to take part in the operation—my biggest so far. Penkovsky described the drop site, in a building near central Pushkin Square with a bookshop downstairs. A theater stood next door to the left, a shoe store to the right and a hospital in front. The drop itself was a container the size of a matchbox lodged behind a radiator inside the entrance. Determined not to tip off the CIA officer, we blanketed the area with surveillance personnel. So many observers were posted in each monitoring zone that eyes would be on the American at all times, without moving people around.

I was stationed in the shoe shop. Pressure mounted early. About two hours before the scheduled time, CIA case officer Richard Jacobs was spotted leaving the U.S. embassy. It seemed the Americans had taken the bait. Jacobs slowly wended his way toward Pushkin Square in an attempt to throw off surveillance. By the time he was two kilometers away, his every step was being closely watched. He eventually approached the bookshop building, opened the door, entered and reached in to take the container. We stormed in to arrest him just as he was about to leave.

After the operation, surveillance detected no movement between the U.S. and British embassies. That is, as far as we knew, the CIA—which probably realized immediately that Penkovsky had been compromised—didn't inform the SIS. So we decided to try to nab a British handler too. The next day, the KGB ordered Penkovsky to signal MI6 for an urgent meeting at the Moscow circus on central Tsvetnoi Boulevard. A KGB officer was made up to look like Penkovsky and sent to wait at the appointed meeting place. But the British didn't show, probably because the Americans had tipped them off without our knowledge. Several days later, Jacobs was expelled from the Soviet Union.

Penkovsky and Wynne were put on public trial by a military tribunal and sentenced on May 11, 1963. Wynne received eight years but was released seventeen months into his sentence in an exchange for Soviet spy Gordon Lonsdale, who was serving twenty-five years in England. Penkovsky was sentenced to death and executed a week later. Following the trial, eight British and five U.S. diplomats were declared personae non grata and expelled from the Soviet Union. GRU chief General Ivan Serov—Penkovsky's mentor—was transferred and then publicly demoted. In the shakeup, some three hundred Soviet military intelligence officers serving abroad were recalled to Moscow.[4]

Penkovsky's exposure was pure chance, chiefly the result of sloppy British tradecraft. He had excellent cover as an intelligence officer detailed to meet foreign intelligence officers, diplomats and businesspeople. He could even travel abroad to meet his handlers and arouse no suspicion. But the operation to run him wasn't properly thought through. While the SIS and CIA used standard and usually secure methods of running their most valuable agent—dead drops, coded signals and undercover meetings in Moscow and abroad—the lack of professionalism was staggering. Penkovsky's dual handling only increased the variables for possible failure.

Couldn't the CIA and SIS officers involved in the operation have devised a better liaison than the wife of the MI6 station chief? The location picked for their meetings also betrayed a lack of imagination. How often do people enter downtown buildings in which they neither live nor work nor have an apparent reason for visiting? The meetings were conducted in broad daylight on a busy street, and in an obvious way. On top of that, Chisholm and Penkovsky entered and left within minutes of each other. Dead drop operations are best conducted at night, when streets aren't busy with pedestrians, and in places less suspicious than random building entrances. The British almost seemed to be playing a game by risking so much and conducting their business so clearly under our noses.

We learned from that mistake. The odds that an agent can be exposed through shoddy tradecraft today are too small to even consider.

Although Penkovsky's characterization of the Soviet leadership was exaggerated, the Cuban missile crisis confirmed one of his main points about Khrushchev. Many members of the Soviet military and political establishment, including Foreign Minister Andrei Gromyko, thought him wildly impulsive and secretly opposed setting up nuclear missile installations in Cuba. But Khrushchev's economic policies, such as his ruinous decision to plant corn in unfertile land all over the Soviet Union, were failing massively. The decision to ship missiles to Cuba in one sense was a time-honored method of distracting public attention. Khrushchev's main mistake was underestimating Kennedy's resolve.

Although Khrushchev survived the crisis, the Cuban failure contributed to his fall from power in October 1964. But it was Kennedy who showed the most visible change in the immediate aftermath of the event. In June 1963, the U.S. president, speaking at American University, called on the Soviet Union to work with the United States to help reduce international tensions and combat the threat of nuclear war, partly through a nuclear test ban treaty. Placing missiles next door to the United States made Washington seriously reckon with Moscow.

Kennedy's assassination shocked the Soviet leadership and put an end to optimism that relations between the superpowers would improve. The Kremlin was also wary about the Kennedy assassin's brief residence in the Soviet Union. Moscow worried it would arouse suspicion, when in fact the KGB had assessed Lee Harvey Oswald as mentally disturbed. He tried to commit suicide shortly after his arrival in Moscow before moving to Minsk. Far from being a target for recruitment, Oswald was suspected as a possible CIA agent, since Langley was known to actively recruit former marines. Oswald was given a residency permit, but there was little interference with his departure when he decided to leave in 1962.

7

In early 1963, in the wake of the Penkovsky case, I was transferred to the First Chief Directorate (FCD), the foreign intelligence wing of the KGB. It was a significant promotion, since the FCD was the KGB's crown jewel. I'd be working in the Fourteenth department, a small group that ran foreign counterintelligence. Later expanded and renamed Directorate K, the department would remain my professional home for twenty-four years. The directorate's chief duties were providing security for Soviet citizens abroad—that is, fending off recruitment and defection attempts— and working against foreign intelligence agencies seeking to establish contacts and recruit Soviet diplomats, military officers and KGB and GRU intelligence personnel. A captain by then, I was assigned to London to keep tabs on Soviet citizens in England. My cover would be as a representative of Sovexportfilm, the trade organization that, as the name suggests, sold Soviet films abroad.

After six years conducting largely routine work for the SCD, I found the First Directorate a welcome change. I'd probably won the London assignment because of my work on the Penkovsky case; I'd also been to England before on an operation that proceeded without a hitch. Transfers between the FCD and the SCD took place frequently. Intelligence officers who were compromised—usually

because they'd become known to foreign intelligence services—
were routinely reassigned to work in counterintelligence at home.
I'd be replacing someone sent back for that very reason. I was given
the KGB files on our comrades living in England—including some
KGB officers—to study closely. I had five months. I also researched
SIS recruitment techniques. I knew something about British intelligence, of course, but had to learn precisely how Soviet institutions
abroad had been targeted. I was also assigned the task of devising a
plan for springing George Blake from prison. Once in Britain, I'd
contact locals who'd pass the information to him.

Blake was the son of a Dutch mother and Sephardic Jewish father from Istanbul, both naturalized British citizens. He served in
the Dutch resistance and the British Royal Navy before being recruited by the SIS in 1944. Posted to South Korea in 1949, he was
captured by invading North Korean forces the following year. He
volunteered to work for the KGB during his detention, and he was
recruited as agent DIOMID. Back in England in 1953, he betrayed
dozens of Western agents. He also exposed the Berlin tunnel, a
five-hundred-meter underground passage from West to East Berlin
used to eavesdrop on telephone lines running out of Soviet intelligence headquarters in nearby Karlshorst.[5] Two years later, in 1955,
he was posted to Berlin.

Blake was betrayed by a Polish defector in 1961 and sentenced
to forty-two years in jail. He escaped in October 1966, aided by
three Irish inmates he'd befriended in jail. Familiar with the intelligence Blake had provided us, I knew how seriously the KGB
leadership took his case. In the end, a KGB plan accomplished
his escape, although I don't know how many of my ideas, if any,
were included.

Three months into my preparation work, the head of my section,
Ivan Grigoriev, called me to his office. "Victor Ivanovich," he said,
"I have some unpleasant news for you. The Central Committee has

decided to reduce the number of our cover positions. Sovexportfilm is one of them." Grigoriev explained that since Sovexportfilm was ostensibly a for-profit entity, the idea was to use it to actually earn some hard currency instead of chiefly providing cover for intelligence. So I wouldn't be going to England after all.

Grigoriev gave me two options. I could return to the SCD or, if I agreed, he'd recommend me for a post in Australia, where a current officer had just been compromised by Australian intelligence. I should actually say *the* intelligence officer, because he was the only one posted there, apart from a cipher clerk. I agreed and then prepared for another assignment abroad. Again I had to familiarize myself with files about the Soviets living in the country in which I'd be posted. I also dug into the archives to study what we knew about the Australian Secret Intelligence Service (ASIS). Meanwhile, I began the paperwork process for the Party's Central Committee to clear me for the job.

In October 1963, Elena and I packed our belongings, turned over our small two-room apartment to Elena's mother and left Moscow with Alyosha, our four-year-old son.

8

We touched down in the Australian capital Canberra. My predecessor met us there and dropped us off in a hotel so we could relax after our long flight. But just when he should have been leaving, he made a proposal. "Victor Ivanovich, I think we should go fishing now."

It was code for talking about business. I flashed a glance at Elena before answering, "You go on downstairs and I'll meet you in a couple of minutes."

Elena exploded the moment we were alone. "Who is this man to tell you to work immediately?" I remained silent. "You're earnest and a hard driver," Elena continued. "I know that. But you're also a husband and father. How can you leave us now?!" she cried. "We're exhausted. What right does he have to tell you to go at a time like this?! Can't it wait until tomorrow?"

I was as calm as I could be. "Look," I said slowly, "I came here to work. You know I have a difficult job. There'll always be lots of work to do, and you simply have to put up with it. That's all—there's simply no other choice."

Elena fought back tears. I washed up in the bathroom, took my coat and briefcase and left.

Making sacrifices for the KGB was difficult, but Elena and I had both agreed to do just that. Back in Moscow, she had to switch out of the SCD because husbands and wives were forbidden to work in the same directorates. She was assigned instead to be a translator in the KGB's political publishing wing. In Australia, she would work as the ambassador's translator and secretary. There was always a lot to do, which kept her mind off things. But she found it hard to adjust to life in a new country.

There was reason to be happy, however. Our living conditions were a marked improvement from Moscow. Leaving snowy Russia, we seemed to have touched down on another planet, amid desert flora and fauna, and with colorful parakeets and parrots flying around our lawns. We lived upstairs in a consulate building, fifteen kilometers from Lake George. I was also given a raise—enough to buy a second suit and pair of shoes in Sydney. Australians, like the English, lived better than we Russians, but the disparity didn't give me much pause. Most Soviets at home didn't think about living conditions abroad; there wasn't much information about it, and in any case they got on with their lives as best they could. It was for their sake I was now adjusting to a completely different environment.

My cover—as it would be for many of my future postings—was as cultural attaché. I had no supervisors and did my work as I saw fit. I filed regular reports about the activities of the embassy staff—despite its tiny number—as well as members of the large Russian immigrant community, many of whom had fled after the 1905 Revolution and World War II. I had no instructions from the Center to establish contacts with foreigners, let alone recruit them.

One of my assignments was to travel with the Omsk Chorus, from the eponymous Siberian region. The group was popular, especially in Sydney, where many Russian émigrés lived. Touring with the singers provided cover for operations such as tracking Vladimir Petrov, a KGB cipher expert who defected in April 1954. Petrov had been posted to Australia by secret service chairman Lavrenty Beria, Stalin's feared henchman. After Stalin's death and Beria's arrest and execution in 1953, Petrov was accused—by the ambassador to Australia among others—of being close to Beria. Recalled to Moscow in April 1954, he made a last-minute decision to defect in order to avoid arrest and possible execution. Requesting asylum, he walked out of the embassy with whatever documents he could lug with him, leaving his wife, Evdokia, entirely in the dark. He later explained that he didn't want to compromise her, allowing her to return to her family in the Soviet Union if she wanted.[6]

Once the KGB realized Petrov had defected, officers seized his wife. But word got out and an angry crowd of Australians gathered at the Sydney airport to protest when she was forced onto a flight home. As the plane stopped off in Darwin, police and the ASIS intercepted the KGB officers, allowing the frightened Petrova to speak to her husband by phone. He persuaded her to stay, and the two were given new identities and a house in the suburbs.

Petrov exposed a large number of KGB agents, including a network of spies seeking to penetrate Australia's nuclear development program. He also described Soviet cipher techniques and gave details about how Guy Burgess and Donald Maclean, two of the famous Cambridge Five group of British spies, defected to the Soviet Union. The Australian public was incensed over the KGB's espionage, so the Soviet embassy packed up and left for several years.

Now, having obtained an address outside Sydney where Petrov was said to be living, I'd try to track him down. During a day off from escorting the Omsk Chorus, I drove out to the house and photographed it. But Petrov had since moved on.

My Australian tour was cut short in February 1964. Yuri Nosenko, a KGB officer serving in the SCD, had defected during a trip to Geneva as part of a Soviet disarmament delegation. Nosenko had worked in the Sixth department—responsible for keeping tabs on American tourists—and sat near me in Lubyanka. Although I'd never worked with him, I'd often seen him in the hallways, so there was a chance he could expose me as a former SCD English department officer.

Continuing fallout from the Cuban missile crisis kept Moscow's relations with Washington particularly tense. To avoid provocations by foreign intelligence services, KGB officers around the world were recalled. The cable ordering me home came just over a year into my tour. When my replacement arrived in November, Elena, Alyosha and I left for Moscow.

_3_

COLD WAR FRONT LINE: BEIRUT

1

The Aeroflot plane taxied down a snow-swept runway, past groves of dark spruce trees and rumbling Soviet airport trucks. I felt pleased to be back on familiar ground, but returning home from Australia would have felt better if it hadn't been for a recent political thunderbolt. A month earlier, in October, a coterie of party functionaries had toppled Khrushchev and installed the uniquely uninspiring Leonid Brezhnev in his place.

Those stolid men represented the mass of Party cadres who were no longer able to countenance Khrushchev's anti-Stalinism. Led by their chief ideologue, Mikhail Suslov, the Brezhnev group put an end to boat-rocking questions about the past, setting up a regime that provided for their mutual security. That arrangement would eventually lead to massive stagnation in the 1970s, when—unable to address the state's inefficiencies—the Kremlin "reformed" by allowing corruption to spread throughout society.

In November 1964 it was already clear that the change in leadership wasn't helping Soviet relations with the United States. Hostile conditions complicate intelligence work, and I worried that the current state of foreign affairs would affect my job reassignment.

Considerations about work evaporated as soon as we entered the airport. A fellow officer who had been waiting for me at the gate took me aside to inform me of a personal tragedy. My brother Pyotr had died of hemophilia. I couldn't believe it. Pyotr was only thirty years old. He'd just sent a lighthearted letter to me in Australia saying he'd recently married. Everything seemed to be going well for him—he was even enjoying his job as an engineer in a factory in Belorussia.

I was granted leave the following day to fly to the funeral in the Belorussian city of Mogilëv. On my return, I was informed that I'd been posted to the Southeast Asia department. My next tour would be in Rangoon.

I knew the weather would be hot in Burma, but I was young and willing to go anywhere. In any case, such decisions were out of my control—I had to accept what I was given. I hoped advancement would come from my resolve to do as thorough a job as possible on each tour, something I also demanded from my subordinates. I'd also learned a key characteristic for remaining in the good graces of my superiors: modesty. Those who were too eager to please the service's leadership often drew its ire instead.

Shortly before my departure, Southeast Asia department chief Anatoly Gusakov called me into his office to discuss a common Lubyanka theme: the KGB's advantage over the CIA. "We recruited our first agent in America in 1923, and they didn't even have an intelligence service before the war," he said. "But they're making up for lost time. They've been stepping up their activities targeting our officers in the past several years." He paused and I nodded.

Indeed, the United States had reorganized its wartime Office of Strategic Services into the Central Intelligence Agency in 1947. By the 1960s, American officers still weren't as experienced as we were in clandestine operations. They were less careful to cover their identities and didn't have nearly as many good Russian speakers as we had English experts. But the CIA was learning, sending out officers increasingly better trained in languages and foreign affairs.

The KGB was adapting too. The FCD's Fourteenth department was recently revamped and renamed the Second service and then Directorate K in quick succession. "We have to stay on top," Gusakov continued. "So a decision has been made to regularize our countermeasures in a systemic approach. The Central Committee is concerned that we don't have enough information on the CIA, particularly after the Berlin and Cuban crises. Chairman Semichastnyi has drawn up plans for a set of special groups to counteract CIA intelligence operations against Soviet citizens."

I wondered how all that applied to me. Had something happened in Burma? Gusakov wouldn't be telling me about the Americans if it didn't concern an operation in which I was—or was to be—involved. "The first group is already being set up," he continued. "It's going to be in Lebanon. You've been picked to go to Beirut. Your main goal will be to penetrate the U.S. embassy and other American organizations and collect information on CIA activities."

So again my plans were thrown to the winds, but this time the choice made sense. I'd be working in a Middle Eastern crossroads, a transportation nexus and financial center. Known to be socially liberal, the city was a playground for diplomatic, intelligence and business communities—the Paris of the Middle East. I didn't know much about the region, but I'd have time to study our files. So much for Rangoon. This prospect was far more alluring.

We left in the fall of 1965. Since Aeroflot didn't yet fly to Beirut, Elena, Alyosha and I took a plane to Damascus, where we were met by my superior officer, who was in charge of counterintelligence in Beirut. Rem Krassilnikov had served in the SCD English department, which he left the year before I joined it. He had then served a tour in Ottawa before becoming deputy *rezident* in Lebanon. In time, he would become a KGB superstar with international billing.

Krassilnikov was friendly, obviously intelligent and had a shy way of smiling. He seemed genuinely happy to see me. Depositing our few bags in the trunk of his car, we set off for Beirut, three hours away. The relatively plush U.S. mission stood on the Mediterranean shore. In contrast, the tiny Soviet compound—where we were to be temporarily housed—was squeezed behind an imposing fence in the downtown area. But its two whitewashed, modern buildings were adequate and came with a children's playground and a soccer field.

The city was fascinating. Much of the boxy new architecture invading the ancient sites was uninspired, but the Beirut peninsula itself, with an embankment stretching for miles along the Mediterranean Sea coast, was stunning. To the north rose Lebanon's famous wooded hills, with their picturesque valleys and ski resorts.

After we dropped off our luggage, Krassilnikov invited us to his apartment in a standard residential building not far from the embassy. His wife, Nelly, to whom I took an instant liking, prepared lunch. (Ninel, her full name, was "Lenin" spelled backward. Krassilnikov's own un-Russian first name, Rem, stood for *revolutsionnyi mir*: "revolutionary world." Many parents gave their children such names soon after the Revolution.)

Once we sat down, Krassilnikov poured me a glass of araq, an anise liqueur, and added ice cubes and water, which turned the liquid milky. I didn't much like the sharp, sweet taste. The Hennessey cognac procured by our embassy in Australia was much better. "Get used to it, Victor," Krassilnikov said. "It's what everyone drinks." Krassilnikov was right, and I had plenty of opportunities to acquire a taste for it. Lebanese food, however, required no such introduction. Restaurants often served twenty to thirty small plates of delicious hummus, baba ganouj, kebabs and other hors d'oeuvres of all kinds. But that would come later. As we sat talking around the Krassilnikov dining room table, my new boss raised his glass for a toast. "Nu, za vsyo khoroshoie," he said (Well, to all things good). I felt certain we'd get on well.

Next morning, Krassilnikov introduced me to the other *rezidentura* officers. The brand-new anti-CIA counterintelligence group he headed was part of the larger Line KR, the *rezidentura's* counterintelligence department. There were four of us, including an officer responsible for counteracting American operations in Beirut's large Armenian community. Besides us, only the *rezident* was informed of the anti-CIA group's existence.

As part of his duties as Line KR chief, Krassilnikov directed operations against the SIS. He'd set up a good network of agents and was running successful surveillance and eavesdropping operations. We had a leg up on the SIS because Kim Philby, who'd defected to Moscow from Beirut only a year earlier, gave us a recent rundown of SIS operations and some by the CIA. Philby had lived in Lebanon since 1956, working as a correspondent for *The Economist* and *The Observer*. But he maintained links to British intelligence, despite overwhelming suspicions he was the "third man" who had helped his fellow Cambridge Five agents Guy Burgess and Donald Maclean escape to Moscow in 1951.

My cover would again be a cultural attaché post. I'd be the sole officer conducting counterintelligence against the Americans, trying to expose and undermine their attempts to penetrate the

KGB. Krassilnikov told me the other operations officer in the anti-CIA group was inexperienced and too timid to do his job properly, which was not unusual. Unlike the Americans, whose lifestyle at home was closer to Beirut's, Russians took longer to adjust. Krassilnikov would be counting on me, which, I supposed, accounted for his apparent delight to see me at the Damascus airport.

He also informed me that I'd have to start from square one. We had no agents, operations, or contacts to go up against the Americans. I'd have to find an apartment for my family, buy a car and get to work making contacts and cultivating agents who might penetrate the CIA. My work was obviously cut out for me. The CIA was especially well plugged into Beirut. On top of the Americans' generally easygoing nature, which gave them an advantage in the city's permissive environment, a number of the agency's officers spoke good Arabic. While we had to work hard to recruit agents, they seemed to fall into the CIA's lap.

Beirut's half-Muslim, half-Christian population generated an atmosphere that differed from the capitals of other Middle East states such as Syria or Saudi Arabia, where Islamic traditions dominated. Its noisy, crowded downtown, packed with markets and street vendors, lit up at night with neon signs. Fashionable crowds flocked to expensive hotels, restaurants, cafés, bars, discos, cabarets, clubs and casinos. Traffic was a nightmare—there were essentially no police. You could operate however you wanted. The Lebanese appeared not to care.

2

Beirut was a wonderful place to do our business. It wasn't a country, it was a Gilbert and Sullivan operetta. It was a country in which you could ski in the morning and swim in the afternoon. And if you were in the espionage and intelligence business, you had access to the PLO, Fatah, Black September, the KGB, the Czech intelligence service, the Polish intelligence service and international banking. Everything a government would want to know about other people's activities that were of interest to intelligence agencies was available in one way or another in Beirut in those days. And it could all be done while sitting on the porch at the St. Georges Hotel and drinking fine wine and eating delicious food.

—*John MacGaffin, former CIA deputy director*
for operations, posted in Lebanon 1969–1972

Beirut was a very seductive environment. It was freewheeling. The Middle East is a place where you grease people's palms every time you turn around. It's a way of life there. We found the Soviets got seduced by that every now and then. They became very interested in money and all kinds of things their government wouldn't have appreciated them doing. That's why I went there—to work specifically against the Soviets and East Europeans—because we felt the environment was favorable to us.

Haviland Smith, CIA Beirut station chief, 1966–1969

The KGB *rezident*, on his last posting before retirement, didn't much care about the day-to-day bothers of counterintelligence. That left Krassilnikov, who proved to be an excellent mentor, effectively in charge of my work. Urging me to operate as independently as I wanted, he offered solid operational advice but never raised his voice to subordinates, much less imposed his opinions. He believed the best training came from relying on one's wits and determination to get the job done. (Not surprisingly, Rem Sergeevich rose to head the SCD's American department as one of the KGB's great generals. In 1985, when I was busy handling Aldrich

Ames and Robert Hanssen in Washington, he acted on their intelligence. The major operations he planned at that time took out the CIA's main agents and operations in the Soviet Union.)

I began frequenting the glamorous Casino du Liban and other nightspots popular with all kinds of foreigners. Many of the customers were men posted to Beirut without their wives. If diplomats were usually reserved in their behavior, businessmen weren't. Out for a good time, they gravitated toward strip bars, loud music and crowds. Gilded Arab youth, come to relax in the permissive environment, helped pack the discos.

I started following Americans home to large, new apartments not far from the U.S. embassy. My attempts to understand Americans would serve me well in Washington many years later, not least in convincing Aldrich Ames to reveal more secrets than he was initially willing to. Poring over embassy directories, I annotated them with basic information about my potential targets. Then I began approaching some of them. I started by using a "foreign flag" cover, posing as a Yugoslav. My legend—the story behind my assumed identity—was that I'd worked in Australia and was now employed by an oil-rich Saudi sheikh.

One of my favorite perches was a bar whose female American bartender turned out to be intelligent, friendly and knowledgeable about her regular customers. I tipped generously for useful information, such as where they worked—one, for example, as a professor at the American University; another for Goodyear tires. All this came in friendly conversation, ostensibly to pass the time. Then I advanced to staging meetings. If I wanted to get to know someone by "accident," I'd come when there was a chance a target would be there alone. Single bar patrons are often lonely. I'd strike up conversations and pose questions. I met one American by asking him to recommend where to buy music—a choice I immediately regretted because it required feigning enthusiasm for popular Western groups. In order to talk about the music, I had to do more research, which included listening to it. Two tedious months of that passed before I realized the contact was useless.

I picked up tidbits this way. One American who worked as an engineer installing telephone lines informed me the equipment his company used came fitted with special outlets for CIA tapping devices. Another technician happened to work for American intelligence. I arranged to pay him $100 for an eavesdropping bug, the kind used to monitor Soviet embassy personnel.

3

Rem and I waltzed around for three years in Beirut. I liked Krassilnikov a lot; he was a good friend and I enjoyed my relationship with him. It was a bantering affair. The people in headquarters told me it was unique, almost strange for its time, that both of us acknowledged who we were to each other. I was very comfortable with that and with him. I was looking to see whether there was any indication that he might be interested in us—and I got absolutely none. So I never pitched him. I tried to make his life as miserable as I could, but I never pitched him. At the same time, I made it very clear by everything that I said and did that I wouldn't be amenable to any kind of overture from him. It didn't seem to matter to him.

I knew Cherkashin as an attractive young case officer, but I didn't see much of him because I didn't want to establish a relationship that Krassilnikov would be able to manipulate. With Cherkashin, it was all sort of cocktail party chatter.

—*Haviland Smith, CIA Beirut station chief, 1966–1969*

A downtown bowling club was especially popular with the American community. The U.S. embassy hired it out two nights a week. It would be an ideal place for me to study the Main Adversary's personnel—the only trick would be to gain admittance on the right days. Suppressing my dislike for bowling, which I found dull, I asked to meet the club owner. The meeting went better than I'd expected. When I professed a heartfelt desire to learn, the owner offered to coach me himself.

I started taking lessons several nights a week. In time, I bowled well enough for my coach to recommend playing with others. To my great luck, he also invited me to watch the Americans play. That enabled me to observe them socializing and practice communicating socially, which would later prove useful. Like listening to Western pop music, however, bowling proved a dead end for my purposes. The bowlers tended to stick together in their groups, which made it almost impossible to develop contacts among individuals. So I gave up that game too.

In general, trawling around the city's nightspots was a work-intensive, inefficient process that yielded few results. It helped to start that way, but as time went on and I began developing a network of agents, I spent increasingly less time on the streets.

My best agents were local Lebanese. Despite Beirut's ostensible alignment with Washington, many Lebanese sympathized with the Soviet Union, largely because Moscow supported hard-line Arab states such as Syria in opposing U.S.-backed Israel and later Egypt. I made contacts with the Lebanese army's counterintelligence wing, the Second Bureau (or Deuxième Bureau, as it was known), and cultivated a handful of agents, including businessmen and policemen. They in turn recruited other agents, most of whom never knew they were working for the KGB.

It soon became clear that the CIA recruited more aggressively than we did. Among the agency's most outgoing operatives in Beirut was named Haviland Smith. A talented, independent and confident officer, he'd often show up at Soviet embassy events and receptions to introduce himself to Soviet staff. It was evident to everyone—he never seemed to hide that—that he was CIA. That was very different from the way I acted. Although I chatted with Smith several times, Krassilnikov was his main interest. The two often met in the city's watering holes, each gleaning information, looking for personality cracks to exploit. It was an unusual case. Each respected the other, and neither made any headway recruiting the other. That relationship was strikingly similar to a later one that would develop between a CIA officer and a KGB officer during my time in Washington.

Among the agents I recruited was a local U.S. embassy employee with a large family who needed an outside source of income. The embassy wouldn't have looked kindly on his having a second job, so I came to his rescue. Posing as the Yugoslav, I secretly employed him to buy office supplies and run errands for me. He came to depend on the money I paid him and didn't raise an eyebrow over my request for a list of embassy staff (ostensibly for the Saudi sheikh to use for lobbying purposes). In time, that agent provided physical descriptions of each embassy staff member, and also his estimate of which ones worked for the CIA. Eventually, my slow upping of the quality of information I wanted from him alerted the likable Lebanese man to what was going on. Never questioning my motives, however, he remained a valuable source, helping me positively identify several U.S. intelligence officers.

Foreign flag cover came with pitfalls, however. Even chance encounters with CIA officers or agents was usually enough to blow the cover—they certainly did their homework. False identities were also difficult to justify to agents. They'd eventually want to know why a businessman needed ongoing access to information on the CIA. Exposure could also lead to diplomatic problems—the Yugoslavs likely wouldn't have been thrilled with my choice of cover. After some time, we decided to stop using foreign flags in Beirut.

4

KGB and CIA officers understood each other's side on a personal level. You could meet for a drink together, laugh over a joke and leave. There were never feelings of malice and operations were never conducted on a personal level.

> —*Yuri Kotov, KGB political intelligence officer, stationed in Israel 1965–1967, Lebanon 1967–1968, Egypt 1968–1971*

We targeted Soviets through agents who had access to them. It didn't matter who they were. Western diplomats, Lebanese, American businessmen. Anybody the Soviets were interested in, we were automatically interested in. Any time we found somebody in touch with a Soviet of interest to us, we would see whether or not we could talk to that person and get him going for us. We were fairly successful. The Soviets were out moving around. Since they were doing that, it gave us the opportunity to get some pretty good looks at them. Ten years earlier, they didn't do anything anywhere. They were all holed up in their embassies, terrorized by the Stalin era and not prepared to talk to anybody in the West by themselves.

If you can generalize about nationalities, the Soviets were not a flexible people. They were pretty programmed and to be set loose in the absolutely freewheeling environment of Beirut was sometimes rather shocking for them. But they had opened up. By that point there was a different Soviet abroad. It was the golden youth. They were educated Soviet officials, most of whom were the progeny of politically important people in the Soviet Union. They did what they damn well pleased. And they were very interesting to us because a lot of them had ideas their fathers had never even considered. It was the beginning of the opening up of Soviet man in effect. That made it a heck of a lot easier for us to get at them.

> —*Haviland Smith, CIA Beirut station chief, 1966–1969*

Beirut was an excellent training ground. I ran operations planting eavesdropping devices in U.S. institutions and CIA officers' apartments, generating propaganda in the local press and conducting liaisons with agents—all of which provided valuable experience that would serve me well for the rest of my career. (Not all the operations were entirely successful. The Americans detected eavesdropping devices planted inside electricity cables in the U.S. embassy.)

I even learned to speak French thanks to an agent code-named PATRIOT, a Lebanese businessman who became one of my most productive agents. On first meeting him, I assumed PATRIOT spoke no English or German—which I'd studied in Leningrad—and addressed him in the broken French I'd picked up talking to local journalists. PATRIOT was gracious enough to compliment me on my language abilities, which turned out to be not nearly good enough. I hired a teacher, practiced hard and my French eventually became passable. When the end of my tour approached several years later, I invited PATRIOT to dinner with the KGB officer who'd be taking over his handling. The new man was trained in English and French, and just as we were sitting down to eat, he asked PATRIOT which he preferred using. To my astonishment, PATRIOT replied that either was fine. His English turned out to be perfect.

PATRIOT was a Soviet sympathizer who supported Moscow's role countering U.S. influence in the Middle East. Recruited by my predecessor, he never accepted a single kopek for his services, and even insisted on paying for some of our meals together. Tall, dark-haired and handsome, the playboy businessman found an obvious thrill in working for the KGB. He was one of the few agents I ran who knew he was working for Soviet intelligence. PATRIOT never refused to participate in an operation, no matter how risky. His name is on a list of especially valued agents at the foreign intelligence museum in the Center.

With many contacts among the local staff of the U.S. embassy, PATRIOT often recruited agents independently. He also had good contacts in the Lebanese army, including the counterintelligence wing, the Deuxième Bureau, which we knew collaborated with the CIA and French intelligence. PATRIOT's almost intuitive understanding of the complicated, shifting allegiances of Beirut politics made him an astute judge of possible recruits and operations. So I believed him one sunny day when we were drinking beers after lunch in a café overlooking the sea. He told me that a contact of his in the Deuxième Bureau had mentioned something worth pursuing. "My friend Hamid says the American embassy has rented a downtown apartment," he said. "The lease is under a false Lebanese name, and no one lives there. There's a cleaning woman who comes around once a week. I guess since they work with the CIA, they're not really interested in the information—but it's been offered to us if we want to act on it."

"Can you find out what goes on there?" I asked. "Could it possibly be a CIA safe house?"

"I'll try to find out."

I wondered why Hamid would have told PATRIOT about the apartment. Surely he didn't think it interested PATRIOT for his own purposes. "Does Hamid know your affiliation? I mean did you tell him?" I asked.

"No," PATRIOT replied.

"You're sure? Is there any way he could have found out some other way?"

"I suppose he could have easily guessed."

If Hamid had worked out PATRIOT's allegiances, that would mean the Deuxième Bureau was playing a double game with the CIA and the KGB. Whatever the motives, the opportunity was too good to pass up. I had the apartment put under surveillance. Sure enough, an agent soon noticed a man we'd identified as working in the office of the U.S. military attaché entering the apartment with different people on several occasions. That backed up the theory that the apartment was used as a safe house. Using my agents inside the embassy, the next step was to identify the man, whom I labeled MARS. It wasn't too difficult. I'd already surmised that since the Deuxième Bureau knew about the apartment, there was a good chance the American was an intelligence contact with the Lebanese. If true, the setup would be highly unusual. It was the first time we'd come across a CIA officer operating under cover of a military attaché office—a circumstance John MacGaffin, the CIA officer assigned to follow me in Beirut, still denies.

I decided to get inside the apartment. We already had our lead: the cleaning woman. Since the presence of a KGB officer would have elicited unnecessary attention, PATRIOT and I agreed that he would approach her. PATRIOT, the ladies' man, was highly suitable for the job. We knew what days the woman cleaned the apartment. Showing up on one of them, PATRIOT rang the doorbell. The cleaning woman answered the door. She was young and not immune to PATRIOT's charm, which he poured on while explaining that he wanted to rent an apartment in the area and moved quickly to chatting her up. She agreed to meet him for dinner.

After a few dates, PATRIOT suggested meeting at the apartment. Several days later, he was in. His carefully disguised observation focused on a sofa with a wooden frame. Later that day, he proposed fixing a bugging device to the bottom. I cabled the Center, which sent a package containing an eavesdropping device to my specifications. It was lodged inside a piece of wood with two sharp metal studs on one of its broad ends. The bug would work for up to a week. PATRIOT would have to find a way to whack the contraption into place under the couch without his new girlfriend noticing.

PATRIOT arranged to meet her at the safe house early one afternoon. When she wasn't looking, he slipped the bugging device
out of a bag and swung it upward underneath the couch. Half an
hour later, I met him in the hills above the city.

"I don't know if I did it properly," PATRIOT said worriedly.
"When I attached the piece of wood, it seemed only one nail took
hold." That meant that the device might be hanging down on one
side—and thereby visible—or have fallen off altogether.

"I think it's best if you go back to fix it," I said. "Or completely
remove it. It's not worth the risk. How long is your friend supposed to be there?"

"Another few hours."

"Okay—go."

Two hours later, we met at another rendezvous point. PATRIOT removed the device from his bag. It had been a very close call. "When
I walked in the door, I could see it lying on the floor," he said. One
of the studs had been badly attached in Moscow and fell off the bug.

Back at the *rezidentura*, we decided on another approach. This
time a technician would make sure our devices worked properly.
Several days later, PATRIOT asked Hamid of the Deuxième Bureau
to obtain a copy of the keys to the apartment, and we soon had a
set. PATRIOT helped us plan the new operation by describing the
apartment's layout. When it was empty one night, two officers
kept a lookout while another installed a miniature camera in a
chandelier and an eavesdropping bug inside an electric socket.

Everything went smoothly and we were soon documenting
everything that went on in the apartment. But the Center decided not to use the information because it deemed the Middle
Eastern political situation too tense. I was soon working on other
cases—with no way of knowing that the information our eavesdropping provided would lead me back to MARS in the West German capital Bonn seven years later.

5

By the time we moved to Beirut, Elena had come to terms with my commitment to the KGB. She later told me that she learned to appear calm no matter what happened. In Lebanon, unsolicited advice the ambassador's wife gave Elena mirrored her own suspicions: "When people here look at you, they don't see you for who you are," she said sternly. "They judge your country by your actions. You should act accordingly."

In August 1968, I took my family for a six-week vacation at a state sanatorium in Kislovodsk, a pleasant resort in southern Russia. Near the end of the month, the radio announced that Soviet tanks were advancing on Prague, the Czechoslovak capital. The object was to crush the liberalization movement called "socialism with a human face." In our own capital, dissidents staged small protests that were quickly broken up. Still, the atmosphere was tense, although most Soviet people supported the move as the media presented it: suppression of rebellion in Czechoslovakia. For my part, I believed the Czechoslovak Communist Party had let the situation spiral out of control. I agreed with the KGB leadership that we had to fight Western attempts to turn socialist countries against Moscow. We had to help the Czechoslovak Party leadership regain its grip on power.

But many countries bitterly opposed Moscow's actions and international relations soured. There seemed a chance our adversaries would take retaliatory measures. When I returned to Beirut, however, work continued with no discernible difference.

As the embassy's cultural attaché, I handled a number of Soviet delegations coming through the Middle East. I escorted poets Evgeny Yevtushenko, Kaisyn Kuliev and a number of sports teams, including Moscow's Spartak soccer club. I also worked with student exchanges, interviewing candidates for study programs in the

Soviet Union. But stepped-up CIA activities in Beirut left me less and less time for my cultural cover work.

One morning, the *rezident*, looking worried, called me into his office. "An urgent case has come up. We have to take Mikhail Ivanov to Damascus right away. I'll explain on the way."

The son-in-law of an influential Soviet minister, Ivanov (a fictional name) was a talented Middle East correspondent for the Moscow newspaper *Izvestiya*. Although the sociable young journalist was on good terms with the KGB, he remained highly independent. Caring little for the opinions of either those in the Soviet community in Lebanon or others back home, he did what he wanted.

"The Americans tried to pitch him," the *rezident* said, meaning he'd been subject to a recruitment attempt. "I've cabled the Center. We need to get him out of the way of any further provocations."

I rushed home to pack a change of clothes. Less than an hour later, the *rezident*, Ivanov and I were making our way southwest toward Syria. Checking in to a Damascus hotel, we holed ourselves up in my room, where I asked Ivanov to relate exactly what had happened.

"If you want me to begin at the beginning," he said nervously, "that would be my setting foot in a casino." I should have known. I liked Ivanov, an eminently decent guy. Gambling was his only discernible vice and was not uncommon among young men let loose in a new environment free of the restrictions imposed back home. Young diplomats, correspondents and other official Soviet representatives abroad grew up in relative privilege, a generation away from the privations of the 1930s and 1940s. Many were shucking the ideological restrictions closely followed by their parents.

"It was all right at first—I guess that's how it always is," Ivanov continued. "Anyway, pretty soon I was losing money. I only had a limited amount because my wife handles the finances. So I began to spend the bureau's cash. I was soon $10,000 in debt. Then you can imagine." Ivanov probably had about a month or so before he'd be found out. Enveloped in scandal, recalled and demoted, he'd no longer be allowed to travel abroad. His whole life would change.

"A contact of mine in the casino took me aside and said he could help."

"Who?" I asked.

"He's Lebanese but works for an American company." CIA, of course, I thought, but didn't say anything. "He said he had some pull with the managers and he'd see what he could do. And he did—he went to them and promised I'd pay off my debt if they'd give me some time. They agreed. At the same time, he said he had a friend who could help me.

"So he called his friend and an American came to meet us. My Lebanese acquaintance left. The American told me he knew who I was, that he's involved in the press and had read my articles. He said he understood my situation and felt sorry for me. Then he proposed to help me think about what to do.

"A few drinks later, he admitted that he was from the CIA. He said he was ready to help me pay my debts in return for political information. 'You can't tell anyone about this,' he told me. 'Especially at the Soviet embassy. They wouldn't be very happy about our helping you solve your problem.' As if I didn't know that!

"I thought those guys could help me. I knew it wasn't the best option, that I'd be taking a chance. But I couldn't think of any other way of coming up with $10,000 at that moment, so I kind of agreed without completely committing. I said it sounded good, but that I'd have to think about it."

Ivanov was pale and clearly worried but maintained his composure. Although I couldn't be absolutely certain, he seemed to be telling the truth. He'd made a mistake by gambling and had tried to correct it without anyone finding out, but there were boundaries he didn't want to cross. He knew he was taking a chance by confessing to me. He could have been arrested simply for speaking to a CIA officer. He must have been relying on his high connections and our good relationship.

"I did think about the offer," Ivanov continued. "But when he began to describe what I'd have to do, that I'd have to meet secretly with the CIA and hand over information, I realized what he was really talking about. I refused and came straight to you."

As far as I could tell, Ivanov's story checked out. We informed the Center, which got in touch with Ivanov's father-in-law, the minister. Ivanov was recalled together with his wife and children. He was given a round dressing down, but his high connections saved him from further punishment. *Izvestiya* paid his debts to the casino and Ivanov continued working for the paper. His was one of many gambling problems in the Soviet community in Lebanon, and not all worked out so well for those in trouble.

6

The Cold War wasn't really cold at all. It was a very hot war, with all kinds of measures used by the opposing sides. In the background were the Korean and Vietnam Wars and other conflicts all over the globe. The Middle East was an especially dangerous, potentially explosive zone. Beirut in all this wasn't a political center, but a stage for propaganda wars. Lebanon was the only Middle East country with a free press. It had newspapers published by all sides in the various conflicts. You could see playing out before you the battle between the monarchist states—such as the Saudis, who were influenced by the West—against those fighting for independence from the West, such as Egypt. We naturally sided with the Arabs to counter Israel's backing by the United States. We supported Palestinian demands against Israel because we thought they were fairer.

> —*Yuri Kotov, KGB political intelligence officer, stationed in Israel*
> *1965–1967, Lebanon 1967–1968, Egypt 1968–1971*

Although civil war between Lebanon's Muslim and Christian populations didn't erupt until 1975, the country began to radicalize in the wake of the Six Day War of June 1967 between Israel and the Arab states of Egypt, Jordan and Syria. The conflict ended in a massive victory for Israel, which snapped up an area four times the size of its original territory, including the entire Sinai Peninsula, all Jordanian-occupied territory west of the River Jordan and the strategic Golan Heights of Syria. The changed power dynamic in the region boosted the role of extremist groups.

The Arab–Israeli war also caused U.S.-Soviet relations to deteriorate over the Middle East after the thaw that followed the successful resolution of the Suez Canal crisis in 1956. Washington said it had nothing to do with the Six Day War. Secretary of State Dean Rusk assured the Soviet government that Israel had decided to attack Egyptian military bases in the Sinai Peninsula and Syria without U.S. approval. We accepted the explanation, and the Americans congratulated themselves on having prevented Soviet ties from worsening.

In fact, however, the KGB informed the Politburo that U.S. President Lyndon Johnson had given his blessing to the Israeli decision to attack Arab targets. Several opinions exist as to why Moscow publicly accepted Washington's line. The most compelling is that if the Soviet Union had officially acknowledged U.S. involvement in the conflict, Moscow would have had to take some kind of action to support its Arab allies—but didn't plan on doing so at the time. In any case, the Six Day War helped turn the Middle East into a permanent foreign policy hot spot.

While the Lebanese government remained essentially pro-American, hundreds of thousands of Palestinians poured into refugee camps in Lebanon. That swelled the membership of Islamic groups there, which began launching attacks against Israel. Those groups included the Palestine Liberation Organization

(PLO), which set up in Lebanon after its expulsion from Jordan in 1970, and later the radical Shiite militia Hezbollah.

If Beirut had earlier been a gold mine for free intelligence searches, providing cover and opportunities at every turn, the city's changing allegiances and lifestyles made information gathering increasingly difficult. The Casino du Liban shut its doors and other bars and nightclubs began to empty as foreign companies pulled out staff.

The nature of my own work changed too, even though there was no longer much need for me to be out on the streets. I'd developed contacts in the U.S. embassy and built a network of agents to plan operations and recruit more people. Following the Six Day War, the Center increased its requests for political intelligence. In the fall, Yuri Kotov, a Line PR officer in Israel, arrived in Beirut to contribute to political intelligence gathering. "Cast-iron Kotov," as he came to be known, was a man of deeply held principles whose mind was difficult to change once it had latched onto something. He became a good friend—after he overcame his suspicions of me. Kotov and many like him believed that counterintelligence officers mainly dug for compromising information on their fellow Soviets.

Working closely with future Russian Prime Minister Yevgeny Primakov, Kotov later took part in highly sensitive Soviet-brokered shuttle diplomacy between Arabs and Israelis. In 1967, however, he was assigned to collect intelligence on Americans in Beirut. In time, his family grew close to mine; we often went fishing in the Mediterranean Sea and drove into the hills for kebab picnics. Since working in counterintelligence meant living in relative isolation from one's own community as well as the local population, I was happy we got on.

In early 1968, Kotov and I were involved in a case that reflected Beirut's increasingly tense atmosphere. It began one evening when shocking news reached the *rezidentura*: Alexander Khomyakov, a second secretary in the Soviet embassy, was visiting the apartment of Soviet trade representative Vasily Vasiliev in downtown Beirut when Lebanese soldiers burst in, firing machine guns. They killed Khomyakov and wounded Vasiliev in the shoulder. There was no indication about what prompted the attack.

As information trickled in about the incident, we learned that it involved an operation by the GRU, Soviet military intelligence, which didn't always keep the KGB apprised of its activities. The Beirut GRU *rezidentura* had come up with a plan to steal a French-built Mirage jet fighter belonging to the Lebanese military and fly it to Soviet territory. Vasiliev and Khomyakov approached a Lebanese pilot and offered to pay him $1 million for the job. He agreed and planning went ahead. The last meeting was scheduled to take place in Vasiliev's apartment. What the GRU officers didn't know was that the CIA had learned about the scheme early on and tipped off the Deuxième Bureau. The GRU walked straight into a Lebanese setup.

The hare-brained scheme amounted to little more than sheer adventurism. The Lebanese air force couldn't have had more than ten planes, most of them secondhand Mirages. Those outdated aircraft would have been of little use as models for technology development. They would also have needed a massive auxiliary fuel tank to safely reach Soviet soil. They would have had to fly through Turkish airspace, a huge risk given Turkey's alliance with the United States and its NATO membership. The GRU compounded its conceptual mistakes with major operational ones. The two Russians should have known Vasiliev's apartment would be bugged by the Americans. But taking that into account wouldn't even have helped, since the pilot whom Vasiliev and Khomyakov had recruited was himself likely a Lebanese agent.

As the three men discussed details of the operation on the last fateful night, Lebanese soldiers fanned out to surround the building. One group climbed the stairs and rang the apartment doorbell. Grabbing his pistol, Khomyakov opened the door, saw soldiers with automatic rifles, and slammed it shut again. It was hit by bursts of machine gun bullets. Khomyakov fired back. The Lebanese detail continued firing, now hitting Khomyakov several times and Vasiliev in the shoulder.

At the time, we only knew that the Lebanese had driven both wounded Soviets away in a car. We were told that Vasiliev was arrested and Khomyakov's body taken to a morgue. By noon the next day, the Lebanese government confirmed that the two Russians had been shot. Vasiliev's wounds were superficial and he was soon released. Meanwhile, the coroner examining Khomyakov had found a weak pulse, and the diplomat was rushed to a military hospital.

By early afternoon, the Soviet ambassador, Sarvar Azimov, demanded permission to see him. I accompanied him to the hospital, where a doctor told us none of his vital organs had been hurt and his condition was stable. We were then allowed to see Khomyakov, who was lying naked on an examining table. He smiled at us weakly. He had five bullet wounds in his shoulder and back. Surprisingly, he hadn't been bandaged. The Lebanese had operated to remove the bullet lodged in his shoulder. Two days later, we were given permission to take him out of the country. We flew him to Moscow, where he had another operation on his shoulder.

No direct proof followed, but PATRIOT's agents in the Deuxième Bureau later told us the Americans had approved the Lebanese operation. The episode worsened relations between Beirut and Moscow. Although no major measures, such as withdrawing diplomatic staff, were taken, the Soviet Foreign Ministry lodged a letter of protest. The incident challenged an unspoken agreement that had existed between intelligence agencies since the end of the war that the adversaries' officers would not be physically harmed. That agreement had protected intelligence staffs from being caught up in spiraling cycles of tit-for-tat attacks. The understanding was questioned again in 1975, when the CIA mistakenly suspected the KGB of assassinating CIA Athens station chief Richard Welch. The attack was later blamed on the Greek 17 November terrorist group. But Moscow's serious reaction to the accusation led to talks between the two sides to resolve the suspicions. The KGB leadership, seeking to calm worries about work abroad becoming more dangerous, took the unusual step of informing lower-ranking officers of the result.

The Middle East situation continued to deteriorate as my tour neared its end. While Moscow tried to do what it thought best there, neither it nor Washington could fully predict the consequences of using proxies in the larger Cold War confrontation. The region's current deplorable stalemate in no small part represents fallout from the failure to address the needs and aspirations of local groups amid a global struggle for influence.

_4_

TREASON

1

On my return to Moscow in 1970, I was promoted to my first major desk job at the Center, evidently thanks to the KGB leadership's approval of my efforts in Beirut. As chief of the Middle East section in the FCD's Directorate K, I'd be overseeing foreign counterintelligence in the region. Instead of operating in the field, often alone, I'd be running an entire division from a Lubyanka office. The Middle East was a growing hot spot. In particular, political tensions in Lebanon were becoming worse, as was the border standoff between Israel, Jordan, Syria and Egypt. It would require diligent monitoring and many trips to the region.

The new job meant that I could afford a bigger apartment. We looked forward to moving out of the two-room flat in the decrepit five-story Khrushchev-era building in which my family and mother-in-law had lived between my foreign postings for over a decade. But the following year, FCD chief Grigory Grigorenko sent me abroad again. I'd be going to India as head of Line KR.

The Soviet school in India only reached to the sixth grade. My son Alyosha, who was about to enter the seventh, had to remain in Moscow. Grigorenko dismissed that concern. So did the *rezident* in India, Yakob Medyannik, who'd asked Grigorenko to assign me to the New Delhi *rezidentura*. But as much as I hated leaving Alyosha behind, I put emotions aside and carried out my duty. Elena had a harder time. She cried for days.

India was impressive but strange. Delhi, with its jumble of cars and bicycles pushing past pedestrian hordes streaming in all directions, felt like the inside of an ant colony. Stray dogs and cows roamed the streets. I was caught up by its energy and that of Bombay and Calcutta. The country's ancient culture could be awesome. Scenes of great beauty were often breathtaking. Agra's hanging gardens and the Taj Mahal, that memorial to undying love. The lost city of Fatehpur Sikri, built in red sandstone by Emperor Akbar.

Although the KGB had a network of contacts there, friendly relations and economic ties between Moscow and Delhi precluded us from running many agents. Quick to display their independence, the Indians often expelled Soviet diplomatic and intelligence staff. When a Line KR officer accidentally grazed Indira Gandhi's parked car, he was immediately sent home. But although the Indian government condemned Soviet spying from time to time, expulsions rarely carried political overtones.

Our embassy complex stood on a main road, sometimes blocking the view of a small sea of squalid shacks. The hardworking *rezident*, Yacob Medyannik, had previously been a deputy director of the FCD and went on to become a top aide to directorate chief Vladimir Kryuchkov. Like Krassilnikov, the demanding yet understanding Medyannik proved to be an excellent mentor.

Number two in the *rezidentura* was Leonid Shebarshin, deputy *rezident* in charge of political intelligence, Line PR. I didn't immediately take to the dark-haired, solemn-looking Shebarshin, who was evidently close to Medyannik. Before joining the KGB, he graduated from the prestigious Moscow diplomatic institute and worked in the Foreign Ministry. Curt and intense, he struck me very much as a career man—until I saw more of him. Then I realized his demeanor, which could easily be perceived as rude, actually indicated he was a determined officer with little patience for superficial niceties. Although he sometimes seemed unwilling or unable to relax, Shebarshin became my close confidante. Soon he'd replace Medyannik as India *rezident* and would continue rising, eventually becoming a long-serving head of the FCD. Much later, his levelheadedness was credited with saving the directorate during the August 1991 hard-line coup d'état attempt against Soviet President Mikhail Gorbachev led by hardliners including then-KGB chairman Kryuchkov. Afterward, Gorbachev briefly appointed Shebarshin acting KGB chairman.

By 1972, Brezhnev and U.S. President Richard Nixon were groping for détente. Wary of upsetting improving relations—and keen on strengthening trade and foreign policy ties with Delhi—the Politburo ordered the Center to turn down most proposals for operations in India. As deputy *rezident* in charge of counterintelligence, I headed security in the Soviet diplomatic community. In addition to my usual counterintelligence work against the CIA, I'd keep an eye on our diplomats' conduct—making sure they didn't defect and that none of their foreign contacts posed a threat of recruitment. I was also responsible for watching the over four and a half thousand nonofficial Soviets in India, many of whom were working on joint construction projects.

Prying into the personal affairs of my fellow countrymen and reporting the inevitable drunkenness and adultery wasn't to my taste. I left that to the other counterintelligence officers, the better to concentrate on operations against the CIA. They were in a mess. Officers scattered all over the country ran a myriad of badly connected sources and agents. My first order of business, approved by Medyannik and Shebarshin, was to shed at least half of our informers.

Shortly before my arrival, the *rezidentura* conducted a recruitment campaign against an ambitious young CIA officer who'd been observed contacting local agents. Some were politicians and military officials, from whom the American was trying to obtain intelligence about Indian political affairs. Oleg Kalugin, then chief of Directorate K in the Center, flew to Delhi to head our pitch, based on threatening to expose the target to Indira Gandhi's government. Refusing to cooperate, the operative informed the CIA of our pitch, prompting U.S. Ambassador Kenneth Keating to protest our activities to the Indian Foreign Ministry.

Of course Keating's objection was disingenuous. In the game we were playing, American intelligence tried no less hard to recruit Soviets. Soon a Russian engineer showed up at our embassy. He worked at a Soviet-constructed steel plant in the industrial city of Bokaro, in the northern Jharkand state—and wanted to report a suspected CIA recruitment attempt. In my office, Sergei described his work overseeing Indian engineers and steelworkers. He'd grown close to his translator, Raj. The two often went out together in the evenings to let off steam.

Sergei didn't hide the fact that he had come to India to make money. Many Soviets who had a chance to work abroad grabbed it, not least because it allowed them to buy coveted foreign goods, some of which they brought home and sold illegally. Sergei's dream of saving enough money to buy a car didn't escape Raj's attention. Offering to help him find moonlighting work, he recommended an American trade representative in New Delhi.

Naturally Sergei was suspicious. Naturally I was too. Although Indians rarely helped recruit Soviets for U.S. intelligence, I knew the CIA had agents in the Bokaro plant. Perhaps Sergei would help. He seemed honest enough, and with no access to secret information, posed a negligible security threat. Those were ideal characteristics for double agents, or dangles. There was no reason, I decided, not to try to find out if the CIA was really trying to pitch him.

Preparing double agents requires painstaking work. Some cases, like Sergei's, arose spontaneously. Most, however, called for meticulous planning long in advance, including research to make sure cover stories were convincing and that any "intelligence" handed over to the other side was correct—if verifiable—but also harmless to Soviet security. To make dangles into attractive targets, we tweaked their résumés, worked on strengthening or playing down various character traits and adjusted the amount of information to which they had access. It was as expensive as it was time-consuming.

Sticking as closely as possible to the truth gave the best results. I told Sergei to be as sincere as he could with potential CIA handlers. "You've nothing to hide about your work—there's nothing classified you can give them. So behave as normally as you can. Answer any questions you're asked and deliver any information you have access to."

I told Sergei to play up his desire to make money and, if it came to that, negotiate hard about what he'd be paid. The savvy engineer made me repeat my instructions. "I want to be absolutely sure I'm getting this right," he said with a measure of incredulity. "You want me to try to establish a contact with the CIA. You want me to work for them as an agent, right?"

"You'll be providing a great service to the Soviet Union," I replied. "We'll be very grateful."

"*Khorosho* [okay]."

Two months later, Sergei returned to Delhi to meet the man his translator had recommended.

After several encounters, the American confessed he was a
CIA officer and told Sergei he wanted him to continue working
for the United States after his return to Moscow. Sergei agreed
and was soon working as a double agent. We fed him false information in the hope it would tie up the Americans in fruitless fact
checking. That was the extent of the operation. As with many
others at the time, we had orders to make sure it didn't harm
U.S.–Soviet relations.

Double agents often provided valuable windows onto adversaries'
motives and intelligence-gathering methods. I scrupulously pored
over Sergei's reports for each tactic used in handling him. I learned
the identity of his handler and the kinds of information that interested him. We used many double agents like Sergei, and so did the
CIA. The dangerous business sometimes created havoc in operations because it opened intelligence services to enlisting double and
triple agents. But it was also unavoidable because recruiting and
running agents was ultimately a case officer's raison d'être. It was
also interesting work. Making the other side believe your agent
was sincere and accepting the disinformation he fed was challeng-
ing. Still, dangles were a double-edged sword, whose specter overshadowed every decision to recruit agents we believed to be real.

The need for intelligence forced me to take risks, but when
Ames and Hanssen approached the KGB in Washington years
later, it was inevitable that I'd suspect the two men, who later became our most valuable spies, of being double agents. Fear of
them caused both the KGB and CIA to turn away countless volunteers. Adolf Tolkachev, a Soviet scientist who became the
CIA's top spy in the 1980s, had to approach the Americans more
than six times in Moscow before they finally put aside their suspicions and met him. Even after the other side recruited one of our
dangles, the possibility always remained that it would find out
and re-recruit him to work against us as a triple agent.

CIA paranoia about double agents reached its peak in the 1950s and 1960s under counterintelligence chief James Jesus Angleton, who was convinced the agency had been penetrated by Soviet spies. Launching a mole hunt operation called HONETAL, he all but destroyed the agency's ability to recruit and handle agents. His natural suspicions were reinforced when a KGB defector called Anatoly Golitsyn told Angleton in 1961 that every Soviet defector after him would be a double agent. Golitsyn made that claim because he'd soon run out of secrets to tell the Americans and wanted to enhance his importance. Angleton swallowed it.

When Yuri Nosenko defected three years after Golitsyn—the incident that forced the premature end of my Australian tour—Angleton became convinced that Nosenko was a double agent. In fact, he was a genuine defector who had already told the CIA the Soviet Union wasn't behind the assassination of either President John F. Kennedy or Lee Harvey Oswald. Nevertheless, Angleton ordered him jailed for almost three years without charge. Locked in an attic room, the Russian was fed only weak tea, watery soup and porridge.[1] He was then transferred to a tiny concrete cell at the Farm, the CIA training center at Camp Peary near Williamsburg, Virginia. His complete isolation included being deprived of all news of the outside world. Lights were kept on to disorient him. More than that, he was given psychotropic drugs.[2] He was also forced to endure rigged lie detector tests and once sat strapped in a chair for seven hours with polygraph equipment attached.

Angleton ruined many careers and all but paralyzed the agency because the paranoia he stoked made recruiting agents—highly risky under any circumstance—nearly impossible. The CIA virtually stopped seeking out Soviet agents and turned away many volunteers, even when the Americans almost certainly knew them to be genuine—because the KGB was too wary to use its own staff officers as double agents. (In the 1980s, the SCD would exploit that perception to great advantage when protecting Ames, feeding the Americans a staff officer double agent who kept them guessing for years.) Dissent against Angleton's policies was drowned out.

CIA failures were legion. When a former KGB case officer in the SCD American department handed over a package of secret documents to the U.S. embassy in Moscow in 1963, the State Department photocopied the documents but returned them to the Soviet Foreign Ministry. The Americans suspected the would-be spy, Alexander Cherepanov, was a double agent offering disinformation. He wasn't: Cherepanov was arrested and executed.

Suspicions about double agents drew the KGB into many mistakes too. In 1976, Edwin Moore, a former CIA officer, left several unanswered notes for Washington *rezident* Dmitri Yakushkin, then threw a packet of secret documents over the Soviet embassy residential compound fence. Suspecting Moore of trying to create a provocation, the embassy's chief security officer, Vitaly Yurchenko, handed the package to the Washington police as a possible terrorist bomb after consulting with *rezident* Yakushkin in his office. Moore was promptly arrested and sentenced to fifteen years in prison. Back at Yasenevo the incident became notorious as a glaring example of unprofessionalism. Both Yakushkin and Yurchenko were at fault for not first sounding out the Center about how to proceed. (Yurchenko would next appear on the CIA's radar screen nine years later, when he defected to the United States. Having provided the CIA with some of the KGB's most sensitive information, he then "redefected" back to Moscow.)

In the end, even the most valuable double agents were rarely worth the intensive efforts it took to run them. Taxpayers on both sides of the Atlantic paid huge sums for very little. More often than not, double agents were scarcely more than balls in the games played by intelligence agencies. Some of the best-known Cold War espionage cases were more about spy versus spy than real issues of national security. Aldrich Ames would arouse great emotion in the United States, not least because the information he gave us led to the deaths of ten U.S. agents. But with few exceptions, most of those executed were intelligence officers involved in the narrow tasks assigned to them, with little knowledge about what was going on in the rest of the KGB, let alone the country. In fact, most of Ames's information concerned secret CIA work against the KGB. It was thieves stealing from thieves, which again raises the question of whether all the years of work and hundreds of millions of dollars were worth it. Any operation, however well protected, could come crashing down the moment a single person—a Hanssen or a Penkovsky—decided to walk into the offices of the adversary and betray his country.

2

The KGB and CIA used roughly the same methods, exploiting the same human weaknesses, and sought to achieve similar goals. But of course, officers on each side were brought up in different systems. The average American and the average Russian behaved themselves differently—that's especially true for intelligence officers. Americans smile too broadly. They laugh too loudly, and often unnaturally. We don't call people we don't know "Mike" or "Bill." We use the full name and patronymic.

—*Leonid Shebarshin, former FCD chief and acting KGB chairman;*
served in India and Pakistan, 1964–1977

I'd have a great deal of difficulty saying, "Okay, we're the CIA and there's a branch of the CIA that runs these political prison camps and historically they're responsible for killing 20 million of my citizens. But that's okay, I've adjusted myself to that." There's where I find the

difference between the CIA and KGB. The position that the CIA and
the whole intelligence community plays in this is far, far different
from being called the "sword and the shield" of the Party that runs
the country.

—*Jack Platt, former CIA case officer*

Much has been written about the antagonism between the GRU
and the KGB. I myself saw little competition between them. The
relatively rare intrigues of the 1950s and 1960s usually took place
in Moscow. Out in the field, the two services cultivated their own
cases and usually didn't interfere with each other. The KGB simply stayed out of military intelligence. While that separation
sometimes led to conflicting operations and contradictory intelligence sent to Moscow, both agencies were encouraged to exchange political intelligence.

The GRU played a large role in India. The Soviet Union sold
India much military technology, and Moscow had good contacts
in the Indian Defense Ministry. Military attachés were among the
Soviet embassy's highest-ranking staff. Although the KGB *rezidentura* usually didn't know what GRU officers were up to and
whom they were meeting, we kept in regular contact about general issues. Officers of the two agencies socialized with one another at parties or played soccer or volleyball together.

The GRU *rezident* in India was a ruddy-faced man named
Dmitri Polyakov, a colonel (soon promoted to general) who stood
out—or rather stood back—because he hardly ever mingled with
KGB personnel or others in the diplomatic community, even
though he lived on the embassy compound. Although intense,
Polyakov was generally calm and unemotional. I saw him blow up
in anger at a colleague only once.

Polyakov suspected his own deputy's friendship with Medyannik
and Shebarshin, warning him to be guarded about what he told the

KGB *rezidentura*. I attributed the colonel's attitude to his natural demeanor. Little did I know that he had concrete reasons for being careful. By the time I met him in 1972, Polyakov had been spying for the CIA for more than ten years as agent BOURBON—and for the FBI as TOPHAT.

Polyakov was recruited in 1961 during a tour in New York. He had access to top state secrets, including valuable information on GRU operations. He disclosed intelligence on military planning, nuclear strategy and chemical and biological weapons research. He also provided documents about Soviet weapons, including antitank missiles; reported on the state of the Vietcong during the Vietnam War; and handed over more than one hundred classified issues of the Red Army's *Military Thought*, which was published for the leadership and discussed top secret plans and strategy.[3]

Polyakov's information on our deteriorating relations with the Chinese in the 1970s helped President Richard Nixon make his historic decision to travel to Beijing in 1972, a major diplomatic breakthrough for the Americans that opened relations with Communist China. Polyakov also exposed a good number of spies.

His information led to the betrayal of at least six American military officers and one British officer who had spied for us. He fingered the Briton by taking photographs of *his* spy photographs of documents about U.S. guided missiles. Using Polyakov's prints, the CIA tracked the spy down to the British Aviation Ministry. I don't know whether the GRU investigated the disclosure of so many of its agents. What's clear is that the agency failed to detect the source of leaked information.

The son of an accountant, Polyakov was born in Ukraine in 1921 and, like Penkovsky, was decorated for action as an artillery officer during World War II. In the 1950s, he served in the General Staff before being posted to New York to work undercover as a U.N. diplomat. He was commended for his efforts and sent back at the end of the decade, this time as deputy GRU *rezident*. After his start spying for the Americans, he went on to serve tours in Burma and India, where he was promoted to general in 1974.

Polyakov spied for the Americans for eighteen years, until he began falling under suspicion in 1978. That year, information about his activities—and those of another U.S. agent code-named FEDORA by the FBI—were leaked to the American press by CIA counterintelligence chief Angleton, who suspected the two were double agents. Soon thereafter, American journalist Edward Jay Epstein published a book about Lee Harvey Oswald. It offered the same evidence, obtained from the CIA or FBI. FEDORA, an agent named Alexei Kulak, had by then died, but Epstein's book led to his posthumous exposure. (Code-named SCOTCH by the CIA, Kulak was a Soviet science and technology intelligence officer who'd been awarded the prestigious Hero of the Soviet Union medal.)

Suspicions about Polyakov were further confirmed in 1979 when an FBI agent in New York contacted AMTORG (the Soviet trade organization serving as a front for the GRU) and handed over a secret FBI list of Soviet diplomats thought to be intelligence officers. The spy also gave information indicating TOPHAT was indeed Polyakov. That FBI agent was a junior officer named Robert Hanssen.

It was impossible not to react to Hanssen's intelligence about Polyakov. In 1980, the GRU recalled the general from an extended trip to Delhi and reassigned him to a Moscow desk job. The agency didn't arrest him, however. Although multiple sources had fingered Polyakov as an American spy, the GRU refused to believe that one of its top officers would commit treason. While the GRU welcomed Hanssen's intelligence, it suspected the FBI operative was a double agent. The information on Polyakov was only circumstantial, and those pushing for a serious investigation lacked hard evidence to convince the doubters. Polyakov's supporters claimed the accusation was an American attempt to discredit the service's officers. More important, perhaps, was the GRU leadership's unwillingness to see one of its own on trial for treason. The KGB, for its part, was kept out of the affair.

Polyakov of course knew the information about him was accurate and managed to confirm through friends in the GRU that he was under investigation. Fearing the probe would close in on him, the general retired soon after moving to Moscow and the GRU closed its investigation. From then on, Polyakov lay low, spending most of his time in the country. That strategy worked. He lived in peace until his new exposure in 1986, this time by Aldrich Ames.

Polyakov was at his beloved dacha on July 4, a Friday, when he received a request to attend a retirement ceremony at GRU headquarters the following Monday. He had reason to suspect his imminent arrest—two ambulances were parked nearby, an obvious sign that he was under surveillance. He showed up at the GRU building on Monday morning in full dress uniform. Approaching the entrance, he was seized, stripped and searched before being locked up in Lefortovo prison, where most spies were held. He was later executed. One of his two sons serving in the GRU committed suicide soon thereafter.

Polyakov was one of many spies put on trial following the KGB's recruitment of Ames and Hanssen during and after the so-called Year of the Spy, 1985. But he occupies a special place on the list because none of the other agents ranked so high in the Soviet intelligence community and none came close to spying so productively for so long. Managing to elude arrest for twenty-five years while working for the FBI, Polyakov was a unique case that spoke to his handlers' professionalism and the ineffectiveness of the Soviet security services in tracking him down.

Like Penkovsky, Polyakov has been portrayed as a "true" patriot who believed Russia had been hijacked by the Communist

Party. Also like Penkovsky, he's said to have made an ideological conversion when his GRU work opened his eyes to the true nature of the system he'd fought to defend during the war. That was also how he presented himself to his contacts in the CIA and FBI, making a point of refusing money and only occasionally accepting presents such as hunting and fishing gear.

There's another similarity between Polyakov and Penkovsky: Their motives for betraying the Soviet Union have been simplified to fit a political line. Most assessments of Polyakov's treason omit one key fact, the fate of his son. In fact, Polyakov became disillusioned with the Soviet Union and the GRU during his second tour in New York. That year, the youngest of his three sons fell ill. Polyakov asked the GRU *rezidentura* to allow him to check in to a New York hospital for a life-saving operation. Permission was denied. Polyakov was desperate, but could do nothing. His son died. Soon after, Polyakov approached a diplomatic contact, a high-ranking U.S. Army officer who directed the Soviet general to the FBI.

Brent Scowcroft, national security adviser to President George H.W. Bush, asked me during a U.S. conference in 1997 why I thought Aldrich Ames betrayed his country—and whether I thought it possible to prevent treason. I replied that the only way to be absolutely safe is to remove people from intelligence gathering. Guaranteeing full security would require leaving espionage to satellites, computers and other technology. That is impossible—human contributions are by far the most important component of intelligence gathering. And as long as people are involved, security threats can never be completely eliminated.

Intelligence agencies do everything possible to avoid the inevitable betrayals, something to which I dedicated most of my career. They start by employing complicated screening processes to hire their officers. The KGB selected candidates thought to be patriotic, loyal to the service and faithful to their families, friends and coworkers. People so heavily vetted for their political trust-worthiness are highly unlikely to become disillusioned with the policies and ideology of their countries simply through sponta-neous changes of heart. (The possibility can't be ruled out, but it's improbable.) That was especially true of Soviet officers, who were perceived to be—and saw themselves as—the cream of society's elite. Consequently, intelligence agency claims that officers com-mit treason because of ideological motives usually fit a disinforma-tion strategy. Such reasoning ordinarily serves a larger propaganda effort to justify the dastardly action of convincing someone on the other side to betray his country. It's an attempt to show that the other guy's political system is bad and ours is good.

In fact, loyalties switch for less elevated reasons than patriotism, ideology and love of country. Often it's not belief in one or another ideology that changes but circumstances, which are usually beyond the control of intelligence chiefs. Rivalries flourish among cowork-ers. Promotions are awarded unfairly. Polyakov was left with bitter anguish over his superiors' refusal to let his son undergo an opera-tion in an American hospital. That inexcusably heartless decision led the general to inflict great damage on his country.

Spies tend to focus on their personal problems, not political ones. Most don't want to betray their countries and refuse to see themselves as traitors. They simply want to solve an immediate problem or satisfy a kindled ambition, and spying offers itself as a possibility. Money is a key motivation. Another is proving self-worth, as in the case of Penkovsky—as well as Aldrich Ames and Robert Hanssen twenty years later. "I'm a good intelligence officer and I'm doing a useful job," a potential agent might say. "But my bastard boss can't see how well I work. He likes flattery and he dis-likes me because I'm honest." Perhaps the boss really is a jerk. But perhaps he has good reasons for disliking his subordinate. Maybe the offending officer is lazy and drinks too much. The fact is that potential spies, with justification or not, often feel slighted.

Betrayal has existed since the dawn of civilization. It's no mistake that espionage, the subject of a chapter in Sun Tzu's *The Art of War* (400 B.C.), is called the world's second-oldest profession. Only later, once the decision to spy has been made, ideological reasons present themselves to justify the choice of treason. At the same time, betrayal will continue to pose as large a threat as it did for intelligence agencies during the Cold War unless society stops viewing the primary motivations for espionage as ideological—that is, unless the public stops buying the stories told by intelligence agencies. As long as punishment for espionage remains as dire as certain imprisonment (it was usually death in the Soviet Union), spies will have greater motives to broaden their activities than to come clean or stop their espionage before it becomes too serious. To pressure Aldrich Ames into betraying most CIA agents in the Soviet Union, I would remind him of the risks he was taking under U.S. law—and give him enough time to consider the consequences of his earlier, far less damaging actions. Thus prepped, as it were, he chose to protect himself by wading irrevocably deeper into the waters instead of retreating.

— 5 —

INTRIGUE AT MOSCOW CENTER

1

In 1975, I was back in Moscow. I'd been promoted to colonel and appointed deputy head of Directorate K's European department. I reported to my old classmate Oleg Kalugin, who had returned from Washington to head foreign counterintelligence. The move was another major boost to my career. I was now in charge of counterintelligence operations against the CIA throughout Europe, including the Soviet Bloc's Eastern European countries. I'd finally be working in an important post in the Center, fighting the Main Adversary in the backyard of its closest allies—especially Britain, France and West Germany.

My office was in the new KGB compound on Moscow's outskirts in Yasenevo, which had opened three years earlier, in 1972. The complex included a twenty-story main building, several wings, conference halls, a gym, a swimming pool and a large park. Aside from inadequate air conditioning, it was a vast improvement over the old offices in Lubyanka. There had been big changes within the directorate, too. In his drive to combat the intelligence agencies of the major capitalist states, above all the United States, KGB chairman Yuri Andropov had beefed up the First Chief Directorate's foreign counterintelligence wing. As I studied our operations in Europe, however, I realized much remained to be done to make counterintelligence effective. Counteracting the CIA wasn't a high priority in most European *rezidenturas;* some KGB stations didn't have a single agent with access to information on American intelligence. *Rezidenturas* instead focused their efforts on penetrating their host countries. The exceptions were the stations in Bonn and Karlshorst, outside Berlin, which did exceptional work, thanks partly to their large size and top-level cooperation with the East German secret service, the Stasi.

I began visiting the *rezidenturas* under my jurisdiction to boost their operative work and ratchet up activities against the CIA, monitoring and exposing CIA pitches to Soviets in Switzerland, Germany and Greece. In the Soviet Bloc countries, cooperation with and trust in the various intelligence services differed in each case, generally reflecting the state of relations with Moscow. We were close to the Bulgarians, respected the Czechoslovaks and had cool relations with the Poles. The Stasi provided by far the best cooperation. Our German "friends" were consummate professionals, planning and executing their operations scrupulously. They also had excellent sources that delivered valuable information on NATO, U.S. military and CIA activities. I regularly traveled to Berlin to oversee joint KGB–Stasi operations.

The American press would later claim that the two services were so close that information gleaned from the Stasi archives after the Soviet collapse led the CIA to Aldrich Ames in 1994. That could not have happened. Despite its unusually strong ties with the Stasi, Soviet intelligence never disclosed agents' identities to officers who didn't need to know them—let alone to foreign services. Files on valuable agents were held in the strictest secrecy. While the KGB often provided intelligence generated by important agents to the East Germans, sources wouldn't have been named, so the Stasi files couldn't possibly have contained documents showing the KGB had a particular agent inside the CIA.

In mid-1977, I received information from the Stasi that an old Beirut target of mine was working on assignment in Bonn. It was MARS—the CIA operative in Beirut who had used the safe house in which we installed cameras and bugs, allowing us to document his meetings with agents. That information had never been used. Perhaps now was the time.

MARS's mistake—the blame for which can be spread around the CIA Beirut station as a whole—was failing to adequately check his safe house for eavesdropping devices. I would try to recruit the American by confronting him with the evidence. There might be a chance that he'd rather collaborate with us than see his sloppy work exposed to his superiors, which might stall his career or precipitate other negative repercussions. Kalugin supported my proposal. It was forwarded to the FCD chief, who also approved it.

Bonn wasn't the best place to pitch a CIA officer. West Germany's ties with the United States were extremely close. If MARS reported my attempt to recruit him, it could have serious consequences for me, including arrest. Moreover, no one in the KGB knew MARS, which would make it difficult to establish first contact. I had to play the operation by ear, hoping to corner him at a diplomatic reception or other such event.

Arriving in Bonn, I started watching for MARS's name on various pilfered invitation lists. Three weeks went by without a sign, and my trip began to look like a waste—until his name was spotted on a schedule for an American corporate presentation in a downtown restaurant. Showing up as a Foreign Ministry official under an assumed name, I spotted the slightly aged MARS and maneuvered toward him to strike up a conversation about international relations. The fair-haired American officer, who was in his early forties, of medium height and a slightly stocky build, was easy to talk to. Our discussion seemed to go well. When I proposed continuing our acquaintance, he readily agreed. I suggested meeting in my hotel.

Two days later, I descended to the lobby to wait for my target. As usual before a recruitment attempt, I was anxious but also excited. The confrontational "cold pitch" was one of the riskiest methods, putting great psychological pressure on a target, and often failed. Even when successful, it often produced agents whose handlers had to maintain constant pressure on them to stay involved. When such agents had a chance to cut their ties—when they were assigned to new posts or when communication with their contacts became risky—they often took it.

MARS showed up smiling. He seemed pleased to be meeting a Soviet "diplomat." We went upstairs to my room and sat in armchairs across a small table. I offered a whiskey, which he accepted. We resumed our discussion about international relations and went on to talk about Bonn's tourist sites. Then I got down to business.

"Let me tell you the real reason for my visit to Bonn," I said. "I've come to convey an offer from the Soviet Union you might find interesting. Please understand I'm doing this as a friendly gesture."

MARS assumed a poker face but didn't reply. "We know you work for the CIA," I continued. "We have information about your activities in Beirut."

MARS had likely suspected I was a KGB officer and may have been expecting some kind of pitch. But he didn't seem to have anticipated my knowing about his Lebanon posting. Nonetheless, he quickly recovered his cool. He could spot where the conversation was going and struggled to manipulate it.

"I don't think the fact that I work for the CIA is particularly discrediting," he replied wryly.

"Yes, working for the CIA isn't particularly discrediting, you're right. But we have other information about you. I don't want to make your life difficult, I want to make you an offer. We can discuss it and do whatever is best to avoid any negative repercussions for your career."

"I don't know what you're talking about," MARS replied.

"How would your superiors feel about your disclosing agents to us?" I pressed.

Struggling to maintain his composure, he remained silent.

"Let's take a look at the facts," I continued, reaching for a folder in my briefcase. I took out photographs of the Beirut safe house MARS had used. They included shots of the interior and close-ups of our hidden video and audio recording devices.

MARS's face blanched. As he examined the prints, I imagined him mentally running through his meetings in the apartment, considering the possible damage our eavesdropping could have inflicted on the CIA. He sat back in his chair. "You're right," he sighed. "This is a serious failure. For me and the CIA."

I said nothing more. Having delivered the damning evidence, I wanted to let off some pressure. It was now up to MARS to decide what to do. He stared at the floor.

"I can't collaborate with you," he finally said with much deliberation. "I've always been loyal to my country and the agency. I love my family. Those have always been my motives for everything I've done, and I can't sacrifice them—even if I have to pay for it with my job." It was the reply I'd more or less expected. Even though we were on opposing sides defending the security of our respective countries, we understood each other as only professional colleagues can. Despite the fact that our jobs revolved around deception, we could now speak more or less openly.

But no matter how hard I tried to persuade MARS that he'd be better off spying for us than ruining his career, he continued to refuse, saying that however badly he'd fumbled on the job, he wouldn't betray his country. "Working for you would be the equivalent of signing my own death warrant," he said. "If I agreed to spy for the KGB, the CIA would find out about it in three days."

The conversation lasted for several hours. When he got up to leave, I wished him and his family well.

MARS reported my pitch to the CIA. Luckily, I made it back to Moscow without incident. But I remained intrigued by one thing he'd said—that the CIA would find out about my recruitment attempt "in three days." I included the detail in my report to the Center and brought it up with Kalugin back in Moscow. Kalugin thought MARS was making it up. The CIA didn't have sources for that kind of information, he said; it was simply an excuse to fend me off. Eight years later, however, I realized MARS wasn't inventing it. Until Ames and Hanssen made their reports, no one ever would have suspected how many KGB sources the CIA had.

Despite my failure to recruit MARS, the FCD praised my operation. Our installation of undetected eavesdropping equipment in the Beirut CIA safe house showed our strength to the Americans. Now they had to worry about how long the bugs had been in place, which of their agents had been exposed and how many operations had been compromised.

2

Diplomatic scandals were an unavoidable part of intelligence work. Most international spats remained low level and quickly blew over. But we deliberately fanned some to discredit our adversaries. The many methods included leaking false information to the press and expelling foreign diplomats. Disseminating disinformation, a favorite KGB activity, was the domain of FCD Section A. Its "black" measures included spreading compromising reports about foreign politicians, other well-known individuals and foreign intelligence services, chiefly by planting articles in the Soviet and foreign press. While KGB counterintelligence rarely took part in smear operations, we did occasionally propose them.

In the summer of 1977, my department assigned me to aid preparations for an international conference of UNESCO—the United Nations Educational, Scientific and Cultural Organization—in the Georgian capital Tbilisi. Moscow wanted the event, which would take place in October, to go flawlessly.

In response to requests to various *rezidenturas* for background information on the conference participants, the Paris station sent word that the American delegation would be headed by a senior diplomat named Constantine Warwariv, the U.S. representative to UNESCO. Several Soviet U.N. diplomats had met Warwariv and reported nothing unusual about the man—aside from one detail. In conversations with undercover KGB agents, Warwariv claimed to have been born in western Ukraine. After the war, he emigrated to the United States, earned a college degree and became a U.S. citizen before joining the State Department.

The Soviet Union annexed the largely Catholic Polish and Lithuanian-influenced enclave of western Ukraine as part of the Molotov-Ribbentrop Pact of 1939. But western Ukrainians resisted Soviet rule and Moscow was forced to fight an ongoing battle to suppress political and religious protesters. When World War II broke out, Ukrainian nationalists collaborated with German forces (which didn't stop Hitler's murderous rampage through the region).

Section A investigated the backgrounds of a number of Soviet émigrés who came to occupy prominent posts in the West. One goal was to show that while countries like the United States denounced Nazism, they actually employed former Nazi collaborators. Warwariv would be the newest target. We'd use blackmail. If the diplomat agreed to collaborate with the KGB, we'd promise not to expose him. But since there was little chance he'd acquiesce, the ultimate strategy would be to discredit him.

Following my request, the Ukrainain KGB dug up documents about members of a Warwariv family said to have collaborated with the Nazis during the war. Specifically, a father and son had been killed fighting the Red Army on the side of the Nazis. There was no other information, and no references to another son who could have fled to the West, so I sent an officer to the small town where the family had lived to investigate further. I sent another to Paris. There was little time to produce evidence, but as the conference drew near, my man in Ukraine sent back promising news: he'd found files on the group of Warwarivs in the local archives. The family actually had *two* sons and a daughter, and both the father and eldest son indeed died in fighting. The younger son retreated with the Nazis as the Red Army attacked German positions in 1944. The daughter, who was deaf, stayed in Ukraine with her mother. But that was the extent of it. There was nothing linking Constantine Warwariv, the UNESCO representative, to the youngest son of a family of Warwarivs who had fled Ukraine.

I conveyed the information to FCD chief Vladimir Kryuchkov, who authorized its use in a pitch to Warwariv in Tbilisi. I was chosen as the point man. Since I was unsure of the Nazi partisan connection, I had to improvise. In the ongoing propaganda battle between the United States and the USSR, tainting a high U.S. official would be a seen as a success. Therefore, simply coming up with insinuations was half the battle. I informed Georgian KGB chief Alexei Inauri about my plans and flew to subtropical Tbilisi three days before the conference was set to begin.

It was still warm and sunny when I arrived. I drove to KGB headquarters before surveying the Intourist hotel where Warwariv would be staying for how many men and what technical equipment I'd need. The day before the conference, I submitted a detailed proposal to Georgian KGB chief Inauri. The long-serving officer was known for imposing strict discipline. His organization was among the most effective of the KGB's regional Soviet branches. So it was a bit of a surprise to hear the veteran, after approving my ideas, propose something rash.

"The hell with it," he said. "Why wait? Why don't we just arrest him as a Nazi sympathizer?" We were all excited about the operation, but Inauri was getting a little carried away.

"We don't have enough information for that," I replied cautiously, repeating what I'd already said. "We have to find out his real identity first."

"*Ladno* [okay]," Inauri grunted, to my relief. The last hurdle was cleared. My work could proceed.

Warwariv arrived the next day with the other delegates. Following him from the airport, local KGB officers kept him in sight at all times. The American took an active part in the first day of the conference, which went off without a hitch. I decided to make my move that night.

Warwariv returned to his room at about eleven o'clock. I rapped on his door minutes later. Speaking in English, I said I was a KGB officer and gave an assumed name. The slim, wavy-haired diplomat opened the door. I demanded to see his passport, which he produced, then asked his title.

He hid any concern or anxiety. "I'm an employee of the United States State Department," he said, giving notice he'd be a tough nut to crack.

"Does the State Department know about your past?" I asked sternly.

"What do you mean?" he replied indignantly.

"Does the State Department know you collaborated with the Nazis?"

"I *what*? I don't know what you're talking about." But his incredulousness bordered on disingenuousness.

"Do you really think the American government would approve?" I continued. "We have proof. There's little point in denying it. We know your family collaborated with the Nazis during the war."

"That's nonsense. You're confusing me with someone else. I don't want to talk to you. Would you please leave?" He walked to his bed and lay down.

"You shouldn't behave like that." Menacingly, I took several steps forward. "You should really be more cooperative if you know what's best for you."

He stood his ground. "You're violating diplomatic protocol," he said, raising his voice. His face was red. "I have diplomatic immunity, so this might have repercussions for you." He got up from his bed.

"I'm not worried about repercussions. Otherwise I wouldn't be standing here. All I'm interested in is establishing justice."

There was no way of telling whether he was protesting because he had something to hide or because he was innocent. But I couldn't retreat without making sure. "We want you to be punished as a Nazi collaborator," I announced.

"Get out! What the hell could you do to me anyway? I'm an American citizen and I don't have to listen to your lies!"

I took a stab. "It's unfortunate you're being so uncooperative. We also have unofficial levers at our disposal. Don't forget your sister still lives on Soviet territory."

Warwariv paused a moment, then smiled. "You're wrong. My sister's in the United States."

He must have thought he'd neutralized my trump—that we could pressure his sister—because she too had emigrated, something the Ukrainian KGB had failed to inform us. But the UNESCO representative had actually stumbled, showing his hand. Admitting to having a sister confirmed his identity. Buoyed, I adopted an even tougher tone.

"Your sister may be out of our reach. But remember, you're on Soviet territory now."

Warwariv realized his mistake and changed tack. "Look, I was young at the time," he pleaded. "I didn't understand what I was doing. I didn't know what each side stood for. Anyway, I never took part in partisan fighting." He began pacing the room.

"Let's see what we can do about it," I said, making my pitch. I told him the State Department need never find out about his past if he agreed to spy for the KGB.

Our ensuing negotiations continued until four in the morning. Warwariv finally agreed to cooperate but claimed to be tired and proposed taking up the conversation the following day. I knew leaving his room would mean only a 50 percent chance of success, but I still felt optimistic. I hadn't expected to come this far. Although we hadn't reached a concrete agreement, I'd succeeded in getting Warwariv to admit to his identity. If all else failed, we'd be able to properly discredit him. If he reported my pitch to the State Department, he'd have to describe the compromising information we used. Either way, he was in a bad situation.

I left the room to let him sleep. The next morning, he showed up at his scheduled conference meetings; nothing seemed out of the ordinary. Around lunchtime, I received a call from the Center saying the U.S. embassy in Moscow had filed a letter of protest with the Soviet Foreign Ministry about a blackmail attempt against a diplomat in Tbilisi. Warwariv had decided not to cooperate with us, but the information about him was out and a scandal brewing. Back in Moscow, U.S. Ambassador Malcolm Toon issued a statement denouncing the provocation against Warwariv and asking for a meeting with Foreign Ministry representatives.

As soon as it became clear that Warwariv had gone straight to the State Department to report my pitch, the Center launched a propaganda campaign, publishing articles in the Soviet press blaming the United States for hypocrisy by employing Nazi sympathizers. Meanwhile, articles in the American press denounced KGB provocations against U.S. diplomats.

All that was predictable. What came as a surprise was fallout from the incident in various Moscow ministries and agencies. The Foreign Ministry sharply criticized the KGB, saying we'd acted improperly by carrying out clandestine activities, undermining efforts at rapprochement with the West. Kryuchkov was seriously reprimanded. Heads appeared ready to roll—mine especially. Deputy KGB chairman Georgy Tsinev—a powerful relative of Brezhnev's and head of the SCD—ordered a full report about the incident, promising that those who'd committed mistakes would be duly punished. He bitterly complained that he, as head of counterintelligence on Soviet soil, should have been informed of my plans. But by the time the requested report reached Tsinev's desk, it was too late for him to do much about it. Kryuchkov and Kalugin protected me by sending me and Directorate K deputy chief Nikolai Lykov to Berlin until things cooled off. Of course, I was grateful for their support. By the time I got back two weeks later, the dust had settled and tempers calmed.

The Americans filed several more protests with the Foreign Ministry. We shot back, publishing a book detailing episodes of Nazi collaboration that was translated and published in the West. Information about Warwariv was of course included. Washington then appealed to the Foreign Ministry to put an end to the affair, but we kept pressing ahead with our propaganda effort. Needless to say, we weren't interested in punishing Nazi collaborators. The entire incident concerned the KGB's operational interests—and in that, it was a great success. The State Department finally threw in the towel. Warwariv, whose continued presence in UNESCO tarnished Washington's reputation, was dismissed.

3

Oleg Kalugin was a fast-tracker. To go from student in 1958 to Washington deputy resident in 1965—it's a span of about six years. You just don't get to be deputy resident in the number-one residency in six years. But he does. That's the measure of Oleg. He's a very productive intelligence officer.

> —*David Major, former FBI supervisory special agent and director of counterintelligence at the National Security Council*

Oleg Kalugin is a traitor and a piece of shit for selling out his country to the Americans.

> —*Leonid Shebarshin, former FCD chief and acting KGB chairman*

After graduating from the Foreign Language Institute, Oleg Kalugin, in 1958, became one of the first Soviet Fulbright exchange students at Columbia University. Assigned to New York soon after, he shone under his cover as a Radio Moscow correspondent reporting on the United Nations. As a Line PR officer in Washington from 1965 to 1970, Kalugin circulated in the highest journalistic and political circles. Under cover as a press officer, he regularly met with columnists Walter Lippmann and Joseph Kraft and senators Robert Kennedy and William Fulbright, along with many other prominent Washington insiders.[1] His news reports about the United States were fascinating.

He got on well with the Washington *rezident*, Boris Solomatin. Kalugin returned to Moscow in 1970 after American journalist Jack Anderson exposed him as a KGB officer. Then Solomatin recommended him for work in Directorate K. Kalugin was soon appointed head of the counterintelligence branch and promoted to general, the youngest in KGB history.

I saw little of my old friend until I returned to Moscow from India in 1975 to work directly under him. As my immediate superior, Kalugin had to approve all my operations, which we often planned together. He was an excellent boss, rarely interfering with my work and usually only to support my actions. Working under him, I was awarded the coveted Honored Officer title in 1977 and the Order of the Red Star in 1979. But by then things had begun to change for both of us.

Kalugin was still serving his first tour in the United States as Radio Moscow correspondent when KGB officer Yuri Nosenko defected from the Soviet Union in 1964. Like many others pulled from *rezidenturas* around the world for fear of possible compromises, Kalugin was sent back to Moscow. (I was, to repeat, recalled from Australia for the same reason.) He had recently recruited his first agent, an American scientist of Russian descent named Anatoly Kotlobai, who provided the KGB with samples of formulas for solid rocket fuel. In his dealings with the KGB, Kotlobai used a pseudonym, Cook. The FBI soon came to suspect Cook and put him under surveillance. He promptly boarded an Air France flight—the French were unlikely to have given him up—and headed to Moscow.

To his surprise, Cook didn't enjoy life in Russia and began openly criticizing our workers' paradise. His complaints weren't well received. Soon the SCD launched an investigation into charges the scientist was actually a double agent working for the CIA. The Second Directorate had a harder time coming up with compelling evidence, however, so Cook soon found himself entrapped in a currency-exchange sting. He was arrested and sentenced to eight years in prison.

Convinced his former agent wasn't a CIA plant, Kalugin took his concerns to Yuri Andropov in 1979. Kalugin was close to the KGB chief, but that wasn't enough to convince him of his argument. Andropov nevertheless allowed him to interrogate Cook. When Kalugin met the agent he'd recruited twenty years earlier, Cook was livid. He cursed Kalugin, saying he regretted the day the two had met. Kalugin left feeling even more certain the man had nothing to do with U.S. intelligence.

Such interference did little to dispel certain clouds that were gathering over Kalugin's head. The young overachiever was fast earning the enmity of many in the FCD leadership, chief among them Vladimir Kryuchkov, the FCD chief and longtime Andropov confidante. Kryuchkov had served in the Soviet embassy in Budapest during the Hungarian Revolution in 1956, when Andropov was ambassador to Hungary. (Moscow's suppression of Hungarian reformers led by Prime Minister Imre Nagy proved a seminal event for Andropov, who subsequently became intent on tackling Soviet critics.)

The outspoken Kalugin never got on with Kryuchkov, whom he privately criticized as an uninspiring careerist. For his part, Kryuchkov was particularly unhappy over Kalugin's close relationship with Grigory Grigorenko, the former head of foreign counterintelligence who was now chief of the SCD. Kryuchkov saw Grigorenko's friendship with Kalugin as a threat to his own control over the FCD. Others in the old guard saw Kalugin as a loose cannon with a playboy lifestyle that reflected a lack of discipline. When rumors began circulating that not only Cook but even Kalugin was an American spy, Kryuchkov did nothing to squelch them.

Kalugin again complained to Andropov—who advised him to back off and suggested he round out his knowledge of the KGB with a short posting to Leningrad to learn the Byzantine ways of the internal service. Kalugin agreed, leaving Moscow in December 1979 to become first deputy chief of the Leningrad KGB, responsible for thousands of officers. He expected to be back in Moscow in a year. But Kryuchkov thought otherwise—and Kalugin's continued criticism played into his hands. Arriving in the former imperial capital, Kalugin was dismayed by what he saw as inefficiency within the KGB internal service. He thought he had the influence to make his criticism heard. However, his appeals to the Party only made matters worse for him—as did a letter he sent to the newly installed Communist Party general secretary, Mikhail Gorbachev, in 1985, urging him to take action against KGB political influence.

As Kalugin fell increasingly out of favor throughout the 1980s, he strengthened his ties with other critics, including his fellow 1958 Fulbright scholar, Alexander Yakovlev. The former Party ideologue headed the Communist Party's propaganda department until 1972, when he published an article denouncing anti-Semitism. It got him posted as Soviet ambassador to Canada, which was banishment from the Party's central apparatus. Yakovlev remained in the political wilderness until Gorbachev—at the time a top Politburo member—met him during a trip to Canada. On becoming the Soviet leader, he brought him back to Moscow to head the prestigious Institute of World Economy and International Relations. By 1987, Gorbachev had made Yakovlev a member of the Politburo and installed him as his top aide.

Kalugin also established ties with the entourage of Boris Yeltsin, fast rising from provincial Party chief to Moscow city boss before being swept into power in regional parliamentary elections in 1990. Despite his maneuvering, however, the odds were against Kalugin. Instead of changing, the system came down on him. Kryuchkov was calling the shots and made sure Kalugin stayed in Leningrad—banished from the Center for eight years, until 1987.

After Kalugin departed for Leningrad, his successor as head of Directorate K, Anatoly Kireyev, compiled a list of officers with ties to Kalugin as part of the effort to attack his predecessor's influence. I knew my name was on the list. Although I felt no fallout from my ties to Kalugin at the time, my connection to him would continue to affect how I was perceived within the KGB.

Kirpichenko later wrote that counterintelligence floundered under Kalugin, who failed, he said, to spearhead any serious operations during his tenure. Kirpichenko charged him with sleeping on the job while the CIA was out recruiting the tens of agents later betrayed by Ames and Hanssen. In fact, most of those recruitments took place later in the 1980s, after Kalugin had left. Actually, Directorate K stepped up its penetration of foreign intelligence agencies under his leadership. Kalugin was right to boast that when he was foreign counterintelligence chief, Line KR—the counterintelligence department in foreign *rezidenturas*—almost doubled in size and nearly tripled the number of recruited agents.[2] He was nothing if not highly active, even aggressive.

Had he really been an American agent, Kalugin would have lost little time in fleeing the Soviet Union. Instead, he squared his shoulders and waded into the rising tide of his unpopularity. When I saw him in Leningrad in the late 1980s in the imposing KGB headquarters on central Liteiniy Prospect, he finally admitted that he'd been banished from the Center because of suspicions by Kryuchkov and Kirpichenko. When I insisted that he take the matter seriously, Kalugin waved his hand dismissively. "Kirpichenko doesn't make decisions according to how they'll play out in the directorate," he said. "He doesn't try to solve problems to address the situation at hand. No. He makes each of his decisions according to how it will look in Kryuchkov's eyes."

How did someone entirely faithful to the Party and the KGB— an officer promoted faster than anyone else in the service and who still might have had a great future—fall from favor so quickly? Kalugin's rise and fall weren't entirely unrelated. His high morale, aggressiveness, tenacity bordering on a sense of invincibility—all that ran afoul of the conservatism of Kryuchkov, Kirpichenko and the rest of the leadership. From 1979, he headed toward an almost inevitable break with the KGB. My own career would follow a different path but remain linked to Kalugin's in a way.

4

Several months before Kalugin left Moscow, I met him in his office. "You know I want to be Washington *rezident*," he said, squinting his narrow eyes at me.

"Yes, Oleg, I know." It was open knowledge that he was up next for the job.

"Well *tovarish* [comrade], I want you to be there too. As my deputy. Line KR."

It was an exciting prospect, but I doubted whether the Americans would give me a visa. They knew me from my previous postings—officers such as Haviland Smith, whom I knew from Beirut, were now posted in Washington—and would spot me a mile away. Surely my involvement in the MARS and Warwariv cases would bar me from the United States. Even if I were somehow able to get there, my history would make me wide open for provocations.

Days later, Victor Grushko, head of the FCD Third department—which oversaw foreign intelligence in the United Kingdom—offered me the post of *rezident* in Ireland. It would be a significant promotion, giving me a major leadership role. But I knew Kalugin was set on my going to Washington. Grushko urged me to talk to him, but he continued to insist.

My family life had changed dramatically since I'd returned to Moscow. My son, Alyosha, graduated from secondary school in 1976 and enrolled in the Moscow State Institute of Foreign Relations (MGIMO), the country's most prestigious college. That meant postings and trips abroad would no longer have a negative impact on family life. With Alyosha now able to be on his own, Elena and I had reached a new stage in our lives. In 1977, she gave birth to a baby daughter, Alyona. With no personal reasons to keep me in Moscow, I was more than ready to jump back into the game with another tour.

In February 1979, I applied for a two-week visa to the United States. Surprisingly, it was granted. I visited New York and Washington, lying low the whole time.

The atmosphere in the KGB *rezidenturas* in both cities was fairly tense. In April 1978, Arkady Shevchenko, a top Soviet diplomat serving as United Nations undersecretary-general, had defected after working two years as a joint CIA-FBI agent. In addition, the FBI had arrested two KGB agents, Valdik Enger and Rudolf Chernyaev, both employees of the U.N. secretariat, in May 1978, accusing them of accepting classified information about antisubmarine warfare from a U.S. naval officer. The officer had been a double agent, working for the FBI and the Naval Investigative Service. Diplomatic immunity saved a third Soviet U.N. employee, Vladimir Zinyakin, from arrest. Enger and Chernyaev were tried for espionage and sentenced to fifty years in prison. Meeting them in a U.N. office after their trial, I was pleasantly surprised to see both men calm and confident that the Soviet government would come to their rescue. Indeed, they were later freed in exchange for the release of five jailed Soviet dissidents.

Despite a snowstorm that severely restricted my ability to check out my future turf, I realized I was looking forward to my new posting. In the fall, Elena, Alyona and I packed for Washington and left for what would be my final tour abroad. By that time, Kalugin was already in Leningrad. He would never become Washington *rezident*. Our paths were already diverging.

_6_

WASHINGTON STATION: THE REDEFECTOR

1

When Cherkashin came to the United States, the FBI was quick to identify exactly who he was. I was on the streets in Washington in 1979, on the KGB squad, and I knew everything we knew about Cherkashin. We knew his reputation. He was considered a heavy hitter, a top gun. You don't get to be the chief of Line KR in Washington DC unless you're important. And generally that means a proven, good intelligence officer.

—*David Major, retired FBI supervisory special agent and former director of counterintelligence at the National Security Council*

The sun baked the Soviet embassy's slate roof several blocks north of the White House one day in late spring 1980. After lunch I was typing a cable to Moscow when the chief security officer knocked on my door. A tall blond with a handlebar mustache, Vitaly Yurchenko was unassuming, chiefly distinguished by worries about his seemingly robust health. This time, Yurchenko was even graver than usual, and almost breathless.

"Victor Ivanovich, there's an American downstairs. He says he wants to give us intelligence documents."

"Who is he?"

"He says he worked for the National Security Agency. He approached the guard and asked to see the head of security, so I went down to check it out."

"What does he look like?"

"Not very well dressed . . . and he has a beard."

A volunteer walking into the embassy was always big news. "Is there anything to confirm what he says?"

"He's brought some papers. I didn't want to look at them before checking with you."

"*Khorosho* [good]. Take him to a briefing room downstairs. Check what he's brought. If anything really looks like intelligence material, bring it here immediately."

Yurchenko disappeared. I resumed work on my cable until he reappeared with a pile of papers several minutes later. "He says his name's Ronald Pelton, and he was fired from the NSA last year. He's willing to give us information he thinks we'll find very interesting. He says he wants money."

Yurchenko stood by as I leafed through the sheaf of papers. No technical expert, I couldn't properly judge their value, but the documents appeared to outline several NSA operations. Although nothing extraordinary, they seemed to support the man's story. At the very least, the sensitive nature of the papers all but ruled out his being an FBI dangle. So did his direct approach—asking for money right away (as opposed to most walk-ins, who claim they want to spy for ideological reasons to prove their sincerity).

"This is interesting," I told Yurchenko without looking up. I had to quickly decide how to handle the case. I didn't want to deal directly with Pelton—if that was indeed his name—until I was surer of his motives and intentions. "We have to find out how he got here," I continued. "Ask him if he thought anyone saw him arriving. Ask him who else knows about his decision. Did he tell his family? Tell him that if he wants money, we're ready to negotiate."

Yurchenko went back downstairs and returned twenty minutes later. "He says the FBI could have spotted him arriving downstairs, but he wasn't sure. He didn't see anyone. He says no one else knows of his decision to come here."

"Good." Needing more time to examine the documents, I sent Yurchenko back down with more questions.

After the walk-in was fully debriefed, it was time to get him out. I again summoned Yurchenko. "Get his contact information. Tell him we'll get in touch about where and when to meet."

The FBI had probably spotted "Pelton" entering the embassy. There would be trouble, however, only if they managed to identify him, the chance of which we needed to do everything possible to minimize. Smuggling him out in disguise seemed the best plan.

"Get a van and a couple of men dressed as maintenance workers," I told Yurchenko. "Get Pelton a change of clothes. He has to look like the workmen. You said he had a beard? Shave it."

The *rezident* approved my plan to smuggle our volunteer to the residential compound on Wisconsin Avenue, keep him there for several hours, and then let him out into the city. When Yurchenko reported that everything was ready, I gave the go-ahead. Pelton and the three men went to a back entrance where food supplies were usually delivered and conspicuously loaded some empty boxes into a van. Then they drove out of the grounds and headed toward the compound. Several hours later, Yurchenko put Pelton in the backseat of an embassy car. Then, as he lay low, an officer named Gennady Vasilenko drove him around the city. When they stopped at a shopping mall, Pelton jumped out and disappeared into a crowd.

Over the next several days, most of the walk-in's story checked out. He'd actually resigned from the NSA after fourteen years of service as a cryptologist. Facing dire financial trouble, he'd decided to earn some money by coming to us.

Androsov and I decided to assign Pelton to Vasilenko, the young counterintelligence officer who took part in his recruitment. Meeting Pelton in a downtown pizza joint two weeks later, Vasilenko handed him a package containing documents outlining our conditions. They described how to load dead drops and communicate with the *rezidentura* using pay phones. They also told him how much we were willing to pay. Our newest spy readily agreed.

2

Soon after I arrived in Washington, Haviland Smith—the CIA officer who had gone up against Rem Krassilnikov in Beirut—made a pass at me. Now CIA Washington station chief, Smith found out about my arrival from the FBI. Saying they didn't have "access" to me, Smith's contacts in the bureau appeared happy to let him have a go. He knew I liked hockey, so settled on taking one of his sons to see a U.S.-Soviet game in early 1980. The FBI even got him tickets. Smith relished the event, laughing at the aversion of his son—an active-duty marine—to the "commies" he saw.

I too enjoyed the game. During a break between periods, I got up to buy a hot dog. Smith slipped into line directly behind me. When I noticed him by chance, he appeared to ignore me. I tried to hide my surprise. After I'd paid, I couldn't avoid turning around again. Now Smith looked straight at me. "Jesus, don't I know you?" he asked. "Who the hell are you? Did you serve in the Middle East, in Tehran?"

That caught me off guard. "No, no, no," I said.

"I know your face," he replied. "I just don't know who you are."

I did everything I could to indicate utter disinterest in Smith's approach. Of course I knew who he was, but I wasn't going to give the Americans an inch. It was better to let them have their work cut out for them.

3

Yurchenko, head security officer of the *rezidentura*, was reassigned to Moscow in June, a little over a month after Pelton's recruitment. I wouldn't see him for five years. When we'd meet again, it would also be in Washington—under circumstances I'd never have predicted in a million years.

Now that I was sure Pelton was a legitimate agent, I decided to meet him myself. One morning I left the embassy compound by car with two other officers. We headed north, turned west on P Street, circled around Dupont Circle and drove toward Georgetown. Our driver spotted an FBI car following us. They were hard to miss because they were always the cheapest American models.

I decided to use a backup plan, which was to drive to the nearest supermarket. One of the officers got out and returned with a six-pack of beer. Then we turned around and headed back to the embassy. Half an hour later, I tried again—this time in a different car with two other officers. As we turned a corner onto 21st Street, the driver slowed and I jumped out, taking a bag I'd brought. It was one of the few times I was out on the streets myself. I walked to the Dupont Circle metro station, took a train north to Cleveland Park and hailed a taxi on Connecticut Avenue. Inside, I checked to see if I was being followed. Then I pulled a jacket out of my bag and put it on. I unknotted my tie and donned a hat and sunglasses. An hour later, I was face-to-face with balding, stocky Pelton. He was nervous but clearly earnest, which was important for my own confidence.

In subsequent meetings, Vasilenko usually met Pelton or loaded and collected dead drops by car, which was the easiest way to do it. The best places were remote—alongside a road or in a field. After loading a drop, Vasilenko would call Pelton from a pay telephone. When Vasilenko had to meet him in person, it was often in a crowded shopping mall. Vasilenko's wife, with whom he'd ostensibly be shopping, often helped him watch Pelton arrive for meetings or unload dead drops.

Six months after his first approach, Vasilenko helped spirit him abroad for the first of several long meetings with top Directorate K officers in Vienna, where they felt safe debriefing foreign agents. I admired Pelton for his bluntness, but running him wasn't always smooth sailing. He disappeared after some months—presumably he felt he'd earned enough money—and turned up again only in 1981 after we found him living in the Virginia suburb of Vienna. Since Vasilenko was one of the few people who knew what he looked like, Androsov had to dispatch him there to find the errant agent.

In one typical rendezvous that followed, ten cars drove out of the Soviet embassy compound in Washington, one after another. Each took a different route. Sitting behind the wheel in one of them, Vasilenko headed north on 16th Street, then turned west on M Street. He turned south on 24th Street and east on K Street before doubling back. After driving three hours that way to shake off any FBI tail, he turned south and headed for Tysons Corner Center, a shopping mall in suburban Virginia. Pelton was waiting for him in the mall's parking lot.

Most of Pelton's information concerned general NSA activities. There was only a little top secret intelligence until he dropped his first bombshell during a trip abroad soon after we reestablished contact with him. It was then that he handed over documents about an NSA operation called IVY BELLS.

Reading about it in the *rezidentura*, I found the information almost too incredible to be true. IVY BELLS was the code name for a highly ingenious, wildly expensive and risky U.S. Navy operation that tapped into a secret Soviet communications cable at the bottom of the Sea of Okhotsk, which separated the Russian mainland from the Kamchatka peninsula. The cable connected a submarine base at the peninsular city of Petropavlovsk to Pacific Fleet headquarters in Vladivostok.

Operating from a specially outfitted submarine in August 1972, U.S. Navy divers clamped a tap containing a battery-operated recording device onto the cable.[1] During the following eight years, American submarines made regular trips at six- to eight-week intervals to replace the tapes, which recorded conversations between the submarine base and naval brass who thought they were safe from prying American satellites and listening posts. The tapes provided intercepts of military command messages and gave technological information, command procedures and operational patterns. IVY BELLS was a major success and Washington—which had spent hundreds of millions of dollars on the operation—was in the process of developing it further. Pelton shut down the whole project for $35,000.

4

As a Soviet naval survey ship searched the Sea of Okhotsk for the American eavesdropping device, Moscow's relations with Washington went from bad to worse. American newspapers directed a constant barrage of criticism at the Soviet Union. Aeroflot had stopped flying to New York after we invaded Afghanistan in 1979. Protestors demonstrated against Soviet policy, often over Moscow's treatment of Jews, and pressured us to let more people emigrate. Every Soviet defection to the United States ratcheted up the tension.

Looming over everything was the possibility of nuclear war. The election of hard-line right-winger Ronald Reagan in 1980

helped convince KGB chairman Yuri Andropov that the United
States was planning a nuclear first strike against the Soviet
Union. He ordered most KGB foreign stations to take part in a
large-scale operation called RIAN (after an acronym for "nuclear
attack") to find evidence of a U.S. plot. Andropov's fears intensi-
fied after he became Soviet leader in 1982.

As part of the operation, KGB officers routinely drove past the
Pentagon, the State Department and other national security institutions to look for outward signs of heightened activity.

By the following year, RIAN had become an intelligence-
gathering priority. No evidence of a U.S. nuclear first strike plan
was ever found, but fears ran especially high in 1983, when
NATO carried out a nuclear launch exercise called ABLE ARCHER.
The program was reported to the Center as a real NATO alert,
and Soviet nuclear forces were placed on the highest alert since
the Cuban missile crisis in 1962.[2]

Despite the tensions, reports that Washington and Moscow
came close to nuclear war are exaggerated.

Apart from the daily stress of operating on the territory of the
Main Adversary, I grew to like the United States. I enjoyed traveling most of all. My family was relatively well-off after my many
tours abroad. With money to spend, Elena, Alyona and I visited
various cities, amusement parks and the Delaware coast to swim
in the Atlantic. We drove to New York City and Niagara Falls.
I'd sometimes combine such trips with work. Before the 1984
Olympics, the Center requested statistical and performance evaluations of American athletes training for competition. The Politburo wanted the information to help decide whether or not to
participate in the event. (Washington had boycotted the 1980
winter Olympics in Moscow to protest our 1979 invasion of Afghanistan.) That prompted a visit to Lake Placid, where obtaining the information wasn't difficult since everything was publicly
available. I had plenty of time left over for sightseeing.

I also enjoyed meeting the American capital's interesting cast of characters. Among our acquaintances was Elena Kamkina, who ran a well-known Russian-language bookstore in Rockville, Maryland. The shop was called Victor Kamkin, after her husband, who'd opened the store. Elena took over after he died in 1974. That Cold War institution—which was subsidized by the Soviet government but nevertheless sold books banned in Russia—attracted all types from students and academics to Russian émigrés and U.S. government officials. Although Kamkina was never in any way connected to my intelligence work, she provided a social outlet, throwing dinners and Christmas parties for the Soviet community. She came from a wealthy Russian family that fled the Revolution in 1917. Although an American through and through, she always remained interested in Russia and enjoyed meeting Soviets.

Meanwhile, my wife, Elena, slowly overcoming her suspicion of Americans, was able to speak to those we knew without worrying about being compromised. But certain incidents put up her guard again. One involved *People* magazine, which Elena enjoyed reading. One day, she received a letter from the magazine saying she'd won $1 million in a lottery. When she told me about it, I joked that a million dollars wouldn't be enough for us. But after that, convinced that the letter was part of a provocation, she wouldn't leave the residential compound without me.

Another incident took place at the same Tysons Corner Center mall in Virginia. When we returned to our car after shopping one day, I noticed a letter behind a windshield wiper. It offered $1 million for my cooperation and provided a telephone number. Knowing I was in plain view and being watched, I tore the paper into little pieces and dropped them into a garbage bin.

That wasn't the only such letter I received or approach by other means. One day, Elena and I were on a Delaware beach with some other embassy couples. When I got up to walk along the sand, several men who had been sitting behind us followed me. We later noticed they were carrying eavesdropping equipment. After that, we swam only at the embassy's country house on the Chesapeake Bay, where no one ever harassed us.

5

Soviet intelligence was the best in the world. Of course in terms of the number of personnel and the amount allocated in budgets, the KGB couldn't compare to the CIA. In 1989–90 the CIA's budget was $30 billion. The KGB's was 5 billion rubles [around $8 billion]. And the KGB included not only foreign and domestic intelligence, but also border guards and other troops. And yet the two agencies went head to head—and the KGB did a better job. Why did we have such an advantage? Because most of our officers were passionate about what they were doing. We were paid good wages compared to the average Soviet citizen, but they still weren't that great. We made slightly more than Soviet diplomats but much less than our colleagues in the CIA. The KGB was really about enthusiasm and patriotism.

—*Leonid Shebarshin, former FCD chief and acting KGB chairman*

In the summer of 1983, the Soviet embassy in Switzerland received a letter accompanying an application for a tourist visa to Moscow. The writer, an American, proposed meeting a KGB representative to hand over information we might find "interesting." As a rendezvous site, the visa applicant suggested Washington's Capitol building—a bold choice but not necessarily a bad one, since the FBI was unlikely to suspect the tourist-clogged site as a KGB venue for meeting agents. The American's name was Edward Lee Howard.

After the Center forwarded us Howard's letter, I discussed his offer with Washington *rezident* Stanislav Androsov. We decided against the meeting because there was no way to be sure it wouldn't be an FBI trap. In the ongoing U.S.-Soviet propaganda war, exposure of a KGB recruitment in no less hallowed a site than the Congress building would go down poorly. We informed the Center, and Howard was turned down.

That, however, wasn't the last I heard of Edward Lee Howard. The former Peace Corps volunteer joined the CIA after working for the U.S. Agency for International Development. Selected for a deep cover Moscow assignment in 1982, the thirty-one-year-old enrolled at the Farm in the most advanced CIA operative training program, the Internal Operations course run by brash ex-marine Jack Platt. Howard's wife, Mary—also a former Peace Corps volunteer in Latin America—was trained to help him.

Howard had a problem, however, which he failed to mention when he signed up with the CIA—heavy drinking and drug use. Instead, he resolved to use his glamorous new job as a CIA operative to turn over a new leaf. According to Platt, Howard, who wanted to be a hero, took his training seriously and diligently. Mary Howard would later tell Platt that the six-week course was one of the few periods her husband abstained from drugs and alcohol because he didn't want to damage his chances of going to Moscow. He relied heavily on his wife and unleashed his frustrations over the exacting training program on her.

To prepare him for running agents and conducting eavesdropping operations, Howard was trained to load dead drops, operate complex eavesdropping equipment and evade surveillance. He was also briefed about several highly sensitive operations in Moscow. After he'd all but completed his training, however, he failed a routine polygraph test, revealing he'd lied about his past drug use. There were other complications too. He'd been caught stealing and cheating on a training exercise. He was fired the following month, in May 1983.

Howard left feeling betrayed.[3] Blaming the CIA for dashing his dream of becoming a hero, he resumed his heavy drinking and made prank phone calls to the U.S. embassy in Moscow. He also nursed dreams of revenge. The CIA kept an eye on him but failed—crucially, as it would turn out for U.S. national security—to inform the FBI that he posed a potential risk.[4] Howard even told a CIA psychologist sent to evaluate him that after he was fired he skulked outside the Soviet consulate in Washington but resisted the temptation to go in.

A year after his first failed attempt to contact the KGB, the Center reconsidered our rejection and issued instructions to contact him. Using the address from his old visa application, we traced him to a townhouse in the Washington suburbs. He'd since moved out and calls to the telephone numbers he supplied got us no closer. Assuming he'd sold his house, we began looking for a real estate agency that might have handled the transaction. Sure enough, we found it. I instructed an officer to ask for Howard's new coordinates by posing as a long-lost friend. We soon tracked him down to New Mexico.

With his new number in hand, I called to remind him of the letter he'd written a year earlier. Although surprised by his claim that he barely recalled it, I was encouraged by his enthusiasm about the prospect of working for us. I told him he'd have to travel to Vienna to meet his handler and that we'd contact him later to inform him when and how to go there. He agreed. The Washington *rezidentura* had finished its job; the Center would handle him from now on, arranging a system of sending postcards to the Soviet consulate in San Francisco for him to contact the KGB.

6

Many intelligence and counterintelligence operations find links, often to the surprise of those involved. Reenter Aldrich Ames. On June 13, 1985, I stepped into a blast of hot summer air, leaving Ames and the neon beer signs of Chadwicks bar beneath Washington's elevated Whitehurst freeway. I soared with the knowledge that I'd just precipitated a momentous day in KGB history.

I was yet unaware of its full significance. Later I'd learn that hours earlier, my old Beirut mentor Rem Krassilnikov—now the KGB's domestic counterintelligence mastermind as head of the Second Chief Directorate's American department—had orchestrated the arrest of a young CIA case officer back in Moscow. That operation too helped turn the tide of the intelligence battle in our favor.

The officer's name was Paul Stombaugh Jr. He was on his way to a park in southwest Moscow to meet a Russian scientist named Adolf Tolkachev. Stombaugh saw him in the distance as he approached. Actually, the figure waiting for him was an actor. Tolkachev was already in Lefortovo prison awaiting a trial that would lead to his execution. He had given Krassilnikov the information needed to set up the sham rendezvous with Stombaugh, who was arrested carrying rubles worth $150,000, concealed miniature cameras, medicine for Tolkachev and other incriminating materials.[5]

The intended recipient wasn't just any scientist—or any agent. Adolf Tolkachev, an employee of a top secret design bureau developing new technology for fighter planes, was the CIA's most important spy since Oleg Penkovsky. Code-named SPHERE (then VANQUISH), Tolkachev provided Langley with tens of thousands of pages of secret documents from the classified library in his office. Photographing them with miniature cameras, he supplied reams of information about Soviet avionics, radar, missile and other weapons systems for fighter aircraft. Using his intelligence enabled Washington to save billions of dollars and many years of research—and achieve superior technology. Tolkachev "paid the rent" at Langley because his services alone saved the U.S. government enough money to justify the expense of all other CIA operations.[6]

All that nearly never happened. Having let Tolkachev slip through its fingers many times, the CIA finally accepted his services thanks only to his unbelievably tenacious and persistent efforts to be taken seriously. He made his first move in 1977. Approaching an American fueling his car at a gasoline station reserved for foreign diplomats near the U.S. embassy, he slipped the driver a note.[7] That man happened to be CIA station chief Robert Fulton. Tolkachev's anonymous message said its writer worked at an institute developing radar technology and promised to give important information.

The CIA didn't respond. Tolkachev left a second note, then a third. But Langley's leadership, caught in a post-Angleton spike of suspicion, had ordered a stand-down, forbidding its operatives to recruit new agents. The agency was convinced the notes were a KGB provocation. It took the arrival of a new station chief the same year—the headstrong Gardner "Gus" Hathaway—to lobby Washington to allow the Moscow station to contact the persistent volunteer. Hathaway, who would become head of CIA counterintelligence in 1985, earned fame after a fire broke out in the embassy. He allegedly blocked a brigade of ax-wielding Soviet firefighters—really KGB officers—from entering the CIA communications area.

Tolkachev continued to leave notes, each disclosing more information about himself. Thanks to Hathaway's persistence, the CIA finally decided to make contact—but missed speaking to him on the telephone when his wife picked up the receiver. Tolkachev's approaches continued. Once he even walked up to the ambassador's residence, Spaso House in central Moscow. He told the Americans he had grown to hate the Soviet system and wanted to do all he could to help bring it down.

Many months later, the CIA finally realized it was dealing with a top scientist who had access to highly sensitive technological information. Tolkachev began working for the Americans in January 1979. He continued for six years, telling no one, not even his wife or son, about his secret life.

When the KGB finally learned about Tolkachev's activities, Krassilnikov organized an arrest using the elite special operations Alpha unit. It took place when the scientist was returning from his dacha one Sunday in April 1985. Alpha men posing as traffic police stopped his car and motioned for it to park near a van whose driver was enduring a dressing-down by one of the phony policemen. Men burst from the van to handcuff and disrobe the spy to prevent suicide. Then they dragged him off to Lefortovo.[8]

The KGB searched Tolkachev's apartment in one of Moscow's seven landmark neo-Gothic "Stalin skyscrapers" built to house the Soviet elite. This one, at Ploschad Vosstaniya (Uprising Square), was for air force pilots and personnel. They found shelves and closets crammed with millions of rubles. Tolkachev hadn't known what to do with his money.

He'd been betrayed by a CIA recruit preparing to take over his handling from Stombaugh. The trainee's name was Edward Lee Howard.

7

Leaving my office late on the chilly evening of November 2, 1985, I drove toward home in the Soviet residential compound, located up Wisconsin Avenue next to the construction site of a new embassy that would replace the old 16th Street mansion. What the Americans would soon call the Year of the Spy had already been strange and momentous, with waves of exposures on both sides. Of course, the CIA didn't realize the central reasons for the KGB's successes—our recruitment of Robert Hanssen and Aldrich Ames—until years later. I thought I was prepared for anything after those coups. But the sight of Stanislav Androsov walking toward me as I parked in the underground garage heralded news I could never have expected.

The *rezident* looked concerned. "Ivanov told me you'd arrived," he said as I climbed out of my car. He was speaking of the watch officer. "Yurchenko's back."

"What?" I stammered. The stunning news was the last thing I expected to hear from Androsov.

"He's upstairs now. He showed up about twenty minutes ago. Says he decided to come back himself."

"I can't believe it! *Sukin syn* [that son of a bitch]!" My mind was spinning. How could Yurchenko possibly be back?

KGB Colonel Vitaly Yurchenko had worked under me as the head of security in Washington until 1980. It was he who handled the walk-in recruitment of Ronald Pelton, the former NSA cryptologist who betrayed IVY BELLS. Sent back to Moscow, Yurchenko was eventually promoted to deputy chief of the Fifth department in my own Directorate K. I hadn't seen him since he left Washington and had heard little about him until four months earlier, on August 1.

I was in my office that day when the *rezidentura* received an urgent ciphered cable from Kryuchkov: *Yurchenko had defected to the Americans during a trip to Rome!* Since he knew about several Washington operations besides Pelton, we scrambled to figure out what he could compromise. One fear dwarfed all others—he may have known about Ames. Yurchenko had no access to information about the top KGB asset, but he may have heard something from the active rumor mill back at Yasenevo. Kyruchkov asked whether it would make sense to exfiltrate Ames to Moscow.

I racked my brains to remember everything I knew about Yurchenko. Before coming to Washington in 1975, he'd been assigned to the Third Chief Directorate, responsible for military counterintelligence. I worked with him regularly for six months after I arrived in Washington. He was a dependable head of security. He handled his team of officers efficiently and was generally well respected by, and on good terms with, the embassy's diplomatic staff. He was experienced in keeping tabs on the Soviet community. He conducted himself unimpeachably in the Pelton case. At the end of his posting in 1980, I'd sent back a positive evaluation of his work.

Yurchenko rarely attracted attention to himself around the embassy but sometimes showed eccentricities that I attributed to stress. Although his athletic body radiated health, he saw any small tic or sickness as a sign of a major, incurable disease. He refused to eat many foods and constantly gulped a variety of medicines.

One sweltering summer day, we were both upstairs in the *rezidentura*: "I'm thirsty as hell," Yurchenko said, speaking for both of us.

I offered him water from a pitcher in my office.

"Is it boiled?" he asked.

"No. But what do you care? It's American."

"It's not filtered properly. I only drink filtered or bottled water— at the very least boiled."

"Okay, whatever you say." Pouring myself a glass, I noted Yurchenko's attitude. It was unusual for Russians, who were used to the worst water pumped by Soviet systems.

Back in Moscow, Yurchenko was assigned to Directorate K's Fifth department, which kept tabs on Soviets and Soviet organizations abroad. He got on well with Dmitri Yakushkin, the former

Washington *rezident*. When his old boss returned to the Center in 1982 to head the FCD's First (American) department, he recommended promoting him and installing him as his deputy. Yurchenko took up the new post in April 1985.

Nothing had prepared the Center for what happened several months later, when Yurchenko engineered a trip to visit the Rome *rezidentura*, ostensibly to sound out a possible agent, a radio operator at the U.S. Navy communications center in Naples who had volunteered to spy for the KGB. Claiming the walk-in, Thomas Hayden, was a CIA dangle, Yurchenko spread rumors in Yasenevo about his unreliability.[9]

In Rome on August 1, Yurchenko told his colleagues that he wanted to visit the Vatican museums. After leaving the Soviet embassy residential compound in the city's western suburbs, he made his way instead to a hotel opposite the U.S. embassy on Rome's Fifth Avenue, the Via Veneto. He phoned the embassy switchboard and was directed to cross the street. He'd decided to leave his wife, daughter and adopted son behind in Moscow. He was about to hand the CIA the highest-ranking KGB officer ever to defect to the United States.

During his initial debriefing in the embassy, Yurchenko told the CIA he'd seen cables sent from the Vienna *rezidentura* describing an American volunteer, "Mr. Robert," who had betrayed Adolf Tolkachev.[10] Yurchenko also told the CIA that, among other intelligence, the KGB was receiving information from a mole in the National Security Agency who had signed up in 1980 and betrayed Operation IVY BELLS. That explained how the Soviet navy located the prized eavesdropping device. Although Yurchenko participated in Pelton's recruitment, he claimed to have forgotten the agent's real name.

CIA Soviet and East European (SE) division chief Burton Gerber and his deputies in Langley still had no idea who betrayed

My family. Clockwise, starting from the top left: me, Petya, Masha, Vasya, mother. (CREDIT: VICTOR CHERKASHIN)

My father, Ivan Yakovlevich, an officer of the NKVD, the KGB's predecessor.
(CREDIT: VICTOR CHERKASHIN)

As a student (on far right) at the intelligence institute in front of the Winter Palace in Leningrad, 1953. (CREDIT: VICTOR CHERKASHIN)

Lubyanka, the KGB's central Moscow headquarters. (CREDIT: GREGORY FEIFER)

Oleg Penkovsky. British and American intelligence compromised their top agent by practicing sloppy tradecraft. (CREDIT: DAVID MAJOR)

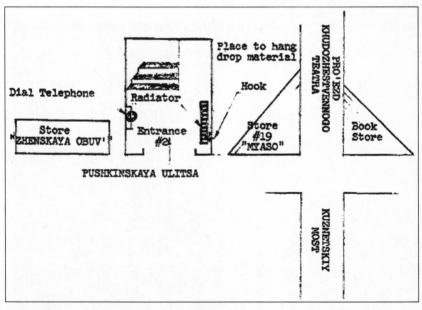

A CIA diagram of a dead drop site for Penkovsky in central Moscow. (CREDIT: CIA)

First tour: Elena and me in Australia (at left) with Antonina Solodova (wife of the Soviet trade representative) and her children Sasha and Tanya, 1963. (CREDIT: VICTOR CHERKASHIN)

With Rem Krassilnikov in Beirut, 1969. Krassilnikov helped teach me the ropes of foreign intelligence operations. (CREDIT: VICTOR CHERKASHIN)

In India, at the presentation of a portrait of Indira Gandhi by Soviet artist Ilya Glazunov. From right: me, Glazunov, his wife and a Soviet embassy official. (CREDIT: VICTOR CHERKASHIN)

Leonid Shebarshin, head of the KGB's First Chief Directorate, whom I got to know when he was deputy *rezident* in India. (CREDIT: LEONID SHEBARSHIN)

Oleg Kalugin, the youngest KGB general and former head of counter-intelligence. Foreign intelligence chief Vladimir Kryuchkov suspected my friendship with my former classmate. (CREDIT: ITAR-TASS)

KGB Chairman Vladimir Kryuchkov (flanked by Boris Yeltsin and Mikhail Gorbachev). Ames helped Kryuchkov detract from the KGB's failures and rise to head the service. He suspected anyone, including me, who knew how he got there. (CREDIT: ITAR-TASS)

CIA Director Bill Casey discounted warnings Langley had been penetrated by a dangerous mole. (CREDIT: AP/WIDE WORLD)

Diplomat Sergei Chuvakhin, who served as the KGB's communications channel to Ames without knowing it. (CREDIT: FBI)

Washington *rezident* Stanislav Androsov. (CREDIT: FBI)

Sergei Devilkovsky, Ames's first KGB contact. (CREDIT: FBI)

Dmitri Polyakov was the highest-ranking American agent Ames betrayed. The military intelligence general, codenamed TOPHAT, was arrested 25 years after he began spying for the United States. (CREDIT: PETE EARLEY, INC.)

Aldrich Ames after his exposure. (CREDIT: FBI)

Valery Martynov. It took months to figure out how to send him back to Moscow from Washington after Ames exposed him as an FBI spy codenamed GENTILE. (CREDIT: FBI)

The FBI recruited Sergei Motorin, codenamed GAUZE, after he sold vodka to buy stereo equipment in Washington. Ames betrayed him in 1985. (CREDIT: FBI)

Elena, Alyona and me at Niagara Falls. We much enjoyed traveling around the United States. (CREDIT: VICTOR CHERKASHIN)

David Major introducing former London KGB officer Oleg Gordievsky to Ronald Reagan in 1987. Gordievsky staged a daring escape from under the KGB's nose in 1985. Sneaking out of Moscow, he met British SIS operatives at the Finnish border, where they smuggled him across in the trunk of a car. (CREDIT: WHITE HOUSE)

The FBI's Robert Hanssen.
(Credit: FBI)

$50,000 left for Hanssen by the KGB under a footbridge in Virginia's Long Brach Nature Center in 2001. It was recovered by the FBI. (Credit: FBI)

Vitaly Yurchenko in 1985. He was the highest-ranking KGB officer to defect to the Americans. Later "redefecting" to the Soviet Union, he helped the KGB play a game that kept the CIA guessing for years. (CREDIT: DAVID MAJOR)

The entrance of the Soviet Embassy compound in Washington, where Vitaly Yurchenko showed up after leaving behind a CIA guard. (CREDIT: VICTOR CHERKASHIN)

The first page of a nine-page June 1989 note from the KGB to Ames. (Credit: FBI)

A torn September 15, 1993, note from Ames to the KGB recovered from his garbage and pieced together by the FBI. (Credit: FBI)

An Ames dead drop site in Little River Branch Park, Bethesda, Maryland. (Credit: Cindy Kwitchoff, CI Centre)

FBI agents arresting Ames on February 21, 1994. (Credit: FBI)

KGB Chairman Vadim Bakatin, who helped dismantle the service after the Soviet collapse. (CREDIT: ITAR-TASS)

Gennady Vasilenko (third from left)—who was imprisoned for six months as a suspected spy—and me (fourth from left) with managers of my Alpha-Puma security company. (CREDIT: VICTOR CHERKASHIN)

At Alyona's California wedding, with grandson Ivan at bottom left.
(CREDIT: VICTOR CHERKASHIN)

Former adversaries: (From left)
The CIA's Milt Bearden, me and
Leonid Shebarshin in Moscow.
(CREDIT: VICTOR CHERKASHIN)

IVY BELLS, but they immediately suspected that "Mr. Robert" was Edward Lee Howard. Yurchenko's defection buoyed the CIA leadership—especially director Bill Casey, the Cold War warrior who'd been seething under an order from Congress to stop aiding the Contra rebels fighting to overthrow the socialist Nicaraguan government.

The Americans flew Yurchenko to Washington and installed him in a safe house in Oakton, Virginia, as I found out in a major stroke of luck several days later. Gerber had assigned SE division counterintelligence chief Aldrich Ames to take part in Yurchenko's debriefing. By then, Ames had been spying for us for almost four months. Desperate to protect him from possible exposure by Yurchenko, I couldn't even contact him to warn of the defection—because Ames was busy debriefing the defector.

Showing up late to meet Yurchenko on the morning of his arrival at Andrews Air Force Base, he nevertheless installed himself first in line to greet him.[11] Like me, Ames tried to guess whether Yurchenko might have been privy to information about him. Even though Yurchenko hadn't mentioned anything about Ames—or anyone who fit his description—during his Rome debriefing, our nervous agent had no way of telling if Yurchenko did know about him.

Although Ames realized there was little chance of that despite Yurchenko's work in Directorate K, he also knew the KGB's strict need-to-know policies couldn't always stop office chitchat. He moved quickly to get to the truth. Climbing into the backseat of the car waiting to drive the defector from the airport, he slipped him a note. "If you have any particularly important information which you wish to provide only to the Director or another senior U.S. official, tell me, and I will take you to him." Yurchenko didn't.[12] Ames continued to press him until the Russian told him about my unexplained trip to Moscow in April or May. My visit had indeed sparked hallway talk that something big had happened in Washington. Happily, nothing implicated Ames or anyone like him.

When Ames finally met his KGB contact, the diplomat Sergei Chuvakhin, several days later, it was clear he was in no danger. The CIA's attribution of what it knew of its huge loss of agents chiefly to Edward Lee Howard had been a lucky break. Only after Ames's safety was assured could I reflect on the significance of his latest assignment: that our best spy was now even more valuable. In the following days and weeks Ames provided us with ongoing reports about what Yurchenko told the CIA. The information was funneled directly to Kryuchkov.

8

After arriving in Washington, Yurchenko began riding waves of conflicting emotions. Escaping the Soviet Union and cooperating with former adversaries who now professed to be his best friends must have given him a massive adrenaline rush. But it was overshadowed by one main concern: Yurchenko believed he was dying of stomach cancer and had only weeks or months to live. That expectation likely played a major part in his decision to abandon his family and Motherland. Yurchenko insisted that the CIA keep his defection secret—chiefly to protect his wife and son back in Moscow. There was a chance his family could be spared harassment if no direct confirmation of his defection surfaced.

Languishing in his safe house during weeks of debriefings, he became increasingly restless and depressed. Hoping to keep him happy, the CIA promised him $1 million on top of a $62,000 annual stipend and a well-appointed house in the Washington suburbs. He was also taken to a private dinner with Casey. His mood improved, but not for long.

Another issue may have played a seminal part in Yurchenko's decision to defect—it was reported that he had a lover, a young woman called Valentina Yereskovskaya, whom he'd met and had fallen for in Washington during the 1970s. That was news to me. Everyone in the embassy had known the two were good friends, but no one suspected an affair. Yereskovskaya, who was married to a Soviet diplomat, had been the embassy pediatrician. In 1985, her husband was posted to Montreal, where both now lived. In a risky bid to assuage Yurchenko's growing unhappiness, the CIA arranged for him to meet his lover to try to convince her to run away with him. Under heavy security, he appeared at her Montreal apartment when she was alone.

Everyone who knew Yurchenko also knew he didn't care for his wife. Having to live with a woman he didn't desire no doubt depressed him. Now he wanted to spend his last few months with the woman he did love. He didn't want to hurt his family (hence his pains to protect them), but had decided to make a last bid for his own happiness. So there he was, in the doorway of his former mistress's apartment. To his great surprise, she turned him down flat. She'd loved a KGB colonel, not a traitor, she told him.[13] Yurchenko's hopes of spending his last days in a CIA-bankrolled union with his beloved vanished. The blow struck hard.

More trouble for the defector and his stewards loomed. Still in Montreal in late September, Yurchenko came across a reprinting of a *Washington Times* story in a Canadian newspaper that broke the news of his defection. More stunning than the leak itself was its almost certain source: no one other than Casey himself, no doubt eager to generate good press for the agency, which was embroiled in the Iran-Contra scandal. For Yurchenko, it was a slap in the face.

His grim mood worsened on his return to Washington. To bolster his flagging spirits, the CIA took him on a holiday tour of the West—where, however, the chaperoned defector felt unable to do anything for himself. In a widening of the probe to track down the KGB agent in the NSA, an FBI agent flew out to meet him with a series of mug shots. Yurchenko finally identified Pelton.[14]

Milton Bearden—the CIA SE division deputy chief who participated in Yurchenko's debriefing—writes that the Russian's mood plummeted after he identified Pelton. He probably realized, to his own surprise, that exposing the former NSA employee might mean that he'd have to testify about the case in court. That would provide incontrovertible proof of his defection, making it impossible for him to return to the Soviet Union—and prompting authorities in Moscow to take action against his family. If Yurchenko hadn't already begun reconsidering his defection, he probably started thinking about how to come back to us then.

Or slightly later, when a beaming Bearden drove to his safe house to convey the momentous news that medical tests showed he didn't have stomach cancer. Yurchenko appeared stunned. He clutched his head. "Oh, what have I done!" he uttered. Far from feeling relief, he began agonizing about what to do with the long life that suddenly stretched before him instead of the few months he'd expected to live.

9

Rezidentura officer Alexander Kukhar was a hot-blooded guy. If he saw an FBI car trailing him, he'd step on the accelerator and try to outrun his tail. He did that all the time—even when he wasn't conducting an operation. The FBI agents assigned to follow Kukhar would have to report that they'd lost their target and of course get reprimanded for that. One day, the KGB officer drove out of the Soviet embassy and found himself surrounded by four FBI cars—one on each side, one in front and one behind. They drove 20 miles an hour, forcing Kukhar along with them. There was nothing our guy could do. He was escorted onto highway 95 and deposited 30 miles outside of Washington. FBI special agent Dion Rankin organized the incident. Kukhar got the picture. He never tried to elude FBI tails again when there was no need for it, which was most of the time. I never thought it was a good idea to annoy the adversary. If worse came to worst, it was always possible to postpone meeting an agent. That's what we were taught—to respect the other side.

—*Gennady Vasilenko, former Line KR officer in Washington and rezident in Guyana*

Jack Platt, who ran the program that trained Edward Lee Howard, had a record as an accomplished case officer, with service in Vienna, Laos, Paris and elsewhere. A Williams College graduate, the Texan served as a marine officer before joining the CIA in 1963. By 1977, he was in Washington, assigned to watch the Soviet embassy. Always on the lookout for interesting cases, Platt's ears pricked up when colleagues told him about a new KGB officer in the Washington *rezidentura*. "He's not your usual Soviet," Platt was told.

CIA and FBI officers could spot most Soviets a mile away. This case was different. The new officer dressed in fashionable Western clothes. He walked confidently. He wasn't wary of meeting Americans. He seemed well educated and well connected. And he was a ladies' man. Platt wanted to find out more, which wasn't too difficult, since the CIA had an agent working in the KGB training institute in Moscow. He'd served as class evaluator for the group in which the new man had graduated.

The officer's name was Gennady Vasilenko, the man I later assigned to run Pelton. Tall and athletic, he was a natural at any sport he took up. He skied, skated, hunted and played basketball. After graduating from secondary school, he enrolled in the Bauman Technical Institute to study for an engineering degree. But his passion was volleyball—he wanted to join the Olympic team. Since the Bauman institute team was mediocre, Vasilenko joined the Dinamo club, not knowing that the Dinamo Sports Association, whose various teams included the famous soccer winners, was sponsored by the KGB. After graduating in 1962, he was offered a position in the secret service.

Vasilenko refused, saying he had no interest in intelligence work. Just ahead of tryouts for the 1964 summer Olympic volleyball team, however, he pulled a shoulder muscle. Unable to compete for a place on the squad, Vasilenko wondered what to do with his life. Prompting from fellow Dinamo members that he sign up with the intelligence service eventually swayed him. Despite his initial misgivings, he soon saw his new job as a great adventure. He continued playing sports during his KGB training.

Vasilenko's gregariousness served him excellently. Arriving in Washington in 1976 to work in counterintelligence, he joined local basketball and volleyball teams and made friends quickly. Feeling completely at ease in the Main Adversary's capital, he soon had five good contacts, including FBI officers. He played tennis with an agent named Pat Matthews. Over a drink one day, Matthews offered Vasilenko and his son tickets to a Harlem Globetrotters game, something that the sports enthusiast was unlikely to refuse.

The gift had been engineered by Platt. Keen to meet Vasilenko, he didn't want to do it the standard way, through the "daisy chain" we all knew about and expected. That scheme had a CIA officer working undercover as a government employee, usually a diplomat, introduce himself to a Soviet. After several meetings, the American would introduce his new contact to an "old friend"—a CIA officer who would assess whether the Soviet target was worth pursuing. At some point, a third American would step in to make a pitch. The timing was almost predictable enough for us to set our watches by it.

Instead, Platt lured Vasilenko to the Globetrotters game. There Matthews introduced Vasilenko to Platt. The Russian took an immediate liking to the blunt Texan, who said he worked for the

NSA. Vasilenko suspected that was a lie, but didn't care: establishing contacts with the CIA was part of a case officer's work.

As he'd expected, Platt also liked Vasilenko, who took to calling him "cowboy." The American began inviting Vasilenko on hunting trips, and the two found themselves becoming friends. Each reported the meetings to his own agency, but—like Rem Krassilnikov and Haviland Smith before them—neither made any headway in his efforts to recruit the other. That didn't put them off; the two rarely spoke about their work. Many of their meetings were also attended by an FBI officer called Dion Rankin, who participated in the recruitment effort on the part of the bureau. Vasilenko was given the cryptonym MONOLITE.

After some time, the *rezident*, Dmitri Yakushkin, began to suspect Vasilenko's motives. When the young officer reported an invitation from Platt for a weekend family outing, Yakushkin gave the go-ahead, then retracted it. More than that, he ordered Vasilenko to cut off his relations with his CIA friend. Vasilenko went anyway and didn't report the meeting, or his future ones with Platt.

For his part, Platt had to brush off criticism at his own agency for having made no headway in recruiting Vasilenko. Part of the thrill for CIA officers was staring across the great divide between the United States and the Soviet Union and trying to understand the other side. Platt genuinely respected Vasilenko, not least for the Russian's devotion to his son Ilya. "He's a real mensch," Platt said about Vasilenko. Platt believed friendship was better than enmity for recruiting agents. Wanting to establish a personal bond that might win his target over, he resisted repeated suggestions to blackmail Vasilenko. "If you succeed, you'll have to re-recruit him at every single meeting," Platt insisted.

The friendship also provided a release from the sometimes crushing CIA bureaucracy. The same Platt who tried to hide his prodigious drinking at the time from the CIA regaled Vasilenko with stories about incidents such as passing out in Paris. His occasional drunkenness initially gave the Russian hope he could recruit him, since he had two children to support. But Platt was resolute. "What are you going to offer me?" he once asked Vasilenko. "Five hours in a bread line? Nine square meters of living space in Moscow?"

Over his wife's disapproval, Vasilenko secretly met Platt three more times after Yakushkin ordered him to stop. During one of Platt's last pitches, Vasilenko cut him short. "Look Jack, let's do it this way. If you want to be friends with me, let's be friends. We have many interesting things to talk about. But let's not interfere with each other's work."

That didn't always hold. In a small Washington restaurant on 19th street in 1981, Vasilenko turned down yet another offer from Platt and Rankin to stay in the United States with his family. By now Platt wasn't asking Vasilenko to become an agent— he was simply offering four U.S. passports and a suitcase stuffed with cash. Vasilenko's reply was, "Look, if you want, I'll take twenty bucks to pay for lunch."

"Your political situation back home is pretty tense," Platt persisted. "You'd do well to stay here."

"Look guys, we've already agreed that I work for my country and you go on working for yours."

Vasilenko was rotated out of Washington two months later. Platt showed up at the airport to see his buddy off. But that wasn't the end of their story. Vasilenko later became involved in a life-or-death struggle involving Platt and Robert Hanssen.

10

Among the stories Yurchenko exposed to the CIA during his months in the agency's safe houses was the fate of French agent FAREWELL. Fifty-three-year-old Colonel Vladimir Vetrov, a hot-tempered officer in the KGB's Line X (science and technology), began spying for France in 1980, during a tour in Paris. The information he provided included documents from the FCD's Directorate T, responsible for overseeing science and technology (S&T) intelligence. They exposed a broad-based effort to steal or buy Western technology deemed crucial to the Soviet Union's efforts to modernize its infrastructure—including information about radar, computers, machine tools and semiconductor technology.[15]

One of the projects Vetrov detailed in his so-called FAREWELL dossier was a plan to build a major natural gas pipeline from Siberia to Europe. Germany and Britain were helping finance the project. It would earn the Soviet Union billions of dollars a year in hard currency and provide Moscow with a means of influence over Western Europe. Like the Americans, French President François Mitterrand opposed the project and secretly told U.S. President Ronald Reagan about FAREWELL during a July 1981 economic summit in Ottawa.

Acting on the intelligence, the CIA later claimed to have slipped the KGB flawed information about pipeline software for controlling pumps and valves. Programmed to malfunction, the computer programs would overload the system. Thomas Reed, a former air force secretary in the National Security Council who helped spearhead the disinformation plan, claimed it was a roaring success. "The result was the most monumental non-nuclear explosion and fire ever seen from space," he wrote. Disruption of the project put into question years of Soviet intelligence gathering on that and other technology.[16]

Those claims have been disputed, but what's clear is the role of the American disinformation campaign in a wider effort to roll back Line X intelligence, on which much of the Soviet industrial and military complex relied. Reagan supporters hailed the actions as a significant contribution to "winning" the Cold War, an exaggerated assessment at best. The blast did delay the project to supply Western Europe. Nevertheless Russia currently provides Europe with a third of its natural gas.

FAREWELL continued informing for the French until 1982, when his espionage ended in bizarre fashion after his mistress found out about it. On leave in Moscow, Vetrov met his lover in a park, where she threatened to go to the authorities with her information unless he agreed to leave his wife for her. Vetrov stabbed her with a knife instead. The story of his subsequent arrest is obscured by myth and disinformation. The woman lived, but Vetrov was also accused of stabbing another of her lovers to death in the park. Vetrov was tried and sentenced to twelve years in prison, but his espionage remained unexposed. Two years later, however, he was betrayed by a prison informant to whom he'd confided during a weak moment. His execution followed. (Despite Yurchenko's account of the case to the CIA, the Americans still believe Vetrov's spying was disclosed by an agent.)

Among other information Yurchenko gave U.S. intelligence was Edward Lee Howard's claim to the KGB that he'd heard of an "angry colonel" who had approached the CIA proposing to spy against the Soviet Union.[17] The information initiated a manhunt, but we weren't able to expose the agent until Ames gave us more information about him—at about the same time Yurchenko was describing the case to the CIA. Ames thus showed once again that almost all actionable intelligence originates from agents, not analysis.

Yurchenko also told the CIA about the fate of Nikolai Artamanov, the captain of a destroyer in the Soviet Baltic Fleet. In 1959 the thirty-one-year-old Artamanov's ship was docked at the Polish port of Gdansk, where he fell in love with a young dental student. The two decided to defect to the West, taking off to Sweden in a motor boat belonging to Artamanov's ship.

Artamanov traveled to the United States, where he was given a new identity—Nicholas George Shadrin—and a job as a Soviet navy analyst for the Defense Intelligence Agency. Adjusting well to his new life, Shadrin attracted the KGB's attention in 1966 as an up-and-coming lecturer on Soviet military affairs in Washington. It didn't take the KGB long to figure out his real identity or approach him with an offer to turn against the CIA as a double agent. The CIA found out about the Soviet plan from the KGB colonel sent to turn Shadrin, who also volunteered with the Americans. The CIA, in turn, asked Shadrin to become a triple agent for the United States by pretending to cave to KGB pressure. He agreed, convincing the KGB he was interested in working against the Americans.

In December 1975, Shadrin traveled to Vienna to meet his KGB handlers. Several days later—as far as the CIA knew—he disappeared. In fact, Artamanov/Shadrin was abducted, injected with sedatives and driven to Czechoslovakia—in the backseat of a car while crossing the Austrian border. When the KGB kidnappers opened the trunk on the other side, they discovered he'd stopped breathing, apparently from a sedative overdose. Attempts to revive him with CPR, brandy and adrenalin injections failed.

Several months later, in 1976, the topic of the missing Russian came up between U.S. President Gerald Ford and Soviet General Secretary Brezhnev. The Americans were told that Shadrin had met with KGB officers in Vienna to discuss returning to the Soviet Union but failed to show for a scheduled second meeting. President Jimmy Carter got the same answer when he later raised the question.

Yurchenko said Brezhnev's lying to two U.S. presidents made the truth one of the KGB's most closely kept secrets.[18] Certain that if the KGB found out he'd informed the Americans about Artamanov, his family would be attacked back in Russia, Yurchenko made it abundantly clear to his handlers that he didn't want the information leaked. In 1985 Artamanov's widow filed a suit against the United States over his death, and the CIA was forced to hand over its files in the case—including Yurchenko's intelligence— which soon became public information. The suit also raised the possibility that Yurchenko might have to appear in court. Bearden believes that the CIA may have thus tried to ensure the problem defector would never be able to go home. When news of the Arta- manov case appeared in the American media despite his strenuous efforts to keep the information secret, he felt betrayed yet again.

On November 2, 1985, Yurchenko found himself guarded by a young CIA security officer, Thomas Hannah. Disliked by more than one superior, Hannah had been given dreaded weekend duty. He allowed Yurchenko to talk him into taking him shop- ping, a clear violation of orders. Yurchenko quietly slipped away at the mall and called the *rezidentura*. Then he convinced Han- nah to take him to a down-market French restaurant in George- town called Au Pied de Cochon.

As the two sat at a table amid the smell of fried food wafting in from the kitchen, Yurchenko spoke up. "What would you do if I got up and walked out?" he asked. "Shoot me?"

"No, we don't treat defectors that way," Hannah replied.

Yurchenko announced he was taking a short walk. If he didn't come back, he said, it wouldn't be the officer's fault. He stood up and walked out, leaving the nervous junior officer behind.[19] After some minutes, Hannah got up to report to headquarters that Yurchenko was missing.

11

"I'm going upstairs to see him," I told Androsov in the parking garage after he informed me about Yurchenko's return. The "rede- fector" was waiting in the apartment of a security officer. He'd just walked the twenty minutes up Wisconsin Avenue from Au

Pied de Cochon and buzzed himself in at the main gates. Androsov told me he claimed to have escaped from the CIA.

Yurchenko looked very much like I'd remembered him, if a little skinnier. He seemed irritated. "*Molodets* [good man]!" I said. I tried as hard as possible to beam widely. I walked up to my old head of security and threw my arms around him. "Congratulations," I said. "Welcome back. You don't know how happy I am you managed to escape," I said. "How did you do it?"

"The bastards," Yurchenko cursed. "They kidnapped me in Rome. They drugged me. I got away as soon as I could. I'm so happy to be back. I just hope I'll be able to find support for my actions here."

Yurchenko sounded convincing. He acted happy to be back but didn't overdo it. He moderated his anger at the CIA, striking an entirely plausible demeanor of frustration and tiredness.

"You'll get our full support," I assured him.

There was no question how I'd treat Yurchenko. Thanks to Ames, we knew exactly what had transpired since his defection. But Androsov and I agreed to buy Yurchenko's story. He was back now, but we didn't know how he'd behave. Maybe he'd want to return to his American friends after a couple of days. Our priority was making sure he didn't defect again before we got him to Moscow as quickly as possible. That meant pretending to be overjoyed to see the prodigal son back on our side while posting security guards to make sure he didn't sneak out. We had to let him feel we trusted him, that we'd support and protect him and that he was among friends. It was a routine decision, made by the book. After about twenty minutes of discussion, I left to find Androsov. We drove back to the embassy to send a cable to the Center.

Yurchenko's surprise appearance came during a barrage of anti-Soviet propaganda in the American press. Even Yurchenko's defection was subordinated to the drive to criticize the USSR. The CIA had arrested neither Edward Lee Howard nor Ronald

Pelton, instead leaking information that inspired numerous newspaper stories about Yurchenko and the intelligence he'd given the CIA and the FBI. The leaks couldn't have taken place without decisions by both the CIA leadership and the White House. By making Yurchenko's defection public and angering him, CIA Director Casey jeopardized his agency's operations together with Yurchenko's future.

Androsov and I agreed that Yurchenko might well have been drugged after his defection to make him more cooperative. But that was irrelevant. Most important was knowing what operations and agents he'd compromised. In addition to information about Pelton and Howard, he told the Americans about KGB contingency plans in case of a large-scale military mobilization. They included a series of 1985 meetings in Karlshorst, the KGB's East Berlin headquarters, to discuss measures such as planting secret arms caches in Western Europe. Yurchenko had been in charge of preparing the plan. He knew which agents were involved and which operations had made it past the planning stage—and he told the Americans about them.

If the initial decision to welcome Yurchenko back was an immediate, temporary measure, it now developed into a larger plan. Thanks to Ames, we were spared guesswork over how to limit his damage. Instead, we decided to fight back from our embattled position on the propaganda front. We'd exploit Yurchenko's return by trying to discredit the CIA and the U.S. government in just the way they were attacking us. Tweaking Yurchenko's story of kidnapping and drugging, we'd unleash it against the United States. We detailed our proposal to the Center.

I met Yurchenko a number of times in the following days. We took meals together and discussed bogus plans about what to do next. He appeared slightly nervous, but mostly happy to be back. It was the perfect attitude to strike, and he did it with confident calm. His story was well engineered: claiming to have been drugged excused him from having to describe exactly what he'd told the Americans while also giving him carte blanche to say with a shrug that he might have told them anything.

Yurchenko had clearly mapped out a detailed strategy for himself, planning for each possible contingency. He had to behave like someone who'd just lived through a major ordeal, when he actually looked like he'd had a comfortable three months. His performance was convincing but not perfect. He wasn't hysterical, didn't get drunk, didn't swear or do other things easily expected of someone who'd just endured months of stress. He also didn't know what we knew about him. Had he known that a KGB agent was telling us everything he'd been doing since his defection, it's unlikely he'd have dared return.

Meanwhile, Androsov and I worked on our priority—getting him back to Moscow. We had to prevent the Americans from attempting to really kidnap him this time. Even though he'd probably told his interrogators everything he knew, he was still important to them. With embassy guards secretly spying on him, his "friends" at the embassy pretended to help him get over his shock while also keeping tabs on him.

One afternoon shortly after his return, several of Yurchenko's acquaintances, including Elena and me, gathered for tea in his apartment. The chief question on everyone's mind was how his kidnapping took place. "It just happened," Yurchenko replied testily.

Someone mentioned that American newspapers had written differing accounts of what they portrayed as a defection. Yurchenko noncommittally replied that he'd read the papers. As his guests talked, he got up to use the toilet. Elena went to the kitchen at the same time. Returning to the living room, she saw Yurchenko gazing into a hallway mirror, combing his hair back. He didn't notice her watching him. He looked confident, as if convincing himself that everything was going according to his plan. Clearly he wasn't afraid.

Connoisseurs of James Bond films and spy novels rarely think about their fictional heroes' steamy affairs. Intelligence officers and agents are usually depicted as putting their lives on the line to fight evil. Love affairs and gambling are therefore understandable and excusable. In real life, people have less tolerance for such activities and support punishment of intelligence officers who dare believe they're more than the sum of their job descriptions and act according to their own wishes. Of course such an explanation has no legal weight, but the fact is that Yurchenko betrayed his country because he allowed himself to act like a human being. Presumably the Soviet intelligence service, its state secrets and its agents were less important to him than his personal desires.

He acted that way all along. Once he fully decided that defecting was a mistake, he chose to take revenge on the CIA for leaking his story. That way he'd save his family from an uncertain future. And he'd have a chance at spending the remaining decades of his life back home instead of whiling away his supposed last months dying in the United States. It was only a matter of time until he returned to the Soviet embassy.

In Washington six years earlier, Yurchenko had told me something that had always stuck in my memory. "I keep telling my son that no matter what situation you find yourself in, there's always a way out."

12

Our plan to bring Yurchenko safely home involved making him discredit himself in American eyes. He had to denounce them—publicly burn his bridges—so he wouldn't be able to go back.

After clearing it with Moscow, the embassy delivered a letter of protest, denouncing Yurchenko's kidnapping as criminal to the

State Department. The letter was based on what he'd told us. The Foreign Ministry in Moscow also lodged a complaint. After polishing the story—that he'd been kidnapped in Italy, drugged and flown back to the United States, where he was forcibly held in a safe house and interrogated—we went to the press.

How Yurchenko would behave was still unclear, so the day after his return, we held a news conference for Soviet journalists only. Since the CIA knew the real story, spinning Yurchenko's kidnapping version was likely to have the greatest impact as anti-U.S. propaganda back home. Yurchenko followed his script to the letter, confirming exactly what he'd told us and damning the Americans for what he said they did to him.

The following day, a Monday, he appeared at a briefing for the foreign press corps in the new embassy compound. There he told his story to a shocked Washington intelligence community. In animated tones, switching between Russian and English, he denounced CIA SE chief Burton Gerber and his CIA handlers as torturers—except for one, an officer who'd introduced himself to Yurchenko as Phil. He was, of course, Aldrich Ames, whom we didn't want to be reprimanded. Yurchenko said the CIA made him look like a willing defector, partly by forcing him to sign a contract promising him $1 million—which the CIA thought would encourage other would-be defectors.

The news conference went swimmingly. If Yurchenko's story wasn't entirely believable, his outrage was. Afterward, I was able to relax because the damage had been done whatever Yurchenko did, even if he somehow managed to escape and return to the Americans. "If he wants to stay here, fuck him—we can't do much about it if that's what he really wants," I told Androsov. "But I'm 90 percent sure he won't."

There was one more step. As it always did in such situations, the State Department insisted that Yurchenko meet with U.S.

representatives face-to-face to confirm his story. The Americans said they had no reason to keep Yurchenko in the United States, but that they needed to know he'd be returning to Moscow voluntarily. We wanted to conduct the meeting in our embassy, but the State Department insisted on its offices. So on Tuesday, the day after his sensational news conference, a Soviet diplomat escorted Yurchenko to Foggy Bottom. There he confirmed his story once again.

The effort went off without a hitch. We won the propaganda battle. Had they wanted to, both the CIA and FBI could have easily countered our version of Yurchenko's previous three months. They had documents, audio- and videotapes to back their story, and could have made them public as some in both organizations reportedly urged. But Gerber ruled out taking action.[20] Part of the reason was our speed in publicizing the kidnapping story. The CIA could have advanced its version for the record, but would have had to engage in a tit-for-tat propaganda battle, which would have been less than effective.

Following Yurchenko's redefection, the CIA had no idea whether its biggest Soviet prize in decades had been a real defector or a double agent all along. The agency would spend years poring over its records, trying to calculate how much it could trust the information he provided and ascertain whether he'd been planted by the KGB to learn important information about the CIA and the FBI during his debriefing sessions. Many differing opinions were offered about why such an operation would be carried out, and whether we compromised Yurchenko's knowledge to hide more important information. He became a hot topic of discussion once again after Ames was arrested in 1994, this time over whether he'd been part of a KGB operation to protect our spy.

I don't know how many Americans believed Yurchenko's kidnap story, but his return hurt the CIA's image regardless. The agency had either been completely taken in by a brilliant Soviet intelligence officer, or allowed one of its top Soviet defectors to slip out of its hands. Reagan summed up American confusion over the event: "I think it's awfully easy for any American to be perplexed by anyone who could live in the United States but would prefer to live in Russia."[21]

Our propaganda coup came on top of two other defections botched by the CIA. The first took place when a Soviet soldier walked into the U.S. embassy in Kabul but was forced out several weeks later, after Soviet troops surrounded the building and cut off electricity and telephone lines. In the other case, a Ukrainian merchant sailor called Miroslav Medved was twice returned to his ship, a grain freighter called the *Marshal Konev*, after he tried to defect on the Mississippi River near New Orleans, once by leaping forty feet.

The Soviet people, on the other hand, accepted the kidnap story—and that had been our most important goal. We showed the CIA was an organization of cynical liars, a portrait newspapers and television sustained for months. That was sweet revenge for U.S. criticism of Soviet human rights violations. Most important, however, by keeping the CIA and FBI guessing, Yurchenko's redefection helped maintain cover for Ames and Hanssen.

13

Five days after he'd showed up at the Soviet embassy, Yurchenko boarded a flight back to Moscow. As he reached the top of the stairs leading up to the plane, he turned, smiled and waved. He knew the CIA was watching his every move. Yurchenko's act surely galled the Americans, but something else worried them even more. Following Yurchenko up the stairs were several other KGB officers from the *rezidentura*—part of an "honor guard" escorting him home. One was Valery Martynov, the Line X officer who had been spying for the FBI since 1982. What the Americans didn't know—but began at that moment to suspect—was that I also knew about Martynov's espionage. Getting him back to Moscow had been one of my chief worries for months.

Yurchenko returned home to a hero's welcome. He was awarded, given a desk in Yasenevo and an analytical job in the FCD. I spoke to him several times after 1986—his dacha isn't far from mine at the KGB plot near Moscow and I still see him from time to time. We're cordial to each other, saying hello but not much more.

Most in the KGB never doubted Yurchenko was a traitor and debated (privately of course) whether Kryuchkov had been right to use Yurchenko's story for propaganda. Most feel the jury is still out. Less understandable was why Yurchenko was given a job on his return. In any case, there was nothing anyone could do. Yurchenko was officially accepted as an upstanding citizen, even as others who betrayed much less than he were shot.

The Americans who thought Yurchenko was a real defector were puzzled. Why wasn't he punished when he got home? Perhaps the biggest reason was Ames. Yurchenko's defection may not have been an elaborate operation to protect the KGB's top agent, but his redefection became exactly that. His arrest would have given the game away. Instead, the CIA was confronted with more questions and uncertainties. We could do nothing to protect the agents and operations Yurchenko had betrayed. But the episode as a whole could still turn at least a little in our favor.

Despite the barrage of criticism leveled at the CIA for letting Yurchenko go, the agency actually did little wrong. In fact, it profited handsomely from the defection, gaining intelligence about two Soviet agents and a number of operations and learning much about the fates of former agents and something about how the KGB worked. Washington also earned points in the propaganda war, however misguided the decisions to leak information about Yurchenko's defection had been for keeping him in the

CIA's hands. Until everything went sour, the media campaign was remarkably successful in putting Langley in a good light.

Not surprisingly, then, it was chiefly in the propaganda war that the CIA suffered as a result of Yurchenko's redefection, but as noted, mostly in the Soviet Union. There was little damage to operations, Yurchenko having already told the Americans everything he knew. After that, he was of little use and much bother. Had he remained in the United States, he probably would have become an analyst, available to write or endorse anti-Soviet literature if necessary. He might also have covered for other agents, claiming to be the source of intelligence that actually came from elsewhere. But all told, the CIA didn't lose much. By letting Yurchenko go, it saved itself the $1 million it had promised him, in addition to a furnished house and countless other expenses.

Unprofessional as it was to release a top defector known to be emotionally unstable, it was a minor mistake. It would have been impossible to keep Yurchenko under constant guard. If he wanted to leave, he'd have found a way sooner or later. The FBI couldn't maintain a platoon of agents to watch every defector whose intelligence potential was largely exhausted. Those most responsible for the security of Soviet defectors were the defectors themselves. The twists in Yurchenko's story further illustrate the nature of treason—that it's most often committed to solve immediate personal problems and is rarely prompted by ideology. Yurchenko never threw away his Communist Party membership card.

14

The CIA has been heavily criticized for sitting on its knowledge that Edward Lee Howard was a potential threat. According to

Bearden, in an account the FBI denies, SE chief Gerber told the bureau about Howard on August 3, 1985, two days after Yurchenko informed the CIA about Mr. Robert, the Soviet agent who fit Howard's description. Bearden writes that the CIA learned only later that Howard had traveled to Vienna in September 1984, when he probably exposed Tolkachev and a CIA eavesdropping operation in Moscow called TAW—actually exposed by Ames in 1985.[22]

On August 9, immediately after Yurchenko's defection, we again flew Howard to Vienna, where, without telling him specifically about Yurchenko, we warned him of a possible threat and told him to make his way to the nearest Soviet consulate in case of trouble.

The FBI had already placed Howard under surveillance. Well trained by Jack Platt to avoid observation, he suspected as much, especially after he was contacted by another man fired by the CIA. Howard had earlier complained to him about his experience with the agency. Now his would-be colleague called to tell Howard that the FBI had come around to question him.

On September 19, the FBI started closing in on Howard. When one of its agents telephoned him to arrange a meeting at the Santa Fe Hilton, Howard agreed. At the hotel, the bureau's officers told him that he'd been exposed, but without naming Yurchenko.[23] Howard insisted on seeing a criminal lawyer before telling the FBI anything. The officers agreed and let him go for the weekend.

Two days later, Howard and his wife, Mary, left their house to drive to dinner. When the Howards' car turned a bend, Howard jumped out and Mary moved a pop-up dummy into his seat. They had learned the "jack in the box" maneuver from the CIA. It turned out to be unnecessary. No one was following them because the junior FBI officer assigned to observe the Howard house from a van at the end of their driveway had failed to notice them leaving.

Howard made his way to the Albuquerque airport (by way of a shuttle bus that stopped at the Hilton hotel where FBI agents were staying and planning to arrest him the following Monday, September 23). He then boarded a plane to Tucson. From there, he flew to St. Louis, New York, and on to Helsinki, where the KGB helped smuggle him across the border into the Soviet Union.

I would see Howard next almost ten years later in Moscow, where he lived in an old, prestigious neighborhood called Chistyi Prudy (Clean Ponds) and ran a small insurance business. He seemed happy.

Ronald Pelton, the other major spy Yurchenko exposed, was less lucky. Arrested on November 25, 1985, he was later sentenced to life in prison.

_7_

WASHINGTON STATION:
THE MOST DANGEROUS SPY

1

In mid-1985, a British journalist "friend" of the KGB contacted me to provide pressing information: the man who'd been picked to head the London *rezidentura*, Colonel Oleg Gordievsky, was an SIS spy. The journalist provided no documents or other proof beyond his word, but the tip-off was credible enough to directly inform Kryuchkov. The FCD chief cabled me to return to Moscow immediately to brief him on the matter, even though I knew very little about the suspected British agent aside from the new information. Gordievsky remained in London, awaiting formal confirmation as British *rezident*.

I took the first plane to Moscow. Back at Yasenevo, I detailed what I knew about Gordievsky to the FCD chief. The information was persuasive, but we lacked hard proof of his spying. Meanwhile, Gordievsky was recalled to Moscow on May 17, ostensibly to formally receive his promotion. Things went badly for him from the start. He immediately noticed that his Moscow apartment had been searched.[1] Taken to a KGB dacha a few days later, he was secretly drugged, interrogated and informed he'd been relieved of his London position. But instead of being arrested, he was given a month's leave. He hadn't confessed under his questioning, and the Center was still looking for incontrovertible evidence. When released, he was kept under close watch, a task that normally would have fallen to the internal counterintelligence directorate, the SCD. To keep the matter internal, however, Kryuchkov made one of his own deputies, Victor Grushko, responsible for watching Gordievsky.

I returned to Washington at the end of the month. Ames also informed us that Gordievsky agreed to spy for MI6. Disclosing various KGB operations and illegal residents, he also provided the British with most of what they knew about Andropov's Operation RIAN, the KGB's search for signs that the United States was planning a nuclear first strike.[2] Later Gordievsky's handlers cunningly helped engineer his promotion. After he was assigned to London, the Foreign Office cleared his way to the top spot by expelling the agent's superiors one by one.

Curiously, the SIS refused to reveal Gordievsky's identity to the CIA. But Langley knew the British were getting information about the KGB from somewhere. SE division chief Gerber ordered Ames, then the SE counterintelligence chief, to figure out where. Ames identified Gordievsky in March, the month before he started spying for us.[3]

Several weeks after Gordievsky was recalled to Moscow, one of the most astounding incidents in KGB history took place. Grushko ratcheted up his surveillance of the British agent, who sensed the KGB was closing in on him. Fearing arrest at any moment, Gordievsky alerted his SIS handlers that he was in serious trouble and requested exfiltration to London. The first attempt took place on June 18, 1985, on Kutuzovsky Prospekt, a busy thoroughfare. It failed when Gordievsky missed meeting his British handlers by one minute.[4] He then made his way to the Finnish border, where he met SIS operatives who smuggled him across. Gordievsky made his daring escape in the trunk of their car, wrapped in thermal blankets to avoid heat detection.

The news shocked me. I'd suspected Grushko had additional information besides my own implicating Gordievsky. However, I had no idea why Gordievsky had been set free on his return to Moscow. Even if there hadn't been enough evidence to arrest him right away, it was inexcusable not to provide enough surveillance to keep him from escaping.

The FCD made another, potentially even more damaging slip. Until Ames gave us his intelligence on Gordievsky, the information we were receiving from the American was analyzed in Directorate K's First (American) department—under which I worked. When Ames told us about Gordievsky, Kryuchkov's deputy Vadim Kirpichenko handed the files to Directorate K's Fifth department, in charge of internal security. But instead of turning over the information on Gordievsky only, Kirpichenko transferred all the Ames files.

That betrayed a stunning lack of professionalism. Alarmed and afraid of losing clout, the First department lobbied for the files to be sent back. In due course they were—but not before the Fifth department officers saw the Ames files. Only a handful of people in the KGB had known about him. But months later, those Fifth department officers were brought into the operations to arrest the spies Ames had betrayed. They could have figured out the identity of our top asset by simply comparing the pattern of arrests to the kind of intelligence they knew the KGB was providing from Washington.

Meanwhile, back in Washington, no one knew the real reason for my Moscow trip. There has been speculation that I went simply to discuss Ames. Although I actually saw Kryuchkov to brief him about Gordievsky, we also talked about Ames and how to handle him. In June, less than a month after my return to Washington, I met him in Chadwicks and he fully committed to the KGB by jotting down the list of CIA agents in the Soviet Union.

2

Ames was said to be a bad case officer. But if he was, I find it strange that he was selected by his agency and accepted by the FBI to run the highest penetration of the United Nations group of Soviets in New York City—the Arkady Shevchenko case. It sort of ruins the theory that he wasn't a very good case officer. I didn't find his personality to be dashing or anything of that sort. But that goddamned CIA had better be a big tent. You need all kinds of people. I've seen the repositioning of history a lot of times. All of a sudden someone turns out to be a bad guy when you find out he's a traitor. But Arkady Shevchenko was a very helpful person to the U.S. government and the CIA. Ames should have gotten credit for that.

—*Jack Platt, former CIA officer*

Just as I was leaving for Moscow in May, an incident took place that helped push Ames toward his momentous decision. On May 19, four days after I first met Ames in the Soviet embassy, the FBI arrested John Walker Jr. after he left a package of classified U.S. Navy documents in a paper bag by the side of a Maryland road outside Washington. He'd been under surveillance by scores of FBI agents and a small plane overhead.

A retired submarine sailor and communications specialist, Walker headed a family spy ring that worked for the KGB for eighteen years. He was first run by Oleg Kalugin, then serving in Washington under cover as press secretary. Walker's ring included his brother Arthur, his son Michael—a sailor on the USS *Nimitz* aircraft carrier who provided the contents of the paper bag—and another communications specialist and old navy friend, Jerry Whitworth. The ring gave the KGB top secret navy communications and codes intelligence that enabled us to decode vital command messages. Walker himself handed over reports on submarine operations, noise-reduction technology and operational manuals in addition to keys for unscrambling navy communications.[5]

The arrest marked the biggest exposure of KGB agents since the Julius and Ethel Rosenberg nuclear espionage scandal in the 1950s. For Americans, news about Walker marked the beginning of the so-called Year of the Spy. Ames worried that whoever had fingered Walker would turn him in too. The FBI claimed Walker's estranged ex-wife betrayed him. But until that version became public, Ames suspected Martynov, the KGB Line X officer in Washington. Ames turned out to be right: by unbelievable chance, Martynov had overheard a conversation about Walker in Yasenevo while on break in Moscow and informed his FBI handlers when he got back. Most published accounts differ dramatically by relying on the FBI's version pinning Walker's exposure on his ex-wife. But while she may indeed have had an important role, Martynov played the crucial one, something documents from his trial support.

Ames has been characterized in the American press as an alcoholic and a mediocre officer who committed treason to make up for personal and professional inadequacies. Milt Bearden, Ames's former boss at the CIA, sums up the general opinion of his colleagues by calling him a "miserable little bastard." Others who knew him disagree.

Aldrich Hazen Ames was born in rural Wisconsin in 1941, the son of a mediocre CIA officer who served in Burma in the early 1950s. The young Ames drank a lot after dropping out of the

University of Chicago, and his driver's license was suspended after his third drunk-driving violation. Still, Ames did apply himself as a new CIA agent. After serving his first tour abroad in Turkey, he studied Russian in Washington and was picked by Haviland Smith, then head of the SE division's Latin America branch, to help handle a young KGB officer named Alexander Ogorodnik. Recruiting Ogorodnik in Colombia after learning about an affair he was having, the CIA code-named him TRIGON. In 1974, Ogorodnik was transferred back to Moscow, where he provided hundreds of diplomatic cables and internal reports.

TRIGON was arrested in 1977 and committed suicide by swallowing a CIA-provided cyanide pill hidden inside a fountain pen. He had been fingered by one of two Czech illegal agents: Karl and Hana Koecher, a husband and wife spy team living in Washington.

"Illegals," as opposed to "legals" like me and others who officially worked in *rezidenturas* abroad, were deep undercover agents planted in foreign countries, many as immigrants. They had complicated legends that took years to create. Often remaining inactive for years while they established themselves as respectable members of foreign societies, they ordinarily worked alone.

Karl Koecher was a translator in the CIA's SE division. He and his wife earned notoriety for their swinging lifestyle and orgies in Washington and New York, sometimes including other CIA employees. Arrested in 1984, they were eventually traded for Soviet dissident Anatoly Sharansky.

In 1972, Smith gave Ames another agent to handle. The new target, code-named PYRRHIC, was Sergei Fedorenko, a brash young Soviet U.N. diplomat and expert on guided missiles. Smith recruited Fedorenko after the Russian approached a fellow weapons expert in New York, asking for an introduction to the CIA. Fedorenko was soon spying for the Americans, passing on information about the KGB's New York *rezidentura* and the Soviet weapons industry. Fedorenko exposed his U.N. colleague Valdik Enger as a KGB officer assigned to pressure him into providing the service with intelligence about his U.S. contacts. (Enger and fellow U.N. secretariat employee Rudolf Chernyaev were later arrested by the Americans for espionage.)

Ames and Fedorenko became friends. Although Ames once stumbled by falling asleep in a subway car—temporarily losing a briefcase with photographs of KGB staff that Fedorenko had provided—he was soon promoted and sent to the New York office. Manhattan was crawling with intelligence officers. The United Nations employed some seven hundred Soviets, providing cover for the hundreds of KGB and GRU officers. The FBI assigned hundreds of special agents to follow suspected Soviet officers. The bureau also worked closely on some cases with the CIA, which maintained a large Manhattan office.

Soon Ames was given another important agent, Arkady Shevchenko, the Soviet ambassador to the United Nations. When Shevchenko contacted the CIA in 1975, asking to defect, the agency persuaded him to remain at the United Nations and work as an agent instead. Code-named DYNAMITE, he informed the Americans about Politburo debates over relations with Washington and other sensitive information. He finally defected in March 1978, helped by Ames.

After Ames moved to New York, Jack Platt gave him yet another agent to handle. Ames met Platt in Grand Central Station's Oyster Bar, a famous drinking hangout, to discuss the plan. Not friendly with Ames, whom he considered abrasive, Platt was concerned the handover wouldn't go well, which was often the case when he didn't know the new handler. To his pleasant surprise, this one went well. Taking Platt's advice about running his new target, Ames showed he understood the work.

After New York, Ames was posted to Mexico City and then returned to Washington in 1983 as counterintelligence chief in the

SE division. The new position gave him access to most of the agency's sensitive Soviet cases. Nevertheless, he was passed over for bigger promotions—despite the important agents he'd handled in New York. He was less successful in recruiting new agents, and sometimes careless. He drank too much, and colleagues complained about his shabby clothes and lax personal hygiene.

He also had financial problems, having collected debts of almost $40,000. And his wife, Nan, was suing him for divorce. Meanwhile, he'd fallen in love with a young Colombian woman, Maria del Rosario Casas Dupuy, who called herself Rosario. They met during Ames's posting in Mexico, where she was working as cultural attaché for the Colombian embassy. The couple married in August 1985.

At some point, Ames began thinking of espionage as a solution to his financial problems. He knew that a Russian source had tipped off the CIA about several KGB double agents who had approached U.S. intelligence with bogus offers to spy for Washington. Thinking of ways to contact the KGB, he stumbled on the idea of telling us about these double agents. By turning them in, he'd be able to demand payment but wouldn't harm the CIA or its real agents.[6] The $50,000 he asked for in his first letter to the KGB would solve his immediate problems. In time, he'd have enough to vastly improve his modest lifestyle.

Members of a CIA and FBI taskforce assigned to hunt for a mole later claimed that Ames gave himself away by spending extravagantly and failing to hide his KGB income. But the commonly accepted story—that clues about his wealth eventually led the CIA to him—are untrue. Ames showed much more cunning than he's usually given credit for, except by the knowing.

Back in 1985, other problems were troubling him too—the ones he mentioned to me during our meetings in the embassy and at Chadwicks. He was incensed by the paranoia of former CIA counterintelligence chief James Jesus Angleton, who betrayed the agency, Ames felt, by exposing American spies he thought were double agents working for the KGB. Among them were TOPHAT and FEDORA, who came to public attention in leaked press reports in 1978. Ames also criticized the CIA for misleading Congress and the American public. To boost the agency's significance and demand more federal funding, it exaggerated the Soviet threat. Helpless to do anything about it, Ames grew angry.

Shortly after Yurchenko redefected to Moscow, Platt ran into Ames in a Langley hallway. Platt mentioned some information about Yurchenko he'd learned from a fellow CIA officer who had seen him in Moscow. It would have been easy for Ames to pass the information along to us, but he didn't even ask Platt the name of the CIA operative in Moscow. Platt would surely have answered a casual question about that. Ames simply didn't care to inquire about such low-level tradecraft—or he was careful to show no curiosity that might have given him away.

3

In 1985 Ames met Chuvakhin about once a month. In May, he provided a number the FBI used to identify one of its sources inside the *rezidentura*—agent 1285. Ames said the bureau was using that mole to channel false information to the KGB.

The intelligence led us to Line X officer Valery Martynov. Ames also exposed former Washington *rezidentura* officer Sergei Motorin, who posed a lesser threat because he'd been rotated back to Moscow. Fingering those two U.S. agents in the Soviet embassy helped establish Ames as an important, well-positioned agent. Although cutting off CIA access to information about the *rezidentura* was also a way of protecting himself, his willingness to divulge information grew after he became convinced that we too were concerned about his security. John Walker's arrest pushed him to consider further protecting himself by exposing most of the CIA's major agents. Sensing his quandary, I played on it during our meetings.

One of his concerns was routine CIA lie detector tests. Training him to pass the tests significantly boosted his confidence in our ability to protect him. Part of our coaching came in four pages of instructions for anticipating the questions he'd face and reacting to them. The recommendations had been drafted by a special KGB clinic in Moscow set up in the 1970s after Soviet officers and agents began having trouble passing American tests. While Soviet and U.S. technology was similar, testing methods differed. In the Soviet Union, only the test administrator was present during an examination, with others eavesdropping from another room. In the United States, several people were often present in the room, possibly making it more difficult to beat the test by increasing a subject's psychological pressure.

Polygraphs measure a number of indicators, including respiratory and heart rates, perspiration, voice level and other movements. The KGB lab's recommendations included how to control physical reactions. Exercises such as yoga improve response management. Drugs also help control physical indicators, as does answering indirectly and playing around questions.

But such tactics are only general measures. Ames's biggest hurdle would be answering standard questions designed to detect foreign agents—such as, Have you recently met a KGB officer? If a subject isn't psychologically prepared to lie, it's important to create conditions that could explain a wrong or suspicious answer. That's why three other officers and I met Ames at a Washington café in May. There was no question that the FBI would observe us. Although Ames knew he wouldn't be meeting Chuvakhin alone, he played along, acting surprised to see me when I walked in. Chuvakhin introduced us. Exchanging business cards, we talked for about ten minutes. Then I left, and Chuvakhin and Ames moved to another table to continue their conversation. Now our agent could truthfully answer he'd met a KGB officer. He took the test in the spring of 1986 before a new posting to Rome. Making use of our meeting, he passed.

Running Ames proved relatively easy. We planned dead drop sites and a system of signals to indicate warnings or schedule meetings. However, during the first year we didn't need to use the ordinary means of communication. We already had an ideal one—through Chuvakhin, a perfectly legitimate interlocutor for Ames. As per their routine, the two spoke about disarmament, Congress, the latest news—"innocent" subjects. Then Ames would hand over a packet of press releases for Chuvakhin and a package of documents for us. Chuvakhin would reciprocate with wads of hundred dollar bills. After the first $50,000 payment, Chuvakhin regularly handed over $20,000 to $50,000 in cash. We told Ames he'd be paid an additional $2 million, to be deposited in a Soviet bank.

Unaware that the KGB was using him to communicate with an agent, Chuvakhin believed he was facilitating a back-channel diplomatic line between Moscow and Washington. His real role came to light only after Ames was arrested in 1994. Ironically, the post-Soviet Russian administration didn't appreciate Chuvakhin's service to the Motherland. He was fired from his Foreign Ministry job by Andrei Kozyrev, the westernizing foreign minister. Completely unaware of his role until then, Chuvakhin was furious. He blamed me for setting him up and refused to meet with me again.

4

The list of CIA informants Ames provided at Chadwicks on June 13 depressed me deeply. Kryuchkov was also taken aback, although he managed to control his reaction. The presence of so many spies deep inside the KGB reflected poorly on him. The potential disaster was worsened by Yurchenko's defection in August, a major blow that threatened to unseat Kryuchkov as FCD chief.

Instead of telling his bosses in the Politburo that a CIA mole had identified eleven American spies, provided corroborating information about others and informed on several CIA eavesdropping operations in the Soviet Union, the head of intelligence took the credit himself. Kryuchkov made it appear that the exposures resulted from hard work by the KGB under his leadership. In return, he received laurels instead of criticism.

To make his story plausible, Kryuchkov had to arrest as many of the agents as he could, as quickly as possible. In his bid to reverse his fortunes, he kept even Rem Krassilnikov—the SCD general who masterminded the arrests—in the dark about the real source of the tip-offs he used to wrap up the CIA's Moscow operations. Kryuchkov's ploy worked, and he was soon made KGB chairman and given a coveted spot in the Politburo. Later he tried to hinder Mikhail Gorbachev's reform policies before taking part in an attempt to topple him. All the while, he knew that I knew how he got to the top, and he held it against me.

Among the first U.S. agents arrested in 1985 was KGB Major Sergei Motorin, one of the two moles in the Soviet embassy in Washington betrayed by Ames. The son of a high-ranking Party official, Motorin was a hulk of a man, a big jock and a ladies' man who ran no agents and knew almost no secrets. In 1980, a persistent FBI agent followed him to an electronics store in Chevy Chase, Maryland, where Motorin tried to buy an expensive television and stereo on credit. He was turned down because of his diplomatic immunity. But after Motorin left, the FBI convinced the store owner to help entrap him by suggesting he pay part of the price with cases of Russian vodka, which he could obtain duty-free. When Motorin returned with the vodka, an FBI video camera caught him on tape.[7] Confronted with the evidence, Motorin faced the prospect of losing his job if exposed or, worse, being charged with "speculation," the Soviet term for engaging in private enterprise. Finally recruiting him, the FBI gave him the cryptonym GAUZE.

Later, I was able to pinpoint when Motorin was enlisted, thanks to the unusually heavy FBI communications chatter we intercepted that day. It came from a group of surveillance cars operating near the office of the Novosti news agency, where Motorin worked. When he went downtown, the FBI followed him in force. We couldn't figure out what prompted such interest in Motorin, so Dmitri Yakushkin asked him about it after he returned to the *rezidentura*. Motorin said he had no idea. Yakushkin advised him to be especially alert in the future and to inform the *rezidentura* about anything in the least bit suspicious.

That Motorin wasn't brave enough to report the recruitment pitch against him eventually had tragic repercussions. The FBI and CIA began feeding him false information to convey to the *rezidentura*. His espionage continued until 1984, when he was rotated back to Moscow and demoted to section A, planting propaganda against the West. To throw off the Americans after his arrest, he was ordered to call a woman with whom he'd had an affair in Washington and assure her everything was fine. The ploy deceived the CIA and FBI, which were no doubt anxious about his disappearance. It was the kind of suspicion-dispelling move we tried to make each time we arrested an American agent.

Colonel Leonid Polishchuk, another agent betrayed by Ames, became the subject of an ornate story fabricated by the SCD. When posted to Kathmandu, Nepal, in 1974, Polishchuk visited a casino and gambled away all the money allotted to him by the KGB. Stepping in, the CIA offered a loan to cover his losses before he was found out by his superiors. Polishchuk took the money and later agreed to spy in return. Before the end of his tour, the CIA (code-naming him WEIGH) trained and equipped him to spy from Moscow.[8] But that was the last the CIA heard from him until he was assigned as a Line KR officer to Lagos, Nigeria, in February 1985. The CIA approached him again, and he resumed spying until he was exposed.

Polishchuk had long wanted to buy a Moscow apartment near his parents, and the SCD arranged for just such a place to become available. The CIA deposited the 20,000 rubles he'd need in a hollow rock in the capital, near the Severyanin railroad station. He was arrested on his arrival in Moscow. Meanwhile, a story was circulated inside the KGB and eventually leaked to the CIA and FBI: The Second and Seventh departments had stumbled on a great find while following a CIA officer. The KGB officers spotted the American loading a dead drop—the fake rock. They then waited patiently to see who came by to unload it. It was Polishchuk, of course. To embellish the account, he was said to have been drunk when arrested at the drop site. It was Martynov who first passed the information to the FBI, saying he'd heard the story from Androsov, who had just returned from a trip to Moscow.[9]

The Center didn't net all the agents Ames betrayed. GRU Colonel Sergei Bokhan spied for the CIA for ten years, informing it of at least two attempts to sell us American military technology. Posted in Greece in the 1970s, Bokhan (code-named BLIZZARD) exposed CIA officer William Kampiles, who walked into the Soviet embassy offering to sell the manual for a U.S. spy satellite.[10] In 1984, Bokhan informed the CIA that a Greek agent had sold the GRU plans for the Stinger missile.

Intelligence from another Soviet agent (whom I'll discuss later) had already put Bokhan under suspicion when Ames fingered him.

On May 21, 1985, the GRU ordered its officer back to Moscow, telling him his eighteen-year-old son was having problems at his military academy in Kiev. Refusing to believe that explanation, Bokhan fled to the United States with the help of the CIA.

Many others weren't so lucky, including Vladimir Piguzov, whom the CIA recruited in Indonesia in the 1970s and code-named JOGGER, and Vladimir Potashov, code-named MEDIAN, a KGB officer working under cover in Moscow's prestigious USA and Canada Institute. Potashov began spying for the CIA after approaching U.S. Defense Secretary Harold Brown during his visit to Moscow in 1981. Potashov was arrested and executed along with nine others betrayed by Ames. Piguzov was eventually pardoned by President Boris Yeltsin.

5

Rick Ames showed us how porous the United States was. You didn't find 20 spies inside the CIA or the NSA or FBI. You found one or two. You found more in the KGB because it was corrupt. The KGB was a good spy organization but a corrupt system. And thank God. Because they had us for lunch with the amount of intelligence they had. The United States was penetrated very broadly but not very deeply. Lots of agencies were losing secrets, but they didn't have huge penetrations.

—*David Major, retired FBI supervisory special agent and former director of counterintelligence at the National Security Council*

If the number of CIA agents in the KGB caused dismay, Ames's information about American eavesdropping operations inside the Soviet Union simply astounded. In 1985, the CIA was juggling several highly complex, technologically advanced, ingenious operations. One had begun in 1979, when, poring over spy satellite photographs, the Americans noticed a construction project near Yasenevo. The CIA narrowed down the possibilities until correctly guessing it was a top secret communications line to a nuclear weapons research institute at Krasnaya Pakhra, in a town called Troitsk twenty-five miles southwest of Moscow. We built the underground communications line to evade their eavesdropping on wireless communications. The CIA had been trying to penetrate the institute for years.

Working jointly with the NSA, the CIA began developing ways of accessing the cable and eventually settled on an operation similar to IVY BELLS. The agency code-named it TAW, the twenty-third letter of the Hebrew alphabet. It planned to clamp a tap on the cable while the project remained under construction. Unlike IVY BELLS, however, the completed communications line wouldn't be easily accessible. Special bunkers sealed with locked metal doors barred maintenance access points. In turn, security alarms and special Sixteenth Directorate KGB guards protected the structures.

The CIA planned to work around the problem by running wires from the tap to a recording device hidden nearby. After building a mockup of the site and training operatives to retrieve and replace tapes, it successfully installed the device in a construction trench. Officers routinely collected tapes from the recording device for five years.

Unbelievably, the CIA also installed eavesdropping devices disguised as tree branches near research installations. The "branches" beamed information back to Langley via satellite.

For its sheer imagination, however, what Ames told us about operation ABSORB amazed us. By the early 1980s, the Americans had essentially located all our permanent ground-based nuclear missile installations. What they didn't know, especially after we began developing MIRVs (multiple independently targeted reentry vehicles) that could hold up to ten warheads, was how powerful the weapons were that each site could launch.[11]

While the United States was building highways in the 1950s—largely spurred by the security need for a national transportation network—the Soviet Union laid railroad track for the same reason. The CIA knew that most nuclear missiles were manufactured in the Soviet west and then shipped on the Trans-Siberian railroad to the Far East for installation in sites aimed at the United States. The CIA developed a plan to smuggle a complex Geiger counter into a train car. Traveling past missile-laden trains on the Trans-Siberian line, the device would count the number of warheads inside by registering the tiny amount of radiation each weapon emitted. By 1983, the CIA had spent almost $50 million on the project. In a test run, the agency hid high-tech cameras behind a fake wall inside a shipping container sent by a Japanese company from the far east port of Vladivostok across the Soviet Union to Eastern Europe. The cameras snapped photos of oncoming trains, many of which were carrying hardware from military manufacturing plants.

The CIA prepared to do the same with its Geiger counter, called a radiation detection device. It sent a container to Japan rigged with complex technology hidden inside a shipment of ceramic vases to be delivered to Hamburg.[12] (The KGB later called ABSORB the "porcelain operation.")

By then, however, Ames had already exposed the project. Although he failed to provide the shipping details, by the time the rigged container arrived at the Far East port of Nakhodka in February 1986, the SCD's Krassilnikov was heading an effort to blanket our ports and stations with surveillance. The CIA cargo was scheduled to be loaded on a train bound for Leningrad, all the way west across the Soviet Union's vast expanse. But KGB officers intercepted the container before it left Nakhodka. Inside, they found cameras, sensors and computer equipment. The technology was designed to register radiation levels, record the location of readings and peg them to images snapped by camera lenses through ventilation slits in the container's side.[13] The apparatus also included radar detection devices to collect information about Soviet air defenses. It was an astounding project, both for the guts it took to put it in motion and its complexity.

Krassilnikov wanted to publicize his success in foiling the CIA mission as part of the propaganda effort against the United States. We had recently used Yurchenko's defection to maximum effect, and Operation ABSORB would give us even more ammunition. But the KGB leadership quashed the idea to protect Ames, who had enabled us to thwart the CIA's investment of many years of research and development costing hundreds of millions of dollars.

6

More cases continued to unfold during the Year of the Spy. In the summer of 1985, a handful of officers at the CIA began to realize their agency was suffering serious problems. Among the leaders was Paul Redmond, an independent-minded, quick-tempered Harvard University graduate from Boston who ran clandestine operations for the SE division.

When he defected in August, Yurchenko seemed to explain why several American agents had disappeared: Edward Lee Howard. But at that critical time, Bearden in the SE division found it difficult to ascertain what director Bill Casey thought about the matter. During a meeting in Casey's office in early August, Bearden pointed out that the CIA had handled Howard's firing badly. "Maybe we deserved it," he said. "We fired him and he was seething with revenge."

"How could we deserve it?" snapped SE division chief Gerber, who resented Casey's close relationship with Bearden, whom many saw as a cowboy. Gerber's subordinates considered him a bureaucratic-minded hard driver. But they also looked up to him as a deep-thinking intellectual. "How could we deserve treason?" he asked.

The enigmatic Casey then seemed to make light of Howard's betrayal, saying mistakes were inevitable. "It only hurts for a day," he offered.

In September, however, Redmond and others in the CIA began to suspect the KGB had another source. Agents Howard couldn't have known about were also being wrapped up. But events moved too quickly. Far from figuring out what was hitting them, the agency's Soviet hands had enough trouble simply staying abreast of what was happening to their assets.

In October, CIA agent MILLION failed to show up for a scheduled meeting. MILLION was Gennady Smetanin, a GRU lieutenant colonel posted to Portugal. Cryptonyms usually stand for something; the CIA came up with Smetanin's after he approached the defense attaché's office in the Lisbon U.S. embassy in 1983 asking to be paid $1 million for his services. He claimed to have stolen that amount from the GRU *rezidentura* and had to return it. A polygraph test indicated he was lying, but he confessed and the CIA signed him up anyway.

Smetanin went on to become a shining example of the CIA's professional handling. Not a top-ranking officer, he had limited access to secret information and probably didn't provide the United States with much useful intelligence. But the CIA hoped he'd become a valuable source after promotions would give him access to better information. For that reason—and also because he obviously had an experienced handler—the CIA did a good job of communicating with him. It proved to us that the Americans had learned the lessons of the Penkovsky case. They kept meetings secret, conducting them in safe houses. They thoroughly checked rooms for eavesdropping devices and always provided backup sites

for meetings. And they gave Smetanin and his wife Svetlana—
who also spied for the CIA—U.S. passports, false identities and
disguises in case they had to escape.

But, as I've already said, even the best handling couldn't protect
against enemy spies. The GRU recalled Smetanin to Moscow in
August, requesting he begin a scheduled home leave early. Com-
plying, he and his wife were arrested as they stepped off a train in
Moscow.

Ames also identified the "angry colonel" about whom Edward
Lee Howard had informed us. The American agent's name was
Vladimir Vasiliev. The GRU colonel volunteered to work for the
CIA in Budapest and operated under the cryptonym ACCORD. He
too was arrested.

In November, the CIA lost track of yet another agent. KGB
Lieutenant Colonel Gennady Varennik worked in the Soviet embassy in Bonn under cover as a Tass correspondent. In April
1985, he approached the CIA in Vienna, saying he needed
money. He was recruited under the cryptonym FITNESS. According to the CIA, Varennik warned the agency that the KGB
planned to damage relations between Washington and Bonn by
bombing U.S. personnel in Germany and blaming local radical
terrorist groups such as the Baader-Meinhof or Red Army Faction
gangs.

President Reagan allegedly took a special interest in intelligence about KGB sabotage operations, which also resonated
loudly among other members of his administration. Bearden
writes that Casey took "the darkest stories of the Soviets at face
value. Arguing against him could be dangerous for a CIA officer's
career."[14]

If discussions of a plot to stage explosions in Bonn did take
place in Karlshorst, they were more likely generated not from
above—as Varennik was said to have claimed—but by a young

officer such as Varennik himself. Aspiring officers often proposed ambitious plans in order to get noticed; I did the same myself. But the KGB's managers considered use of terror unacceptable. Although the Soviet Union aided national liberation movements and other groups that committed terrorist acts, Soviet intelligence itself didn't resort to terror.

Mobilization in case of war would be something else. For that, the KGB planned sabotage and other fifth column actions. We trained special forces for diversion operations and, as already mentioned, deposited supply caches in various countries. The KGB held annual meetings to discuss updating war mobilization plans. But the intelligence leadership would have ruled out the type of peacetime proposals Varennik is said to have described. Had we really planned acts of terror, discussions about them would have been highly secret. They would have taken place in Moscow, not Berlin, and lower-ranking officers such as Varennik wouldn't have been privy to the debates.

Ames provided no precise intelligence about Varennik, requiring the Center to conduct its own significant analysis. That was often the case. Ames frequently gave indirect information, either confirming what we already knew or sparking new drives to identify agents. Varennik was arrested after his exposure. The KGB recalled his wife and children to Moscow several days later, telling them he'd slipped on ice and hurt himself.

Ames also exposed Major Sergei Vorontsov, a counterintelligence officer in the local Moscow branch of the SCD. The gruff, street-smart officer contacted the CIA in February 1984 by dropping a letter through the window of an embassy car. Code-named COWL, Vorontsov told the CIA about practices we employed to track American agents in Moscow, including use of a chemical substance the KGB had developed decades earlier to track targets in Moscow. The CIA called it spy dust.

The uncommon substance contained nitrophenyl pentadien (NPPD), which could be used in small amounts. The KGB placed the chemical where targets were likely to come into contact with it. Traces would stick to anything they touched. If we wanted to confirm whether a KGB officer was meeting a CIA operative, for example, the chemical could be deposited on the passenger seat of the Russian's car. If it later showed up anywhere the American had been, we knew we had our man (or woman). The CIA long suspected we used the chemical, having found traces of it on one of its officers. But the agency wasn't sure until Vorontsov provided a sample. After his defection, Yurchenko also confirmed the substance's existence. Shortly thereafter, in April 1985, the CIA decided to inform Moscow embassy employees about the news. It raised a media stink. The Americans feared NPPD was carcinogenic—which was potentially true.

Vorontsov also told the CIA about Father Roman Potemkin, a KGB operative working under cover as an Orthodox priest. (Most of the Orthodox hierarchy was in some way connected to the KGB at the time.) Potemkin had tried to win the confidence of American journalist Nicholas Daniloff—Moscow correspondent for U.S. News and World Report—by claiming to oppose Soviet religious oppression. When Daniloff showed the CIA a letter of technological information sent to him and addressed to the agency, the CIA contacted the priest—mistakenly thinking he'd written it. Nothing came of the exchange, but Daniloff later found himself at the center of an international scandal. Set up by a source of his who gave him photographs of the Afghan war, he was arrested and imprisoned. That was Moscow's reply to the FBI's arrest of a Soviet physicist at the United Nations on spying charges.

U.S. Secretary of State George Schultz met Soviet Foreign Minister Eduard Shevardnadze to discuss Daniloff's arrest. Burton Gerber also used a back channel to the KGB to meet counterintelligence chief Anatoly Kireyev in Vienna about the issue. Daniloff was soon released.

Meanwhile, Vorontsov was arrested and used to entrap his CIA handler. When an American called Vorontsov's KGB office at an appointed time in March 1986, Vorontsov was on the other end, ready to arrange a meeting. SCD officers arrested the handler, Michael Sellers, when he showed up to meet his agent, and expelled him from the Soviet Union.

By early 1986, Redmond was no longer in the minority of CIA officers convinced the agency harbored a mole. In January, SE counterintelligence chief Gus Hathaway—the former Moscow station chief—and SE division head Gerber approached CIA case officer Sandy Grimes about the previous year's failures. Grimes headed SE operations in Africa at the time but had also handled one of the CIA's vanished agents, Leonid Polishchuk. Hoping to safeguard agents not yet compromised, Gerber assigned Grimes to handle two new spies recruited in Eastern Europe.[15] The same month, Hathaway, Gerber, Bearden and Clair George, chief of CIA covert operations, briefed director Casey about their ongoing losses.

One of their major theories was that we were intercepting CIA communications. To pinpoint a leak, the CIA sent internal cables about a fictitious agent in Moscow, then monitored communications links to ascertain whether the cables were the source of information to the KGB. Langley sent another series of cables to Moscow's CIA station falsely claiming that our unpopular *rezident* in Lagos, Nigeria, was taking part in a fictitious U.S. operation. The Americans then waited to see if the *rezident* would be summoned to Moscow. He wasn't.

The CIA also sent a counterintelligence deputy chief to Moscow to meet the station chief in the CIA's secret work area on the top floor of the U.S embassy. Dubbed the "yellow submarine," the cramped enclosure, sealed inside a metallic box floating on cushions of air, had a self-contained power supply. (No electric devices or manual typewriters were permitted inside. That directive came after a 1984 incident, when the CIA discovered we had intercepted thirteen electric typewriters shipped to Moscow and installed tiny transmitters inside them. Placed in secure areas of the embassy, although not those used by the CIA, the typewriters broadcast every typed word to a listening post outside the embassy.) Testing for KGB penetration of the premises, the two men discussed another fictitious operation against the KGB, but again nothing came of the conversation.

Early in 1986, Casey asked John Stein, a top CIA officer, to examine files from the SE division for signs of a leak. Stein concluded that the agency had a major problem, but probably not caused by a Soviet agent inside the CIA. At the same time, Casey continued to disregard advice from Paul Redmond and others to launch a mole hunt.

Meanwhile, Ames underwent polygraph testing in preparation for his posting to Rome. Scheduled for May 2, it was his first since 1976 and he was deeply worried about it. When the test administrator asked him if he'd been pitched by a foreign intelligence service, his negative answer registered fluctuations on the machine. The examiner pressed on, trying to find out why Ames appeared to be lying. Replying to the administrator's questions, Ames explained that the nature of his work meant *he* was involved in pitching Soviets. He also claimed to be afraid of possible recruitment attempts in Rome. After the test, the examiner again asked Ames to explain his response. He replied that the question made him nervous because he knew the KGB was always trying to recruit CIA officers. "We know the Soviets are out there somewhere, and we're worried about it," he said.

That seemed to settle it. The examiner accepted Ames's explanation of his suspicious response and believed he was telling the truth. According to procedure, however, he again tested Ames, asking the same questions about being pitched. This time, Ames responded evenly, registering nothing to indicate he was lying. He was on his way to Rome, thrilled that the KGB had helped him pass the test and evade exposure.

Meanwhile, the CIA revamped its security procedures, tightening rules about sending communications, cutting down the volume of sensitive information broadcast electronically and reducing files on new agents that a mole might intercept. In May 1986, Hathaway asked Jeanne Vertefeuille, station chief in Gabon, to head a special task force to investigate the 1985 and 1986 losses. But the Iran-Contra affair soon distracted the CIA from its search for a leak. The scandal blew up after Nicaraguan troops shot down a U.S. military cargo plane carrying weapons to the Contra rebels seeking to overthrow the socialist Sandinista government. The news exposed the CIA's—and especially Casey's—violation of a Congressional ban on supplying arms to the rebels.

In December 1986, Casey was hospitalized with a brain tumor after suffering a seizure in his office. His acting replacement, Robert Gates, later said he was never told about the importance of the 1985 losses. The agency failed to put together the evidence about its exposed operations—and continued to do so until a Russian betrayed Ames to the CIA. Meanwhile, as the FBI formed its own group to investigate the losses of bureau agents Motorin and Martynov, the CIA continued learning about yet more disappearances.

7

Of the agents and operations Ames betrayed, I can confirm only those he exposed through the *rezidentura* when I was stationed there. As I've said, he provided circumstantial evidence about many spies, often not giving names because he didn't know or wasn't yet prepared to provide them. He also identified agents already implicated by others. Because new handlers ran Ames after I left Washington in 1986, I can't say exactly how many agents he fingered.

In early October 1985, the CIA pulled Ames off the Yurchenko case to begin studying Italian in preparation for his new posting as Soviet branch station chief in Rome in 1986.

Meanwhile, late in 1985, the Center planned a meeting with Ames outside the United States. He suggested Bogotá, where he and his wife, Rosario, planned to spend Christmas. Ames met a KGB operative introduced to him as Vlad in the Colombian Soviet embassy.[16] Ames learned his KGB cryptonym was LYUDMILA and agreed to sign his notes to the KGB as KOLOKOL, after the nineteenth-century liberal journal published by philosopher Alexander Herzen.

In July 1986, after passing his lie detector test, Ames took up his new post in Rome. Now he and Rosario began spending their KGB money liberally—although both purport she didn't yet know the source of the funds. Vlad flew to Rome to introduce Ames to his new go-between, Rome diplomat Alexei Khrenkov. Ames then exposed Sergei Fedorenko and Soviet scientist BYPLAY, whom he'd briefly handled in 1978.

Fedorenko had been rotated back to Moscow in the late 1970s after spying in New York, where Ames had handled him. The Russian cut off contact with the CIA after the 1977 arrest of TRIGON, another agent Ames had handled. However, Fedorenko wasn't arrested after his exposure by Ames. The KGB never found evidence of his espionage, despite heavy surveillance and searches of his apartment. Fedorenko was sent back to the United States in 1989 after working on a committee advising Mikhail Gorbachev. Ames met him in Washington and then informed on his old friend to the KGB once again, but Fedorenko defected before we had time to act on the information. He began lecturing at the Naval

War College in Newport, Rhode Island, near where the FBI bought his family a house.

In December 1986, the SCD arrested another agent Ames fingered. KGB Lieutenant Colonel Boris Yuzhin was a nuclear scientist sent to study at the University of California–Berkeley in a 1975 exchange program. Tasked with recruiting agents and gathering science and technology intelligence, he was instead recruited by the FBI under the cryptonym TWINE. Yuzhin gave the bureau information about KGB recruiting efforts and described what kind of information we were seeking on the West Coast. In 1978, three years after his exchange program ended, the KGB sent him back to San Francisco to operate under cover as a journalist.

One evening, a cleaning woman found a cigarette lighter on the floor of a Soviet consulate office in San Francisco. It contained a miniature camera. The device belonged to Yuzhin, who'd left it by accident. Naturally suspecting the Americans had recruited one of our officers, we launched intensive investigations. Having narrowed the possibilities to Yuzhin and another officer, we sent both back to Moscow in 1982. Installed as an analyst in a research institute, Yuzhin was kept under close watch.

Only after Ames named him did we finally pinpoint our man. He was arrested and tried but not executed. A court sentenced him to fifteen years hard labor, perhaps as a reward for his quick confession, or because Kryuchkov was feeling generous. Boris Yeltsin granted Yuzhin amnesty in 1992, and he moved to the United States.

Among the other agents Ames is credited with unmasking after I left Washington was a radar scientist the CIA code-named EAST-BOUND. He fell into a KGB trap by accepting an offer of amnesty and then helped set up his CIA handler, Erik Sites, who was arrested in May 1986.[17] In 1989, Ames identified MOTORBOAT, a Bulgarian he had recruited after the agent volunteered at the Rome embassy.

Ames is said to have exposed as many as twenty-five U.S. agents, a claim nearly impossible to verify. Some of the names chalked up to him were double agents—loyal KGB officers who made the CIA and FBI believe they spied for them. One particularly interesting case involved Alexander Zhomov, an SCD officer who staged an elaborate double-agent operation in Moscow in the late 1980s to protect Ames. The CIA gave Zhomov the cryptonym PROLOGUE.

To give the impression it had solved its problems and to rationalize its failures, the CIA also accused Ames of betraying agents about whom he couldn't have known. Other names incorrectly attributed to him in the press may be of agents the FBI and CIA had invented to obscure the number of spies they actually ran and to control the information about Ames filtering into the public domain.

Those kinds of actions were hardly unique. The SVR, the Russian foreign intelligence agency that replaced the FCD after the Soviet collapse, did the same. Organizations on both sides of the Atlantic continue to play complex propaganda games, making the task of confirming details about the agents Ames betrayed— even for someone heavily involved, like me—almost impossible at this time. However, my best knowledge leads me to concur with published reports that Ames was the first to provide the names of eleven U.S. agents: Leonid Polishchuk, Gennady Smetanin, Gennady Varennik, Sergei Vorontsov, Valery Martynov, Sergei Motorin, Vladimir Potashov, Boris Yuzhin, Vladimir Piguzov, Dmitri Polyakov and Vladimir Vasiliev.

Some of those names were already known to us, as I've said. Others were found only after the Center tracked them down from indirect information provided by Ames. For example, the KGB was already looking for Gennady Varennik when Ames offered information about him. And there were others named by Ames during the time I handled him who were already in our sights. I knew Gordievsky was a British spy when Ames fingered him (which he did after we asked him to provide more information about the suspected SIS agent).

8

I met Ames for the last time on June 13. I continued handling his case in Washington until he left for Rome—and I returned to Moscow—in the fall of 1986. During a meeting with Vlad in Rome, Ames expressed dismay at the sudden spate of arrests that followed our meeting in Chadwicks. He was angry but not livid because he understood we had to do something about the moles in our system. Still, he rightly felt that arresting the agents posed a major threat to his safety.

To assuage his displeasure, he was told that the arrests were the direct result of a Politburo decision over which the KGB had no control. While that explanation may have technically been true, I've never seen a directive confirming the claim. But I also doubt the arrests were truly at the Politburo's bidding. If Kryuchkov had reported to his political bosses what had actually happened—that a Soviet spy had exposed more than ten CIA agents passing Washington reams of information—the Politburo would have likely fired the KGB leadership immediately, depriving its members of their pensions. The news represented total disgrace. What, after all, was the KGB paid for if not to prevent such staggering security breaches?

But far from losing jobs, the KGB leadership handed out dozens of medals. That differed markedly from the CIA shakeup after Ames's disclosure in 1994. The KGB issued no censures because, as already noted, Kryuchkov refused to tell the Politburo that a KGB agent in Washington was responsible for all the exposures.

Instead, he said the KGB's own hard work had uncovered the agents—which reflected much better on the top brass. By that logic, it was a shame we'd been penetrated by so many moles, but at least KGB counterintelligence officers were obviously doing their jobs well. Still reeling from Yurchenko's defection and other problems, Kryuchkov was able to serve up a string of huge successes instead of one massive failure. Ames could have sunk Kryuchkov's career—but the FCD chief saved it with his manipulation. Naturally, the disinformed Politburo responded by approving plans for arresting the exposed agents.

Aside from his motivations, Kryuchkov can't be entirely faulted for the arrests he authorized. He had to do something about the moles—he couldn't allow them to remain in place and pass information to the Americans. Of course the arrests got the Americans thinking. The FBI and CIA formed commissions to investigate their leaks, which gave us some tense moments, to be sure. But if we'd allowed the U.S. agents to remain in position, what would have been the point of all my counterintelligence work?

Some arrests were covered up. Others were hushed up while we carried out a number of separate operations to protect Ames. Ultimately, the stories and operations were successful. After launching its mole hunts, the CIA concluded it hadn't been penetrated by the KGB—despite much evidence to the contrary. Our own mistakes notwithstanding, Ames—and later Hanssen—weren't exposed by detective work and continued to spy until they were betrayed by CIA agents.

If the Politburo had reacted differently—if it had asked why there were so many spies inside the KGB in 1985—it would have concluded that Soviet intelligence was riddled with major human resources problems. Any intelligence service has elements of patronage. At the KGB, however, the problem was especially serious. The awards given to tens of KGB officers in the face of obvious failure spoke to the substantial impunity officers like Kyruchkov enjoyed.

Although the KGB had many honest and decent officers, it protected those whose good relations with their bosses enabled them to get away with almost anything. Why weren't measures taken to stop risky activity, which in the end compromised not only a single individual but the entire agency?

Some KGB officers landed their jobs and promotions through patronage. Good connections often came with immunity to bad evaluations. Thus a number of potential traitors weren't stopped before it was too late. Perhaps just as damaging, however, some hardworking officers who saw others wrongly favored found justification for committing treason.

In Washington at the time, I found out about many of the arrests of agents Ames exposed only in 1986. Some have said I reacted angrily. I know I was upset that wrapping up almost the entire network of CIA agents in Moscow might have easily led the Americans to Ames. In fact, I said nothing about it then. I did—and do—disagree to some extent about how the moles were seized. But it wasn't my place then to criticize the arrests, which were carried out by another department with different responsibilities than my own. There were also unspoken rules. It was up to the Center to decide how to use the information I provided from our agents. I was never asked what I thought and I never volunteered to make it known. My criticism came much later.

In the final analysis, while it would have been absurd to let CIA agents in the KGB continue providing the Americans with intelligence, not all of them should have been arrested. Some moles could have been recruited as triple agents to pass along disinformation to the CIA. In other cases, officers could have been demoted and assigned to jobs that would have cut off access to classified information. Still, the exceedingly difficult job of turning double agents into triple agents could have worked only in a few isolated cases. Despite his motivations, therefore, from an operational point of view, Kryuchkov didn't commit a serious mistake in arresting the agents Ames betrayed.

Another question altogether is what happened to them after arrest. Maybe it's worth repeating that I think execution was wrong and entirely unnecessary. Martynov may have damaged us by exposing John Walker. But what about someone like Motorin, his colleague in Washington, who also was shot? He knew practically nothing. He couldn't have told the Americans much more than that I was a counterintelligence officer and Stanislav Androsov was the *rezident* in Washington at the time—which the CIA already knew. I remained deeply convinced that the spies Ames betrayed should have been fired and deprived of their pensions, but no more. What further harm could they have done?

Ames, meanwhile, ended his tour in Rome and returned to Washington in 1989 to head the western branch of the SE division. In October 1990, he became an analyst at the CIC, the CIA counterintelligence center. After the Soviet collapse in 1991, he continued spying for Russia until his arrest on February 21, 1994.

_8_

WASHINGTON STATION:
HOW TO CATCH A SPY

1

The bombshell dropped on a typically mild autumn day in Washington. Leaving my apartment in the residential compound that Saturday morning in October 1985, I visualized the pile of work waiting in my office. The *rezidentura* was largely empty. With Androsov on vacation in Moscow, only his deputy and a duty officer were at their desks when I arrived. It fell to me, as the station's second in command, to deal with the usual communications arriving from the Center. Other concerns were decidedly not routine. At the top of my list was how to handle fellow Washington KGB officer Valery Martynov, whom Ames had exposed as an American spy months earlier. I'd been agonizing over how to get him back to Moscow, but hadn't figured out how to do it without risking him taking flight.

That problem was about to worsen—but in a way that marked the start of one of the KGB's greatest successes ever. The cipher officer delivered the day's cables. Several minutes after I sat down to read them, the deputy *rezident* knocked on my door. He held an envelope in his hand. "Degtyar received this by mail," he said. "Have a look at it."

The envelope was addressed to Victor Degtyar, a midlevel intelligence officer in the *rezidentura*. It had been mailed to his apartment in a Virginia suburb, dropped in front of his door by a letter carrier. It was postmarked "Prince George's Co, MD." A second envelope inside gave me a moment's surprise. "DO NOT OPEN," it read. "TAKE THIS ENVELOPE UNOPENED TO VICTOR I. CHERKASHIN."

Nothing on the envelope indicated who had sent it, but clearly the writer understood something about KGB procedures. He must have known the FBI relaxed its otherwise unrelenting surveillance of our officers when they were at home—and used that to minimize risky direct contact. Addressing the envelope to me also revealed that the sender knew who was who within the *rezidentura*.

I silently removed the sensational letter that would come to shame and haunt the guardians of American security. I couldn't help thinking that the surprise delivery revealed mistrust of me among some of my colleagues back at Yasenevo. That suspicion must have included someone in the Washington station, for despite the envelope's strict instructions, it had already been opened.

"Dear Mr. Cherkashin," the typed letter began. "Soon I will send a box of documents to Mr. Degtyar. They are from certain of the most sensitive and highly compartmented projects of the U.S. intelligence community. All are originals to aid in verifying their authenticity. Please recognize for our long-term interests that there are a limited number of persons with this array of clearances. As a collection, they point to me . . . "

Our long-term interests? Who had sent the stunning message? What manner of entrepreneur was claiming an array of clearances for the U.S. intelligence community's most sensitive projects?

Obviously someone who knew something important. More than that, someone critically placed because—as I read further—the letter went on to betray several CIA and FBI moles inside the KGB: "I trust that an officer of your experience will handle them [the documents] appropriately. I believe they are sufficient to justify a $100,000 payment to me. I must warn of certain risks to my security of which you may not be aware. Your service has recently suffered some setbacks. I warn that Mr. Boris Yuzhin (Line PR, SF), Mr. Sergey Motorin, (Line PR, Wash.) and Mr. Valeriy Martynov (Line X, Wash.) have been recruited by our 'special services.'"

The letter went on to provide information about recent Soviet defectors to the United States. It also discussed a number of highly sensitive U.S. technical operations against our spying in the United States. And it included data about the sums the American government was spending on intelligence, including the NSA, FBI, CIA and military intelligence. The following day, I learned the envelope also contained an attachment—removed by the deputy *rezident*—providing intelligence about espionage projects in the U.S. space program.

There was no signature.

It seemed too good to be true. The overriding question was whether the offer was real or a provocation to trap the KGB through a double agent. Recruiting Ames had been more than enough success for a lifetime in intelligence, justifying all my work as a KGB officer. Receiving such a letter just six months later was exceedingly improbable. Most likely Ames had sent it to cover his tracks. If communications from the *rezidentura* to the Center were intercepted, the "evidence" that we had more than one source, he may have thought, would prompt the Americans to lay less blame on him.

It took me—and everyone else in the KGB—sixteen years to learn the real name of the letter's sender: FBI special agent Robert Hanssen.

Alone in my office, I wrote my thoughts in a cable to be sent on my private link to Kryuchkov. The line had been set up in May after my first Moscow briefing about Ames. Since I'd agreed to undertake no action concerning our new spy without the FCD chief's sanction, there had to be a way of informing him about the case while keeping it secret from everyone else, including the cipher officers who normally handled communications.

Only Androsov knew about my line to Kryuchkov. It was a unique situation; I've never heard of another secret communications link between a *rezidentura* deputy officer and the FCD chief. In most cases, only the *rezident*—or one of his authorized deputies if he was away—could contact the head of foreign intelligence. Others could send personal letters only by mail; as for encrypted communications, cipher clerks simply wouldn't accept messages from anyone else. I used my private line to Kryuchkov only on rare occasions. October 5 was one of them.

2

I struggled to contain my anger as I composed my cable. I had days to think about the brand-new volunteer's letter and its implications before working out a response. Dealing with the information it contained about American agents, however, couldn't wait. Motorin and Yuzhin were safely back in the USSR, but Martynov still sat in the office next to mine. Ames had already exposed all three spies, but no one in the *rezidentura* besides Androsov had known about them. Now that someone else had seen the letter addressed strictly (and wisely) to me, the secret was out in the open. More embassy personnel would inevitably know, making it harder to trap the traitor into returning home for interrogation—and execution. Martynov could now be tipped off and slip through my fingers. I was livid, but had to conceal all signs that I'd seen the letter had been read and that I was doing anything about its information concerning Martynov.

I'd been trying to find a way to get Martynov back to Moscow for five months. The easiest way would have been to send him home on vacation. But he'd just returned from a holiday to Moscow in the spring—when he happened to hear about John Walker. Having him take another break was impossible, a red flag to Martynov that he was under suspicion. There were other possibilities, such as sending him home to receive an award or inventing family trouble in Moscow that would require him to return. The trouble was that Martynov, as an intelligence officer, knew about such ploys. He'd detect the faintest whiff of something irregular and go straight to the FBI. It was also almost impossible to control the actions of his wife and children, who lived with him off compound and would be able to escape quickly. Meanwhile, Martynov had the benefit of the FBI's analysis in addition to his own. If the bureau stumbled on something suspicious, it would act to protect its agent. My only option was to do nothing while waiting to find a plausible excuse to send him home. Doing nothing was probably the hardest course to take, however, not least because I liked him.

Martynov was in his early thirties in October 1980, when he arrived in Washington on his first tour. He had a son and a daughter on whom he doted; I'd often see them playing at the embassy's Chesapeake Bay complex. The children attended the embassy school with my daughter, Alyona.

Martynov's Line X assignment to Washington was highly prestigious. It provided a chance to make a name for himself collecting science and technology intelligence. The American East Coast boasted countless engineering companies and libraries from which an enterprising young officer could glean information. It also hosted conferences and presentations on a myriad of scientific topics, giving excellent opportunities to make and develop contacts.

With his excellent prospects, the ambitious Martynov looked forward to a great career. His main mistake was overestimating his abilities.

A year into his tour, his superiors in Line X decided against giving him an agent to run, which would have been a crucial career step. The assignment went to another young Line X officer assigned to Washington at around the same time. The decision riled Martynov, who thought himself more qualified. Unlike Sergei Motorin—the other Washington KGB officer working as an FBI spy, who was often out chasing women—Martynov was a hard worker. But his inexperience showed when he met an American at a science conference in 1982 and, failing to notice a classic FBI trap, saw him as a promising target. The two met several times to speak about general topics and become acquainted. I later learned that Martynov became entangled in the FBI's Operation COURT-SHIP, its drive to recruit Soviets in Washington in the early 1980s.

The Center also failed to notice the obvious, perhaps because Martynov convincingly embellished his picture of his new American contact. That was strange because Yasenevo usually made a point of warning its field officers to watch for double agents. Perhaps this time the Center felt pressed for results. Meanwhile, Martynov got along well with his new American friend. Believing he was hooked, the FBI turned around and pitched *him*. As enticement, the bureau offered up a fictitious agent to recruit, through whom Martynov would receive disinformation to feed the Center. The fake intelligence would sound real enough to convince us he'd scored a huge success. He agreed with little persuasion, which was unusual in pitching agents.

Martynov was back on track in the KGB. Code-named GENTILE by the CIA and PIMENTA by the FBI, he met CIA officer Rod Carlson and FBI special agent Jim Holt twice a month. They used various safe houses for their fifty-odd meetings, often in the Virginia suburb of Crystal City. Martynov gave the FBI a running commentary of the goings on in the *rezidentura*, including operations and targets, instructions from the Center and rumors from Yasenevo. He also singled out likely recruitment targets for the FBI. Some of his information about our activities came from the wall map of Washington pinned inside the *rezidentura* offices to help process the FBI communications we were intercepting.

The FBI's plan to provide disinformation to the Center worked: Martynov was soon rewarded, becoming Line X deputy head after his superior had been rotated back to Moscow. Apparently, he didn't seriously consider the possible consequences of his actions. The FBI and CIA say he spied for the United States because he'd become ideologically disillusioned with the Soviet Union. He was also said to be dissatisfied with his intelligence work and sought the spice he felt his job should have given him. Martynov was paid some $200 to $400 a month for his services, clearly indicating he wasn't in it for the money. In fact, his priority was still his KGB career, not least because he wanted to provide for his wife and raise his children well, which spying for the FBI enabled him to do. In other words, he found it acceptable to betray his country for his family's sake. Espionage was part of a business arrangement he thought would never come to light because he was certain the KGB wouldn't be able to recruit agents who could expose him.

The most valuable intelligence sources have access to information unavailable elsewhere. Top agents also deliver intelligence regularly. By those standards, Martynov was hardly the most important of agents. Aside from general information and what he knew about his own S&T operations—not the most critical area for the FBI and CIA—he had only limited access to information. His espionage was essentially irrelevant to national security policy and international relations. The intelligence he gave—on the layout of the *rezidentura*, its personnel, routines and other general information—was valuable chiefly to counterintelligence officers operating against us. By dumb luck—and, to repeat, contrary to most accounts—he overheard a KGB general boasting about John Walker, enabling the FBI to catch one of our most valuable long-term spies. But Martynov's spying was ironically limited by the complex FBI counterintelligence operations that made work in Washington difficult for the KGB. Perhaps more so than in any other *rezidentura*, only those who truly needed to know about operations had access to sensitive information. Still, the Americans had high hopes Martynov would continue collaborating with them as he rose up the KGB hierarchy.

3

I was shocked to learn Martynov was the mole I'd been seeking for over a year, ever since we'd realized the FBI was trailing KGB officers around the city, leaving "clean" diplomats to go about their business. Yasenevo had to be informed, but I had to do it carefully. The Center treated defections and spying for the other side as an unfortunate fact of life. Traitors were dismissed as misguided—people who either believed the enemy's lies or had developed grave delusions of their own. Many in the KGB didn't want to seriously consider the constant danger that agents could penetrate Soviet intelligence. That would be an admission of weakness. Such simplistic but pervasive thinking made getting the top brass to look hard at counterintelligence issues a tough sell.

After much consideration and hesitation, I drafted a cable to Kryuchkov in April 1984. I didn't provide the names of officers I suspected as possible FBI or CIA agents or offer suggestions for how to find a mole in the *rezidentura*. I stuck to my analysis of the FBI radio intercepts and the homing devices we'd found, elaborating on my assumption that we'd been penetrated. The kind of information the FBI had gathered couldn't have come from simple outdoor surveillance of our activities, I argued.

When I showed the cable to Androsov, he said it could have serious repercussions. No one in Yasenevo wanted to hear that kind of news, he warned. His suggestion was to sit on the information until one of Kryuchkov's deputies, scheduled to visit Washington in May, could vet it. When the general arrived, we laid out my argument. The deputy dismissed the analysis as unconvincing, saying I hadn't provided enough evidence to support my accusations. He assured me Kryuchkov would react the same way, accusing me of spy phobia and whipping up mistrust. Restating my point only irritated him. His increasingly angry demeanor suggested he felt I'd put him in a delicate and unenviable situation by making him read the draft of my cable. By insisting on our view, we were forcing him to make a decision about a course of action. Given a good chance he'd make the wrong choice, the deputy preferred to do nothing instead. Since my argument would clearly find no support in Moscow, I didn't send it.

When Ames confirmed Martynov's espionage, I found no pleasure, only more tension, in having been right about a mole in the *rezidentura*. Now I had to come to terms with the fact that a colleague I liked had been selling us out for more than three years. And I had to find a way to catch him. Androsov was on vacation again; until he came back, I couldn't share the information with anyone. That night, I could hardly sleep. The next morning, I tried to convince myself that the whole unhappy matter was only part of my work. Why should it upset me?

Back at the office, my rationalization offered little comfort. I had to act as if nothing had happened. I struggled to recall my normal manner with Martynov. How did I usually greet him? Did I smile? Grip his hand hard when I shook it? I found I could remember none of it.

Since the air conditioning in the *rezidentura* worked poorly, I usually kept my office door open to circulate air, even when I handled top secret documents. Martynov kept his door open too. We often discussed politics and Washington's operational situation. It would be a tough day.

I'd already cabled Kryuchkov when Martynov showed up for work in the morning. Concentrating on the papers on my desk, I pretended not to notice him. Twenty minutes later, I had no choice but to speak to him. I got up and tapped on his door.

"*Dobroie utro* [good morning]," I said, trying to make my voice businesslike but not severe.

"Hello," the youthful Martynov replied, looking up from his desk.

"We intercepted FBI talk yesterday evening about activity near the Pentagon City zone," I said. "Are you sending any of your boys around there today? Warn them there will probably be surveillance."

"I don't think anyone's going there, but I'll check."

"Good. Line PR said Yuri was shopping there yesterday and didn't notice anything, so let me know. Maybe it's just a coincidence. He didn't tell anyone he'd be there, so maybe they were trailing someone else."

Martynov appeared to see no change in my behavior. Relaxing, I walked back to my desk. Soon he informed me that none of his officers had noticed anything at Pentagon City, and we both went back to work.

Watching Martynov like a hawk during the following weeks and months, I became attuned to his moods. I took his signs of stress as probable indicators of meetings with the FBI. At least that's what I thought. How much my constant watchfulness colored my perceptions is difficult to say. Martynov had been living a double life for years and was used to it. I also had to watch for changed behavior in his wife and children in the residential compound and at the Chesapeake Bay complex. But I was aided by the fact that no other embassy staff knew about his spying, eliminating the chance his family would sense an estrangement.

Returning from vacation, Androsov joined me casting around for a way to get Martynov back to Moscow. We relayed our thoughts to Kryuchkov at the Center, which was also working on the problem. Our ideas included inventing an agent for Martynov to run in Mexico, where we could nab him more easily. We dismissed that story as too suspicious. If giving Martynov a new agent had really been under discussion, the possibility would have been raised during his recent trip to the Center. Even if we managed to get him to Mexico, the FBI would probably set up some kind of protection for him. For starters, it would keep him under surveillance so he could signal at a sign of danger.

Pretending not to know about his spying included not curtailing his access to classified information. Officers were given no instructions to maintain extra secrecy. There were no changes in the *rezidentura*'s operations schedule. Work continued as usual, with Martynov receiving the same ciphered cables from Directorate T. As for the intelligence he received from his agents, I had no control over that. He was able to investigate any issues the FBI asked him to raise with his fellow officers, who of course had no inkling of his real intentions. By the end of the summer, his colleagues included several new officers brimming with Yasenevo gossip and eager for tips on Washington operations.

Experience told me I had to continue doing nothing to change the situation if I wanted to stay in the game against the American special services. When I saw that the letter from the agent I later learned to be Robert Hanssen had been read, I was afraid the game might be up. Luckily, however, nothing happened.

A month later, Yurchenko showed up at the gates of the embassy residential compound—and I had my way of sending Martynov home. Yurchenko would be accompanied to Moscow by an "honor guard" (ostensibly a formality to emphasize the importance of his return) to help make sure he didn't escape. Martynov would be one of the group's four members. If he didn't immediately suspect the real reason for his inclusion, the plan had a good chance of working. Because the FBI and CIA knew what was going on in the *rezidentura*, I also feared the Americans might suspect our motives and warn their agent. We decided to go ahead anyway. The Center approved the idea and sent a cable—for general consumption in the *rezidentura*—outlining a plan to send Yurchenko home accompanied by four officers with unimpeachable operational backgrounds. All would receive state awards in Moscow.

The next two days were even more nerve racking. I had to make sure Yurchenko safely boarded the special Aeroflot flight chartered to bring him home, and that Martynov was on the same plane. On November 7, the day before Yurchenko's return, Martynov left the office for several hours. Assuming he was meeting his FBI handlers, I grew nervous. But he showed up at the embassy at day's end looking calm. Everything seemed to be going according to plan. Nevertheless, I could barely sleep that night. Had Martynov appeared calm on purpose? To lull me into thinking nothing was wrong? Maybe he was planning an escape the following day. Surely he'd been poring over the possible reasons for his selection for Yurchenko's honor guard. Perhaps his confidence actually came from a resolution *not* to board that plane to Moscow.

My worries began to abate the following morning. Martynov showed up at the embassy on time lugging a small suitcase. The plan was still working. He, Yurchenko and the rest of the honor guard drove to Dulles airport together with some of the embassy staff—including Elena and me.

Elena had learned about Martynov while translating a cable about him several days earlier. She hurried to my office to hand the communication to me. "You know nothing about this!" I told her. I never doubted Elena's discretion but feared the slightest involuntary glance in the wrong direction might tip Martynov off. "You've never laid eyes on this cable."

Elena looked down at the floor. "Of course not." She also liked Martynov, so it was a supremely difficult moment for both of us. But she understood my priority was the task at hand.

Arriving at the airport, our group made its way to the Aeroflot plane on the tarmac. The travelers said their good-byes. Martynov walked up to shake my hand. Not noticing him, I turned away before he reached me. But Elena did see him. Her feelings stirred by his action, she walked up smiling and tugged on my arm.

"Valery Feodorovich wants to say good-bye to you," she said. I turned to shake his hand and—according to polite custom—look him in the eye. Elena and I knew that Martynov, a gentle man we both liked, was boarding a flight to his death. It was one of the events in my career I most questioned. Was doing my job on behalf of my country the right thing to do? I decided it was. Martynov was an American spy. Someone had to stop him from further betraying the Soviet Union.

Meanwhile, FBI agents mingled with the airport staff preparing the plane for takeoff. But as Yurchenko and Martynov walked up the steps to the cabin, I knew that whatever happened, there was nothing the Americans could do. My job with both men was finished.

On its way back to Moscow, the Aeroflot plane refueled at Shannon Airport in Ireland. Passengers usually got off to wait in the lounge for the hour or so it took. This time, a KGB officer from the Ireland *rezidentura* ordered the travelers to stay on board to prevent any possible provocations against Yurchenko. Ten hours later, the flight arrived in Moscow's Sheremyetevo 2 Airport without incident. Arrested as soon as he got off the plane, Martynov was driven straight to Lefortovo prison.

Two weeks later, Martynov's wife and children were informed that he'd hurt his leg. They too returned to Moscow. Now the Americans would almost certainly know their agent had been caught. Years later, Martynov's wife told journalists that her husband had expressed no concern about his final trip home and even seemed happy.

The CIA filmed Yurchenko's departure at Dulles. Watching the footage the same day, several officers, Paul Redmond among them, saw Martynov and immediately suspected he'd been exposed.[1] The FBI learned about his exposure a year later. FBI special agent Jim Holt, who worked with Martynov, later told me the bureau became concerned about his disappearance in the spring of 1986 and finally heard of his arrest from an informer that fall. The bureau launched a six-person probe called ANLACE to explain the loss of Martynov, Motorin and other agents. But ten months trying to find a leak produced nothing. The group was disbanded in September 1987, near the time of Martynov's execution.

Back in Moscow when he was tried in 1987, I was called as a witness. Pleading guilty, Martynov detailed his spying activities. After his execution, I was among several officers reprimanded for failing to expose him earlier. It was my only reprimand in forty years of service.

4

The Year of the Spy, 1985, was a watershed in espionage, a stunning succession of recruitments and betrayals for both sides in the Cold War. The immediate effects came later, the exposures of spies leading to arrests in 1986 and after—and to repercussions still playing out today. Much still remains unknown to both sides.

The main facts, however, are clear. One wave of betrayals that took place against us included the exposures of the Americans John Walker, Ronald Pelton and Edward Lee Howard. Although the revelations actually hurt the KGB, news of their espionage struck a stunning blow to U.S. intelligence, initially defining the Year of the Spy for the Americans. Among the agents exposed in

1985 was a spy with whom we had nothing to do: U.S. Navy intelligence analyst Jonathan Pollard. One of eleven agents the FBI arrested in 1985, he sold classified information to Israel. He and his wife were arrested on November 21, 1985, outside the Israeli embassy in Washington while trying to gain asylum. He was sentenced to life in prison; his wife, Anne, received five years. The case became a cause célèbre. Pollard claimed to have passed along intelligence vital to Israeli security, which the Pentagon had been withholding. It included information about Soviet arms shipments to Arab countries, chemical weapons in Syria, a Pakistani project to build a nuclear bomb and Libyan air defenses.

Pelton, Howard and Walker were exposed by Soviets—Yurchenko and Martynov, who dealt the KGB heavy blows. Having spied for years, their stories and fates entwined in 1985. It would have been an extraordinary time of high-stakes twists and turns even without Ames and Hanssen, who provided the year's third wave of betrayals. Their intelligence exposed the extensive network of CIA agents in the KGB and the GRU. That shocking fourth series of revelations defined the Year of the Spy for us, resulting in the arrests that would continue to baffle the CIA for many years.

So much had happened by the October day on which I received Hanssen's letter that I didn't believe it possible another once-in-a-lifetime recruitment had come my way. But exactly that had happened. The provider of the promised extraordinary secrets turned out to be real enough. Hanssen's unsolicited approach, his astounding "walk-in" self-recruitment, began a spying stint during which he betrayed more FBI secrets than anyone else in the agency's history. So much of his information also concerned the CIA that when U.S. counterintelligence officers began tracking down the source, they looked first to Langley. Hanssen allowed us to penetrate U.S. intelligence to such a degree that we came to regard him as our greatest asset, surpassing even Aldrich Ames.

_9_

WASHINGTON STATION:
THE BIGGEST CATCH: HANSSEN

1

Operational intelligence work conjures images of clandestine meetings, dead drops, disguises and other means of evading and penetrating the other side's agencies. Actually, as I've suggested, at least 90 percent of my job consisted of routine, including hours at my desk reading everything from newspaper articles to agent files and cables from the Center. Even active case officers rarely met with agents. Operations were usually preceded by weeks of detailed planning and coordination with the Center. Everything had to be written up in volumes of reports to Yasenevo. Venues had to be found, security and countersurveillance provided, supporting officers picked to participate. In our trade, the more contingencies were anticipated and provided for, the less risky the operations.

Some cases, however, didn't afford the luxury of time. The opened letter delivered to Victor Degtyar that exposed Martynov demanded quick action to stem further security breaches. In Androsov's absence, Degtyar, to bypass me, could only have taken the letter to Androsov's second deputy, whom I suspected of unsealing it. That would mean both he and Degtyar had probably seen its contents. I knew I couldn't rely on either's sense of ethics. I couldn't tell them we already knew Martynov was collaborating with the FBI, or that we were preparing an operation to get him back to the USSR. I also couldn't prevent them from talking to others about the letter. That meant I could no longer guarantee that Martynov, who was still in the *rezidentura,* wouldn't find out he'd been fingered. Even if the letter were seen as a joke, a single word about it in the embassy would tip him off.

Writing to Kryuchkov, I described exactly what had happened and proposed inventing a cover story to obscure the letter's nature and make sure all future communications from the anonymous volunteer would come directly to me. I suggested the Center send the *rezidentura*'s second deputy a cable saying the KGB was cooperating with the Bulgarian intelligence service, the DS, in an operation meant to provide cover for one of its agents.

Since I'd recently worked with the DS *rezident* in Washington, it was a natural cover. I proposed saying that our Bulgarian "friends" had asked us to assist them in checking the sincerity of their agent by gauging his reaction to information fed to him by a source in his network. If the agent was cooperating with the FBI, the bureau would find out about the letter. The Center would have to make it clear that the information about Martynov was invented, part of a ruse to see whether the FBI would follow up on the message, thereby verifying a leak. According to the cover, the operation had nothing to do with the KGB; we were participating only to help the Bulgarians.

I suggested that the Center order all other *rezidentura* officers to hand all messages directly to me, since I had the best relationship with the DS *rezident.* I included the plan in my secret cable to the foreign intelligence chief—a communication I was sure no one else could possibly access—and gave it to the head cipher officer to send. The same day, an order arrived from the Center instructing all officers to do exactly what I'd proposed. It ordered that all unsolicited messages be handed to "Alexei," my alias at the time. Since the idea was completely untraceable to me, there was no suspicion that it was anything other than what it purported to be—a new dictate out of the blue directly from Yasenevo. That also discredited the information in the previous day's letter.

The plan worked. The wily second secretary handed me documents he'd removed from the envelope sent to Degtyar (which he'd previously withheld). I never had a problem with that particular breach again.

Next, I got to work analyzing Degtyar's letter. There was little doubt the volunteer was an intelligence officer. That was clear right away because to prove his "bona fides," he betrayed three agents about whom only an intelligence officer would have known. His motives, however, remained unclear. I soon ruled out a move by Ames to help provide cover for himself. There were too many nuances about which he couldn't have known, and not enough overlap between what I pieced together about the letter writer and what I knew about Ames. He wouldn't have known so much about NSA activities and finances. The letter also made me think its sender was located in New York rather than Washington. My best guess was we were dealing with an FBI agent. Back at the Center, Kryuchkov agreed with my conjectures. His standing with the Politburo had dramatically improved thanks to Ames, and he was thrilled that we appeared to have pulled off the impossible by recruiting someone else potentially just as valuable.

On October 15, a week and a half after Degtyar received the anonymous volunteer's letter, he found another package from the same sender. As promised, it contained a large number of classified documents. The following day, the FBI had its first clue that something was up when surveillance officers spotted Degt-yar showing up for work with a large canvas bag. They noted that as unusual, but the report was never followed up.[1]

Coming on top of his first letter, the new documents proved the volunteer wasn't fainthearted. He'd made a decision to spy and was doing it in full measure. From the little I could tell from his two deliveries, he was highly professional. That was why he was being so careful to obscure his real identity. He knew that CIA and FBI agents inside the KGB posed his greatest risk.

In his initial letter, the volunteer provided a simple code to set up meetings and dead drops: "I am open to commo [communications] suggestions but want no specialized tradecraft," he wrote. "I will add 6, (you subtract 6) from stated months, days and times in both directions of our future communications."

That and other aspects of his approach were unusual because he was dictating to us how to run him. It was also highly pragmatic. The volunteer had approached me because he'd seen my FBI file and knew who I was. He also seemed to trust me, which was rare in espionage. That was flattering—and a good move on his part because it made me more inclined to believe what he said. It also made his approach feel more human than a general appeal to the KGB. Above all, it provided more evidence of his experience, reinforcing my instinctive sense that my best course of action would probably be to agree to whatever he said. If the volunteer wanted to run his own case, I wouldn't stand in his way. My most important concern was for him to deliver valuable intelligence to the KGB.

2

The report [on Hanssen's espionage by the Office of the Inspector General of the Department of Justice, 2003] calling Hanssen a mediocre agent just gets it wrong. Bob Hanssen was diabolically brilliant. We would sit in my office and talk about the vulnerabilities of intelligence officers and agents and what the weaknesses were in tradecraft. Bob Hanssen knew this business. When I later read about how he operated, I said, "You diabolical bastard! You did exactly what we were talking about." The people who say he wasn't a master spy are those who aren't close to what his operation was and how very, very clever it was. He never let the Soviets run him because he knew about the operational mistakes they made. Bob just turned that on its head. He knew everything we knew about what the Soviets did—and we knew a lot about how they operated. He also knew what we did. So he could operate within the cracks.

—David Major, *retired FBI supervisory special agent and former director of counterintelligence at the National Security Council*

Robert Philip Hanssen was born in 1944 in Chicago to a police officer and a housewife. He attended Knox College, a small school in Illinois, where he studied the Russian language. On graduating, he enrolled in a dentistry program at Northwestern University. However, he soon decided to take up accounting and earned an MBA from Northwestern. He worked as an accountant before signing up with the Chicago Police Department as a financial investigator.

In 1968, Hanssen married Bernadette Wauck, who called herself Bonnie. She was a devout Catholic and a member of the highly conservative, secretive Opus Dei organization, said to exert influence on Pope John Paul II. Hanssen, a Lutheran, converted to Catholicism and joined the group.

He started work with the FBI in 1976 in a white-collar crime unit in Gary, Indiana. He was transferred to New York two years later to take part in accounting-related investigations. In 1979, he signed up with the New York field office intelligence division to help create an automated counterintelligence database to track Soviet intelligence officers. Hanssen was a computer and electronic technology whiz. In addition to helping create the computerized database, he worked with technicians installing eavesdropping bugs and video surveillance.

Soon the junior FBI special agent began his first stint as a spy. Hanssen walked into the New York office of AMTORG, the Soviet trade organization serving as a front for the GRU, and volunteered to provide intelligence. During the following months, he exposed Dmitri Polyakov and gave the GRU a secret FBI list of Soviet diplomats suspected of being intelligence officers. The following year, in 1980, his wife discovered him writing a letter to the GRU in the basement of their Scarsdale house. She suspected he was hiding evidence of an affair. To convince her otherwise, he confessed to spying but told her he was tricking the GRU by providing worthless information. Still a devout Catholic, Bonnie made Bob confess to their priest. Hanssen refused to come clean to the FBI, however. Instead, he agreed to give the money the KGB paid him, about $30,000, to charity and promise never to spy again. He spent years paying installments to Mother Teresa.

In 1981, Hanssen was transferred to the intelligence division at FBI headquarters in Washington, where he soon became a supervisory special agent. Then he was moved to the budget unit, where he helped draw up the agency's classified intelligence budget requests to Congress. In 1983, he took an assignment to head the unit analyzing FBI information on Soviet intelligence operations in the United States. He also served on a special committee in charge of coordinating technical intelligence projects against Soviet intelligence. Much of the information to which he was privy came from the CIA.

Hanssen was posted back to New York in 1985. He'd been promoted to supervisor in counterintelligence, giving him greater access to secret information. He'd be conducting technical operations against Soviets stationed at the United Nations and the

New York Soviet consulate. Ten days later, he sent his first letter to Degtyar. Until his exposure, the KGB never knew that agent B (or "Ramon Garcia," as he signed some of his notes) had spied for the GRU six years earlier. We gave our new agent the cryptonym KARAT but often referred to him as "the Source."

3

When Johnnie Walker spied, he lived in Norfolk. For ten years, he left Norfolk and drove to where he spied. When Bob Hanssen started spying, Cherkashin said, "We'll pick a place out here." And Bob said, "Bullshit!" He said, "I'm not going to be walking around, sliming around in the mud wearing a suit out here." Bob had to have cover for action. Cherkashin said, "You'll come to us." And Bob says, "No. You come to me." Cherkashin was smart enough to let him run his own operations. The Soviets would find the sites—and Bob would approve them. Hanssen's first dead drop was across the street from his house. They were all within four or five miles from his house. He would set the signal and then go in and fill the drop. Then a Russian would come in, read the signal, clear and fill the same drop and go home. It would take one act. Then Bob would return, clear the drop, set another signal and then leave. So Bob had four or five operational acts and the Russian had one. Read and then fill, clear, then go home and the next day come out and see if the signal had been set to show it had been cleared. That minimized the officer's action and maximized the agent's action. No one else spies like that.

—David Major, *retired FBI supervisory special agent and former director of counterintelligence at the National Security Council*

On October 24, Degtyar received a third letter at his house. The envelope was postmarked "New York, NY," which seemed to confirm at least one of my assumptions. The message indicated a drop site for the sender's payment under a footbridge in a northern Virginia state park. I had to admit that was a good spot—isolated, but not so much that a Russian's presence there would arouse any suspicions. The Source asked that we signal each other with white tape on a pedestrian crossing sign near the park's entrance. A vertical strip would indicate he was ready to receive the drop. After loading it, we would tape a new strip in a horizontal position. He would later affix another vertical strip to signal he'd unloaded the drop. His letter indicated the operation should take place on November 2 and specified times for the signals. The Source was calling the shots. The KGB almost always designated dead drop and signal sites for our agents and did most of the preparatory work. This time the tables were turned. All *we* had to do was drop our package and mark a signal.

Writing my first message to include in our package for the Source, I decided to see how far I could go toward running the agent on our terms. Although the site he'd picked was a good one, it was new to us. I proposed different ones. I'd already picked some for such occasions, and I was familiar with them. I also suggested a more complex system of communications, including high-tech radios called burst transmitters that emitted signals in short, intense spurts that were hard to intercept and decode. Finally, following Kryuchkov's instructions, I suggested meeting outside the United States—which we were soon to do with Aldrich Ames.

There was also the question of the money to be included in the drop. The Source had asked for $100,000, which was a lot for a first take. He'd delivered top-quality intelligence, to be sure. But we'd already known about the agents he exposed. Moreover, there had to be limits to what he dictated to us. The amount was our call. We sometimes negotiated with agents, but in the absence of meetings, we had to come to our own decision. I consulted the

Center. We settled on half of what the Source had asked for. Our initial payment to Ames had also been $50,000.

I selected a *rezidentura* Line KR officer to handle most of the operational work. He's been identified as Alexander Fefelov in previous accounts of the Hanssen case, and I'll continue calling him that. The young officer had never taken part in an operation before, so he couldn't be identified by the FBI. Planning this one with him required elaborate care because despite all our security measures, we tried to minimize discussions involving agents. To avoid eavesdropping, we conducted some of our meetings outdoors and others in loud bars.

Eventually, Fefelov drove to the drop site—under that bridge in Nottoway Park—which we code-named PARK. Taking a car never before used in operations to minimize FBI attention, he and his driver checked the location and noted its surroundings for security. He spent several hours walking around the park. Meanwhile, other officers—who weren't told the real reason for the operation— drove past the park entrance to check for surveillance and warn Fefelov if they saw anything suspicious.

On the designated Saturday, he drove to the site again, this time with a plastic bag containing stacks of hundred dollar bills I'd counted out in my office. Other officers trailed him to provide heavy security. After loading the site without incident, Fefelov marked the pedestrian sign the Source had indicated. He later returned to check whether the agent had signaled having unloaded the drop. Yes!

Six days later, on November 8, Degtyar found another letter addressed to me in his mailbox. "Thank you for the 50,000," it read. "I also appreciate your courage and perseverance in the face of generically reported bureaucratic obstacles. I would not have contacted you if it were not reported that you were held in esteem within your organization, an organization I have studied for years. I did expect some communication plan in your response. I viewed the postal delivery as a necessary risk and do not wish to trust again that channel with valuable material. I did this only because I had to so you would take my offer seriously, that there be no misunderstanding as to my long-term value, and to obtain appropriate security for our relationship from the start."

The Source went on to reject the communications plan and dead drop sites I'd proposed. Instead, he asked to use the same PARK site on September 9 for our next exchange. The "6" coefficient code he'd set out in his first letter indicated he wanted the operation carried out on March 3, 1986.

He also gave more information that revealed his motive. "As far as the funds are concerned, I have little need or utility for more than the 100,000. It merely provides a difficulty since I can not spend it, store it or invest it easily without triping [sic] 'drug money' warning bells. Perhaps some diamonds as security to my children and some good will so that when the time comes, you will accept by [sic] senior services as a guest lecturer. Eventually, I would appreciate an escape plan. (Nothing lasts forever.)"

If the Source was to be believed, his motive must have been professional. He was either unhappy with his job or simply bored. The lecturing tone of his correspondence seemed to confirm that he liked showing off his expertise. There was also more indication that he worked for the FBI. (If true, he'd have to be in counterintelligence.) About Yuzhin, Motorin, and Martynov, he wrote, "I can not provide documentary substantiating evidence without arousing suspicion at this time. Never-the-less, it is from my own knowledge as a member of the community effort to capitalize on the information from which I speak. I have seen video tapes of debriefings and physically saw the last, though we were not introduced. The names were provided to me as part of my duties as one of the few who needed to know. You have some avenues of inquiry.

Substantial funds were provided in excess of what could have been skimmed from their agents. The active one has always (in the past) used a concealment device—a bag with bank notes sewn in the base during home leaves." Finally, the Source provided details about a new NSA eavesdropping technique.

I was infinitely pleased. Even though the Source had batted away my proposals, I remained happy to let the man run himself. My pride wasn't going to get in the way of what finally seemed clear: We'd hit it big again.

4

David Major left his post as director of counterintelligence programs in the White House National Security Council in September 1987. The following year, he returned to FBI headquarters, housed in a central concrete monolith with a horizontal extension on top—ironically reminiscent, I thought, of the flourishes of late Soviet architecture. As deputy head of the CI3 section, Major was responsible among other things for strategic and operational analysis, policy and budget formulation and counterintelligence training.

Robert Hanssen—deputy chief of CI3's A unit, which performed Soviet analysis—was first to greet Major in his office on his first day at work. Major knew Hanssen from earlier assignments and considered him an unusual FBI agent. He'd observed Hanssen's eerie way of quietly entering an office and waiting until he was noticed. He often whispered, which Major thought showed security consciousness. Hanssen also liked to tell inside jokes, snickering about them afterward. He wasn't a "guy" guy, as Major would say. He never wanted to talk about sports or women or other standard topics for banter among bureau agents. Major never saw him at the FBI gym, the focal point of the bureau's physical fitness culture. More work was sometimes done downstairs at the gym, networking among agents, than anywhere else. Hanssen had a locker, but it was one of the few collecting dust. Unlike other agents, he also almost never carried a sidearm.

Major liked to wear a different tie to work each day and sometimes joked with others about their own tie choices. "Those are the ugliest paisley ties in the world, Bob," he once said to Hanssen. "What are you doing?"

"I've got six kids," Hanssen replied. The somber dresser often wore dark suits reminiscent of the Hollywood-eulogized "G-man" uniform of the 1950s. The quiet introvert was more like an NSA employee—the intelligence community version of a geek, Major thought. But he also knew Hanssen was smart and keen on working hard to improve the bureau. He was the last person Major thought would be a spy. Hanssen also didn't suffer fools well. He often complained about management policies he thought were ill conceived, and Major found himself admitting that Hanssen was right more often than not.

After Hanssen's exposure, most people didn't understand how he could work both for and against the FBI. Major did. He realized Hanssen wanted to be a great wizard, to offer and glean information from intelligence agencies on both sides of the Cold War front line. He certainly had the opportunity to do that, since he saw everything that came in on the Soviet program. As manager of the program's analysts, he got a copy of every communication they wrote. He was like a funnel, Major found himself thinking after his arrest. Everything went in to him and out from him. He was senior enough to have wide access and, because he was a deputy, junior enough to read it all.

He also eschewed intraoffice politics. Major knew that when Hanssen showed up in his office to talk, he would speak his mind—and have something interesting to say.

"You know why the FBI can't beat the KGB?" he once asked Major.

"Bob, what's the answer?" Major replied.

"Because they don't practice the theory of OODA loops."

"Oodaloops?" OODA, a term used in the air force to describe a conditioned decisionmaking process, stands for observation, orientation, decision, action. Carried out repeatedly, the procedure becomes the OODA loop.

"Yes, jet pilots understand that," Hanssen replied. "If you're in a dogfight, and you go to Top Gun school, you learn that you have to see your environment and react quicker than the person who's pursuing you. If you do, you can turn quicker. You can get behind your adversary and beat him. Pilots understand that looking at your environment, assessing the situation and changing quickly will let you win.

"The FBI is too bureaucratic. Before it wants to do anything, it has to study it and have meetings on it. We're just walking in mud. If the bureau could look at a situation and respond quicker, we could beat the KGB."

Major thought Hanssen was right. The FBI was a big bureaucracy in which everybody had to sign off on everything. Later he learned that Hanssen was speaking from practical experience, not just a theoretical standpoint. When he read about Hanssen's espionage tactics, he saw how his former subordinate changed his operating environment at will—the very advice Hanssen had given Major. In most operations, the adversary targets the intelligence officer (IO)—the known entity—as opposed to the secret agent. So it made sense to maximize the agent's action and minimize the IO's. Major later saw that was precisely what Hanssen did; he practiced OODA loops, testing us each time, and we responded to his tactics. It was ironic, Major thought, that selling the theory of OODA loops to a massive bureaucracy like the FBI was almost impossible. But we bought it.

5

Running an agent whose identity you don't know is not the best idea. As with Ames and my other agents, I wanted to know as much as possible about the Source. Trying too hard to identify him, however, posed a risk of compromising him, and I wasn't about to jeopardize the information he was giving us. So we began quietly collecting physical evidence that might lead us to him. Despite my caution, two of the scraps we managed to collect helped expose the Source fifteen years later: a tape-recorded telephone conversation and a plastic bag he used for wrapping classified documents, which we dusted for fingerprints. Both were stored in Yasenevo, along with his file.

But trying to identify KARAT came later. For the time being, it was enough to have two brilliant sources on my hands. I had helped penetrate the heart of counterintelligence in both the FBI and the CIA in the Main Adversary's nerve center. Handling the goose's golden egg, my priority was to make sure both agents were as secure and happy as possible. Consequently, after Fefelov loaded the PARK dead drop on March 3, 1986, according to the Source's own instructions, I was extremely upset to learn he failed to unload it.

That kind of thing happened all the time. The slightest hint of danger caused agents to miss meetings and leave drops untouched. Ames became well-known for failing to show up for rendezvous. Although I could only hope that was also the problem this time, I had no way of telling if we'd lost one of our top two agents. I waited for the Source to send a signal. Days turned into weeks, then months. Eventually, I had to admit the possibility that he'd decided to give up, if only for the time being, or that he was suspected or under investigation. I could do nothing but wait.

In late June, almost six months after I'd last heard from him, the Source sent Degtyar another letter. It brought a major sense of relief. "I apologize for the delay since our break in communications," the letter read. "I wanted to determine if there was any cause for concern over security. I have only seen one item which has given me pause. When the FBI was first given access to Victor Petrovich Gandarev, they asked . . . if Gundarev knew Viktor Cherkashin. I thought this unusual."

Victor Gundarev was a Line KR officer who had defected to the United States in Athens on February 14, 1986. I didn't know him and couldn't imagine what prompted the FBI's question—besides wanting to provide more information about me for the bureau's files.

The letter continued, "I had seen no report indicating that Viktor Cherkashin was handling an important agent, and here-to-fore he was looked at with the usual lethargy awarded Line Chiefs. The question came to mind, are they somehow able to monitor funds, i.e., to know that Viktor Cherkashin received a large amount of money for an agent? I am unaware of any such ability, but I might not know that type of source reporting."

The Source then said that if we wanted to continue running him, we should place an advertisement in the *Washington Times* the following month. He'd call the telephone number we were to provide in the ad and leave another number with a 212 (New York City) area code. We were to call that number an hour later with a message for him. The letter was signed "Ramon." If the contact went ahead as the Source had dictated, it would be our first communication with him outside of typed messages. I was anxious to glean anything I could about him, which meant I'd be sure to tape the conversation.

We began preparing another package for the Source. It included $10,000 in bills, which I again counted out and wrapped myself. I still wanted to acquire as much control over the agent as I could without upsetting him. Although he'd flatly turned down my previous suggestions, I proposed two new dead drop sites. I also provided a means of contacting the KGB in Vienna, advising the Source to use it in an emergency.

During the appointed four days in July, we posted the exact advertisement the Source had asked us to submit to the *Washington Times*: "DODGE—'71, DIPLOMAT, NEEDS ENGINE WORK, $1000. Phone (703) 451-9780 (CALL NEXT Mon., Wed., Fri. 1 p.m.)."

We gave the number of a pay telephone near the Old Keene Mill shopping center in suburban Virginia. It was also near the PARK drop site, to make loading easier once we'd communicated. At the fixed time the following Monday, Fefelov was sweating in the booth. The telephone rang. He picked up the receiver and heard a steady voice reciting precisely what the Source had written he'd say. "Hello, my name is Ramon. I am calling about the car you offered for sale in the *Times*."

Fefelov also stuck to the Source's script. "I'm sorry, but the man with the car is not here. Can I get your number?"

The Source gave a number and hung up. Fefelov loaded the PARK drop site before returning to call the new number and say the package was ready. Since the Source was in New York, it would take him at least a day to unload the drop. All we had to do—again—was wait.

We heard nothing for two weeks. Then another note arrived at Degtyar's house. To my great dismay, the Source wrote that he hadn't found the package. He said he'd call the same pay phone at the Virginia shopping center at an appointed time about ten days later. I didn't panic. If the FBI had found the bag of money and our correspondence, I could do little about it now. That it was missing made me highly nervous, however. For a second time, there was a chance the Source had been compromised.

Meanwhile, accompanied by all the officers I could spare to provide him security, Fefelov raced to the PARK site to search for the package. When he returned, his news made me both relieved and furious: Fefelov had recovered the dead drop—from the wrong corner under the bridge. Wisely, the Source hadn't spent time looking around for it. Our stupid mistake could have compromised all our intensive work, but at least nothing had been lost.

When the Source called again on August 18, one of three dates he'd given in his letter, Fefelov was waiting. It was our first non-scripted communication with our agent. I would listen to it again and again in the following days, trying to catch any clue about his identity and character.

His voice sounded muffled. Fefelov explained what had happened with the dead drop. "The car is still available for you and as we have agreed last time, I prepared all the papers and I left them on the same table. You didn't find them because I put them in another corner of the table."

"I see." The Source sounded annoyed.

"You shouldn't worry, everything is okay," Fefelov said, trying sound as reassuring as possible. "The papers are with me now."

"Good."

"I believe under these circumstances, it's not necessary to make any changes concerning the place and the time. Our company is reliable, and we are ready to give you a substantial discount which will be enclosed in the papers. Now, about the date of our meeting. I suggest that our meeting will take place without delay on February 13, one, three, 1:00 P.M. Okay? February 13."

It sounded strange, of course—a meeting "without delay" to be held in six months. I knew that the conversation would be highly suspicious to anyone listening in. But like the Source, who had taken a gamble by communicating by mail, I knew the chances that the FBI was eavesdropping on the conversation were slim.

The Source was confused, which seemed strange given his high degree of professionalism. "February 2?" he asked Fefelov.

"Thirteenth," the Russian replied. "One, three."

"One, three?"

"Yes. Thirteenth. 1:00 P.M.," Fefelov said, to make sure.

"Let me see if I can do that," the Source said. "Hold on."

"Okay. Yeah."

Fefelov waited. He heard the Source whispering to himself, "Six . . . six," adding the coefficient to figure out the meeting's real date and time—7:00 A.M. the next day.

Fefelov grew nervous. "Hello? Okay?"

But the pause continued until the Source answered at last. "That should be fine."

"Okay," Fefelov said. "We will confirm to you that the papers are waiting for you with the same horizontal tape in the same place as we did it at the first time."

"Very good."

"After you receive the papers, you will send the letter confirming it and signing it, as usual. Okay?"

"Excellent." The Source sounded a little more confident, but Fefelov wasn't sure he'd understood everything.

"I hope you remember the address," he said—even though the Source had provided it himself. "Is . . . everything is okay?"

"I believe it should be fine and thank you very much."

Fefelov finally relaxed slightly. He'd delivered all the information about which I'd coached him. "Heh-heh," he chuckled. "Not at all. Not at all. Nice job," he said, speaking to himself now as much as to the agent. "For both of us. Have a nice evening, sir."

"Do svidaniya," the Source said in heavily accented Russian. The newly assured tone sounded like the man I thought I could decipher through his notes. Like many volunteer agents, he was probably self-conscious. But to try to cover it, he, also like many others, developed an assuredness that he was right about everything. From his behavior and accent, and judging from what I'd seen of other Americans, I guessed he was from the Midwest.

After speaking to the Source, Fefelov loaded the PARK dead drop with the package I'd prepared. Several days later, Degtyar showed up at the *rezidentura* with a note, this time handwritten. "Received $10,000. Ramon."

6

I was soon back in the Soviet Union, but the Source continued to spy for Moscow, on and off—including a yearlong hiatus after my departure and another after the Soviet collapse—until his arrest in February 2001. He was caught one evening, minutes after leaving a dead drop under a footbridge at Wolftrap Creek in Foxstone Park, near his house in Vienna, Virginia. FBI agents also found $50,000 the Russian Foreign Intelligence Service (SVR, the post-Soviet successor to the FCD) left for him at another site. Sentenced to life in prison without chance of parole, the Source is now locked in so-called supermax conditions—underground solitary confinement without visitors or reading material. I first learned his name several days after his arrest, when I saw it on a news report.

In the following days, the American press reported that the KGB and SVR paid Robert Hanssen a total of $600,000, diamonds and a Rolex watch. Of that amount, I myself had counted out $60,000 in hundred dollar bills to be deposited for him at the PARK drop site. The Center allocated a further $800,000 to be deposited under his name in a Moscow bank.

In all his years of spying, Hanssen never had to take a polygraph test. As part of a plea bargain cut by his defense lawyer, Plato Cacheris, he would now have to take them on demand to determine whether he was telling the truth about his espionage. But his wife, Bonnie, was given a widow's pension of about $38,000 a year.

The information Hanssen provided Moscow was worth tens of billions of dollars. He supplied the KGB and then the SVR with thousands of documents, many on twenty-seven computer disks containing information downloaded from FBI servers. The intelligence helped expose some of the NSA's most expensive and technologically advanced eavesdropping programs, the most shocking of which was a tunnel the agency built with the help of the FBI beneath the Soviet embassy compound in Washington. A technological wonder, it was packed with equipment to listen in on conversations. Special sound-conducting materials helped. On orders from the FBI, American contractors had installed them during the compound's construction. The project had cost almost $1 billion.

Ames is called America's "deadliest" spy because he unmasked the CIA's human intelligence network, leading to many deaths. But Hanssen was even more important to us because his disclosures went to the heart of Washington's intelligence infrastructure. He gave us documents about the national MASINT (measurement and signature intelligence) program, revealing American spy satellite technology. He provided information about how the United States intercepted the satellite transmissions of other countries, including the Soviet Union. And he passed along documents on the American continuity of government program meant to secure the country's political succession in the event of nuclear war. The program included measures to track cabinet officials and evacuate them, together with the president, to command centers in massive underground bunkers.

Among other information Hanssen provided from the CIA, NSA and NSC was the FBI's effort to recruit double agents. He also gave us documents detailing what the FBI knew of KGB recruitment operations against the CIA and our efforts to acquire U.S. nuclear secrets. Various CIA and FBI analyses of the KGB, as well as the budget for the FBI counterintelligence program, came our way.

Among the operations Hanssen betrayed was an FBI investigation of Felix Bloch, State Department director of European and Canadian Affairs. Bloch fell under suspicion of spying for the KGB in 1989, after he received a telephone call from Reino Gikman, a KGB illegal agent in the United States who was being tracked by the CIA.

When Bloch subsequently traveled to Paris, French intelligence helped the CIA observe him dining with Gikman in the Hotel Meurice on May 14, 1989. Two weeks later, they were spotted together in Brussels.

Hanssen didn't like Bloch, who was widely criticized as stiff and arrogant. In one note to the KGB, he called him a "such a shnook." But wanting to protect Gikman, he informed us of the FBI investigations into both men. Tipped off, Gikman soon boarded a plane for Moscow. But Bloch remained uninformed of the probe into his activities for some time.

Early one morning at the end of June, Bloch received a telephone call from someone identifying himself as Ferdinand Paul. He said he was calling on behalf of a man named Pierre who "cannot see you in the near future.

"He's sick," the caller said, adding that "a contagious disease is suspected.

"I am worried about you," the caller said before hanging up. "You have to take care of yourself."

Bloch finally knew he was in trouble. "Pierre" was what he had called his contact Gikman.

The FBI was listening in on the conversation. Its investigation compromised, the bureau brought Bloch in for questioning that day. He refused to confess and appeared at work during the following days. Hounded by the FBI and—after his story was leaked—the press, he finally resigned from the Foreign Service. Among the details the FBI investigation revealed at the time was Bloch's penchant for sadomasochistic sex, and that he allegedly paid a prostitute while he was the U.S. embassy's deputy chief of mission in Vienna. But the FBI failed to gather enough evidence for an arrest, and Bloch was never charged.

I never met Robert Hanssen and, although I guessed that he worked in FBI counterintelligence, I knew almost nothing about him until February 2001. When a picture of the man began to emerge, I reacted to the characterizations as I would have to those about a complete stranger. I knew the FBI would publicize the most damning information about him while covering up flattering details. The U.S. Justice Department report about his espionage activity is just one case in point. A good intelligence officer, Hanssen was characterized in it as mediocre.

As a child, he was treated roughly by his police officer father. In a letter to the SVR in March 2000, he wrote that he'd been influenced by *My Silent War*, a book by Kim Philby that describes his spying exploits for the Soviet Union. In fact, Hanssen was twenty-four when the book was published in 1968.

As an adult, Hanssen lived in Spartan conditions and dressed in cheap clothes despite the money he was getting from us. He reportedly denounced communism as "godless" and railed against Marxist infiltrators in the United States. As David Major points out, that was part of his success—he was able to compartmentalize his life, spying for the KGB while remaining an outwardly pious, devout and disciplinarian father of six.

Among the motives attributed to his decision to betray his country was wanting to be perceived as an active FBI agent instead of the nerd analyst image he projected. Hanssen's colleagues nicknamed him "the mortician" for his dark suits and humorless demeanor. He was also called a misogynist. Stories emerged that he encouraged his best friend, a childhood pal named Jack Hoschouer, to observe him having sex with Bonnie via a secret closed-circuit videocamera set up in his bedroom. Hanssen also posted erotic stories about Bonnie on the Internet, even disclosing his own name and e-mail address. And he became friendly with Priscilla Sue Galey, a stripper he met in 1990 in a Washington club.

Making it his mission to reform Galey, Hanssen gave her tens of thousands of dollars of his KGB funds. He bought her jewelry and a used Mercedes. He paid the bills of an American Express credit card he gave her to cover her car expenses. But he spurned her sexual advances. Two years later their relationship fell apart and she moved to her hometown—Columbus, Ohio—where she became addicted to crack cocaine. Dismayed by her credit card bills, he drove out to confront her and take away her card. When she was arrested on drug charges and called him for help, he didn't respond.

Hanssen also had disciplinary run-ins at work. He once hacked into the FBI computer system and downloaded a file from the computer of Ray Mislock, head of the Russia section. He did that, he said, to show the system wasn't secure. In 1993, he was suspended without pay for five days after a young typist named Kimberly Lichtenberg claimed he attacked her after she walked out of a meeting during which another typist's work habits were being discussed. According to Lichtenberg's account, Hanssen ordered her to return. When she refused, he approached her from behind and threw her to the ground. The allegation was never proved.

Reading newspaper stories about the Source's personal life made me realize how little it mattered to me. I didn't care about his secret lives, only his brilliance as an agent.

7

Robert Hanssen wasn't only the last person David Major thought would spy against his country. He was also the last person Major thought would invite his best friend to watch him having sex with his wife. Others in the FBI who knew Hanssen well also told Major they'd never have suspected that. But when the details emerged after Hanssen's arrest, Major understood that his public and private lives reflected his espionage—both were completely compartmentalized. Major agreed with the CIA's Paul Redmond that once he began spying for the KGB, he didn't alter his public persona. Dr. Jekyll simply turned into Mr. Hyde, letting loose his inner demons in a way no one could have imagined.

At work, Hanssen was seen as a perfect support agent. Always remaining in the shadows, he was never put in control because he wasn't gregarious and didn't have the skills necessary to manage people. Socially, he behaved in a similar way. Major's wife told him Hanssen was sexually unappetizing. He never took the limelight at parties. That was the role of his wife, Bonnie, whom many compared to the actress Natalie Wood. Attractive and personable, she never talked about work, only family matters and religion. Hanssen often stood back, basking in her glow, prompting acquaintances to ask, "What's this geek doing with this beautiful woman?"

Major believed Hanssen didn't spy for money or ideology, but because he wanted control—maybe with a hint of Darth Vader, the villain of the 1970s film *Star Wars*. Hanssen too started out "good" before turning to his dark side.

8

It's worth repeating that no amount of sleuthing by the CIA or FBI unearthed either Ames or Hanssen. In 1989, after it became clear that the post-Soviet Russian SVR couldn't have gained access to information about the FBI's Bloch investigation—and other intelligence—from Aldrich Ames, the bureau assigned over sixty agents in the Washington field office to search for a mole. The hunt continued throughout the 1990s. In 1996, the bureau arrested counterintelligence agent Earl Pitts on charges of spying for the KGB and SVR from 1987 to 1992. He was sentenced to twenty-seven years in prison. But it soon became clear that Pitts's relatively insignificant spying couldn't explain the bureau's losses.

According to an account by writer Ronald Kessler, the CIA stumbled on Aldrich Ames after he was betrayed by a retired high-ranking SVR officer who had previously fled Russia. The agent's cryptonym was AVENGER. After giving the United States information pointing to Ames, AVENGER led the CIA to another retired top-level KGB officer. The second man handed the Americans a gold mine in November 2000: the KGB/SVR files on Hanssen.[2] Kessler writes that the new agent, who also defected, was paid over $1 million for the documents. Clearly he too must now be outside Russia under FBI protection.

The files on Hanssen stolen from the KGB archive contained documents from 1985 to 1991. That indicates they must have been taken in 1992 or 1993, while being moved following the post-Soviet reorganization of the KGB. The evidence given to the FBI included correspondence and the black garbage bag Hanssen used to protect the materials for a dead drop—the one we had kept to try to identify him. The file also held the tape recording of Hanssen's telephone conversation with Fefelov after he'd missed our package. In short, the Hanssen file contained everything except his name, which, of course, we didn't know.

I can't name the agents who exposed Ames and Hanssen. Never having worked for the SVR, I've seen no documentary evidence of their identities. But uncovering them wouldn't be difficult. Precious agents such as Hanssen and Ames were known to a very small number of people. Both cases were kept under strict control. Items such as the black plastic bag were kept in special containers in the files along with the paper documents. Hanssen's file could have been retrieved from the archives only on the authority of someone directly involved in the case. Access was restricted to the heads of several departments, including foreign counterintelligence, and some of their deputies. All those men have remained in Russia. Some are retired and some have died.

As for Ames, the number of KGB officers who knew he was a Soviet agent has been put at five to seven. Actually, it was probably closer to twenty. Among those who knew about Ames in 1985, when I was involved in the case, are KGB chairman Victor Chebrikov, FCD chief Kryuchkov and his deputy Kirpichenko. Others are the Directorate K chief and his two deputies, Washington *rezident* Androsov, four cipher officers in the Center and one in Washington.

Within a year, the head of Directorate K's American department joined the list. (Each successive foreign counterintelligence chief would have to be informed for the ongoing drive to find American spies in the FCD.) There were also officers such as Vlad, who met Ames in Bogotá and Rome, the Rome *rezident* and more cipher officers who worked in various locations and times.

People further down the list would have known fewer details about Ames. A few, such as the SCD's Krassilnikov—who tracked down and arrested many of the spies Ames exposed—knew about intelligence he provided without being privy to its source.

One thing is clear: AVENGER couldn't have worked on the Ames case because the officers who did are known. Therefore, the agent must have had indirect access to the information. One explanation is that while top secret files were officially handled only by directorate heads and deputies, subordinates also worked with them—often illegally. If the source exposing Ames and leading to Hanssen wasn't the foreign counterintelligence chief or another directorate head—all of whom, as I've said, remained in Russia—he must have been a subordinate entrusted with the files. Still, in the final analysis, blame for the leaks about both Ames and Hanssen lies at the top level because bosses are responsible for the actions of those they authorize to carry out their work.

The cryptonym AVENGER described in Kessler's book wasn't given by chance. It refers to someone who perceived himself as harmed in some way and wanted revenge. Since he spied after the Soviet collapse, his motivations couldn't have been ideological—as many in the West like to attribute to KGB turncoats. AVENGER was punished, demoted or fired—in some way treated badly. The SVR leadership knows who he is, as do I, but is probably sitting on the information because he remains out of its reach.

As for Hanssen's file, the FBI made a conscious decision to disclose that it came from an agent. By releasing its affidavit detailing the file's documents, the bureau probably wanted to show the SVR the extent of its knowledge, to flaunt that it could get its hands on detailed information from the heart of Russia's intelligence structures. However, the affidavit masks the file's source, partly by incorrectly attributing some of its evidence to vigilant neighbors or intrepid FBI agents digging through garbage. The SVR also knows who stole the Hanssen file. As David Major put it, it was someone's "insurance policy" after the Soviet collapse. To find the culprit, it would be enough to check who among the tiny number of SVR officers with access to the file left Russia for the United States around November 2000.

9

Russia hasn't caught the people who betrayed our most valuable agents. And the United States still hasn't found at least one other Soviet agent in the CIA or FBI responsible for some of the losses of 1985. In other words, another Ames or Hanssen remains at large. In his book, former CIA SE division chief Milt Bearden calls him or her the "fourth mole," after the three who were exposed—Edward Lee Howard, Ames and Hanssen. As evidence, Bearden cites the case of Sergei Bokhan, the GRU colonel stationed in Athens who

eluded a KGB trap to get him to Moscow. He did so by defecting to
the United States in May 1985, before Ames composed his list of
CIA agents.[3] Bearden also cites the case of Leonid Polishchuk, the
KGB officer in Lagos who was lured home with the story that a
Moscow apartment had come on the market. Finally, Bearden
includes the 1984 execution of Vladimir Vetrov, the Directorate T
(science and technology) officer code-named FAREWELL by the
French, as proof the KGB had information that couldn't have come
from Howard—who wouldn't have known about agents in third
countries—Ames or Hanssen, whose spying began after Vetrov's
execution.

It's very likely the sources who delivered information about
Ames and Hanssen to the CIA also revealed some about other So-
viet and Russian agents. That the KGB ran a "fourth mole" is un-
deniable. It's also true that the CIA ran agents we never caught.
Meanwhile, the intelligence agencies of the United States and
Russia continue to recruit assets all these years after the end of the
Cold War.

My own forty-year experience with intelligence taught me that
there can be no real disclosures of information without agents.
Despite the billions of dollars spent on counterintelligence, almost all exposed spies are betrayed by other agents. To quote an
old saying, spies catch spies. If that weren't true—if the CIA had
managed to develop special technology or come up with a better
catching system—agents would be much less important than they
are today. Exceptions to the rule, such as the exposure of Oleg
Penkovsky, are incredibly rare. The CIA didn't find Ames when
it was actively searching for moles in the 1980s. It caught him
only in 1994, when the operational situation vis-à-vis Russia was
relatively quiet.

The FBI and CIA deserve criticism for failing to catch Ames
and Hanssen. Some of the blame can be attributed to both agen-

cies' risk-averse nature, which encourages the tendency to protect their own and the belief that they are incapable of harboring moles. Information is often kept secret supposedly because its exposure would harm intelligence-gathering capabilities and help adversaries. In fact, intelligence agencies want to avoid criticism that would result in firings, demotions and the taint of scandal. If that's natural for all bureaucracies, it's even more so for those steeped in the practices of secrecy.

But critics should also remember that catching even sloppy moles is incredibly difficult, notwithstanding the many mistakes of the FBI and CIA—including lax policies for administering routine polygraph tests. The public was bombarded with lists of obvious signs of espionage *after* the arrests of Ames and Hanssen. Ames bought new houses, cars and clothes he couldn't possibly have afforded on his CIA salary. Hanssen left telltale records of searches he ran of the FBI computer database for signs of investigations into his activities. But given the thousands upon thousands of possible suspects engaging in similarly suspicious activities, identifying the agents—if possible at all—would have taken more time than executing a mission to fly to Mars. AVENGERs continue to exist in Russia, the United States and everywhere else. As long as emotional needs and frailties exist, so will spies. And as long as intelligence services exist, so too will the temptation to find more about what the intelligence services of their adversaries are up to.

─ 10 ─

THE FINAL YEARS OF THE KGB

1

Ames left Washington for his tour in Rome at the end of July 1986. I handed over his files to my successor, and the following month, after more than six years in Washington—and almost two longer than originally planned—I returned to Moscow with my family. Those additional unexpected months had turned a good tour into a spectacular one. As the Aeroflot plane took off from Dulles Airport, I was conscious of it also being my last posting overseas.

The major coup I helped pull off put us squarely on top of the Cold War intelligence battle. One result was a worsening of foreign relations. Although the Americans sensed something was going on, not knowing exactly what increased their nervousness. In two months, Gorbachev would meet with Reagan in Reykjavik to propose drastic nuclear cuts. The summit would be seen as a failure when Reagan, loath to give up his Star Wars antiballistic missile project as part of the package, walked out.

But if the Cold War showed no signs of abating, that didn't
mean things weren't changing. Gorbachev had begun to kick-
start the campaign begun under Andropov to combat corruption
in state institutions, forcing grossly corrupt Party bosses to resign.
In April 1986, a reactor exploded in the Chernobyl nuclear plant
in Ukraine. When the world's worst nuclear accident spewed
out radioactive matter, Gorbachev chose to publicly announce
the catastrophe. Although the decision took some days to make,
it heralded a new level of openness on the part of the Soviet
government.

Relations between Gorbachev and Reagan would soon improve
dramatically, pushed along by British Prime Minister Margaret
Thatcher's declaration that the Soviet leader was someone she
could "do business" with. But the rapprochement began amid the
backdrop of an increasingly tense security standoff.

In May 1985, following the arrest of John Walker, Reagan—
who felt fighting the KGB and GRU was an integral part of winning the Cold War—announced he wanted twenty-five Soviets
working at the United Nations to leave the United States. They
were finally expelled in September 1986 in an operation called
FAMISH. My replacement as Washington Line KR chief, Vasily
Fyodorov, was among them. Especially concerned about the number of Soviets spying on their territory, the Americans said we
had more intelligence officers in New York, Washington and San
Francisco than they had FBI agents to cover them.

We weren't about to take the expulsions lying down. Toward
the end of October, the Foreign Ministry kicked five CIA officers
out of Moscow. Days later, Washington declared fifty-five Soviets
personae non grata and ordered them out. We followed by withdrawing all Soviet personnel staffing the U.S. embassy in Moscow.
That virtually paralyzed the work of the American mission, including the CIA.

2

As that diplomatic battle unfolded, we worked to protect Ames and Hanssen, employing measures that included confounding the CIA with our cooked-up story about Yurchenko's redefection. Another measure was conducted by the SCD's First department, responsible for tracking foreigners in the Soviet Union. It knew nothing about our Washington agents but indirectly ended up helping them. The target was Clayton Lonetree, a marine guard in the U.S. embassy in Moscow. He fell prey to a classic "honey trap" sex entrapment scheme. An attractive young interpreter convinced him to pass information about embassy operations to a man she introduced as her "Uncle Sasha." Lonetree continued spying after his transfer to Vienna in 1986. He eventually confessed to the CIA in December, prior to a secret trip to Moscow the KGB planned for him. A court-martial sentenced him to fifteen years in prison.

The Marine Corps' image took another blow in March 1987, when several more guards were arrested and accused of spying for us. Those charges were eventually dropped, but the incidents deflected American attention from investigating a mole in Langley. Instead, the CIA spent precious months scouring for security breaches in the Moscow embassy.

Other operations were executed with the sole purpose of protecting Ames and Hanssen. In March 1986, the KGB delivered an anonymous letter to the mailbox of a CIA case officer in the West German capital, Bonn. It offered to explain how Gennady Varennik—one of the CIA agents Ames betrayed—had been exposed. The letter asked for $50,000 in return. The fictitious writer claimed to be a KGB officer who had been friends with Varennik. As "proof" of his identity, he identified Varennik's handler as CIA officer Charles Leven. The letter also hinted

that the KGB had penetrated the CIA's electronic communications link to its Moscow station.

The CIA was susceptible to such tactics because the KGB had
previously been loath to disclose any significant operational information. Back at Langley, counterintelligence chief Gus Hathaway,
SE chief Gerber and SE clandestine operations chief Paul Redmond
decided to pay the money, which a KGB officer picked up from a
dead drop in Austria. The CIA dubbed the letter writer "Mr. X."

Several days later, the KGB sent a follow-up letter giving more
specific information. It said Moscow was intercepting cables sent
from the secret CIA communications center in Warrenton, Virginia, and it asked for more money. To make the information
seem more credible—as well as to further stir up the CIA—it accused CIA officer Leven of skimming money from payments to
Varennik. The KGB sent up to six more anonymous letters in
1986. The CIA was simultaneously testing its communications,
leading Gerber and Hathaway to eventually decide the letters
from Mr. X were fakes.[1] I later learned what clinched the argument: The CIA officers refused to believe that Leven, whom they
trusted, had been stealing. The KGB had miscalculated by failing
to perceive the cultural difference between Soviet and U.S. intelligence. Nevertheless, the operation helped distract the Americans from investigating the source of their real problems.

Even after the CIA exposed our misinformation campaign, the
Americans couldn't be completely certain of their conclusions.
The possibility always existed that something had gone unchecked
or been misinterpreted, or that key facts remained unknown. In
that sense—spreading uncertainty and tying up resources—the
KGB's post-1986 operations were highly successful.

Of the double agents we ran to protect our American assets, one
in particular shone as an example of boldness and professionalism.
In 1987, an officer in the SCD American department called Alex-

ander Zhomov approached Moscow CIA station chief Jack Downing with an offer to spy for the CIA. The KGB knew the CIA was all but certain that we never risked dangling one of our own staff officers. Because Zhomov was a precisely such an officer, we believed the CIA would almost certainly take him for a real spy. It did, giving Zhomov the cryptonym PROLOGUE.

Zhomov provided false information about the arrests of some agents lost in 1985. In each case, the KGB was shown to have found the moles through sheer luck and hard work. Zhomov continued his operation until July 1990, when the CIA tried to exfiltrate him to the United States for proper questioning. Of course Zhomov wouldn't leave the USSR for the USA. That game was up.

3

I was long accustomed to the routine following an overseas posting. Complaints about my work were rare. My reports and evaluations were all pro forma, and I always knew in advance about my next assignment. The year 1986 was different, however. Even before arriving from Washington, I found it odd that my replacement as U.S. Line KR chief could tell me almost nothing about my prospects.

Back in Moscow, I had to wait two days before speaking to Directorate K chief Anatoly Kireyev. He also had no idea about my future. "Kryuchkov's dealing with it," he said in answer to my questions about my next assignment. "I'm sorry, but that's all I can tell you." It was a cold reception, but I should have expected it. Returning officers were almost always met with suspicion by Yasenevo staff officers. I knew that the few KGB bosses who were aware of my stunning successes in Washington would be especially difficult. There was also the question of my old friendship with Oleg Kalugin, on which I knew Kryuchkov frowned. I'd never considered myself Kalugin's supporter or anyone else's, for that matter. But as he had drifted further from the KGB leadership's good graces, I knew that—fairly or not—I was seen as a member of his camp. Despite my fast-sinking expectations, however, I wasn't prepared for what lay in store.

By now a specialist in actions against the Main Adversary, I believed I was still most useful in anti-CIA foreign intelligence. I knew the top KGB positions were closed to me, but I expected to at least be named head of the FCD's First (American) department. (My successor in Washington, Vasily Fyodorov, had occupied that job before replacing me.) But the days went by and I heard nothing. Then I was told to put my personal affairs in order.

Nonwork matters indeed needed attention. My daughter, Alyona, had to be enrolled in a new school. My son, Alyosha, had married, and his wife moved in with us in our five-hundred-square-foot apartment. So did Elena's aging mother. With six of us now living together in cramped quarters, it was time to look for a new place. (Little did I know that it would take years to find one.) There was also the question of our dacha. Before leaving for Washington in 1979, I'd been allotted a plot of land outside Moscow in an area reserved for KGB officers. Away in the United States, I'd been unable to build a dacha—a tricky and laborious process that required procuring construction materials from wherever they could be scrounged. After returning, I was dismayed to find my plot had been assigned to someone else. Although I eventually managed to secure another plot in the same area and, in time, set about building my dacha, it was an ominous sign.

A week after my return to Moscow, I received a telephone call from Yasenevo asking me to attend an awards ceremony. Showing up at headquarters the following day at ten in the morning, I was surprised to see so many people—about two hundred, representing each KGB department—filing into a hall to attend the ceremony, presided over by KGB chairman Victor Chebrikov. After the standard laudatory speeches, the recipients' names were read out, and I began to realize I was taking part in what was essentially theater. Around fifty decorations were awarded, all to officers in Directorate K.

Ten or so got the Soviet Union's highest honor: the Order of Lenin. Mine wasn't a surprise. My successor in Washington, Vasily Fyodorov, had told me about the decision to add to my awards, which already included the Order of the Red Star, the title of Honored Officer and about thirty lesser medals, certificates and letters of gratitude.

The ceremony might have been one of the brightest days of my career—had I not grasped the spectacle's main purpose: to publicly attribute the wave of arrests of CIA agents to the hard sleuthing of KGB counterintelligence. I could have approved of the measure if it had been staged mainly as another way of protecting Ames and Hanssen. But the ceremony's main purpose was to cover up the massive KGB failures and advance the careers of Kryuchkov, Kirpichenko and a handful of others. The counterintelligence officers being awarded medals they didn't deserve were the actors in the show—and those from other departments were the audience. After the ceremony, I went straight home. If there was a dinner afterward, I wasn't invited.

I wore my Order of Lenin only once—in 1986, when I was asked to do so for a KGB institute graduation ceremony in Yasenevo. I sat on stage as a member of the presidium along with a number of other officers and Kim Philby, the star of the ceremony. I'd spoken to him once before, shortly after my return from Washington, and found him friendly and modest. Although he knew how valuable he'd been to the Soviet Union, he didn't show it. I'd met his wife, Eleanor, in the late 1950s as an SCD English department officer. She'd traveled to Moscow from Beirut to join her husband, who was visiting the Soviet Union. I made the arrangements, booking a room in the Metropol Hotel, and picked her up at the airport.

By the end of September 1986, my "vacation" was over and I reported at Yasenevo again. Again I was told the top brass were still dealing with my reassignment. The situation was plainly becoming absurd. Feeling I was making a fool of myself, I decided to retreat home, lie low and wait.

In late December, an old colleague named Alexander Bykov telephoned to wish me a happy New Year. Bykov worked in the First Chief Directorate's department of operations on Soviet territory—Directorate RT. We spoke about general matters, including how I was adjusting to life in Moscow. I told him I'd more than settled back in.

"Good," Bykov said. "When do you think you'll be coming in to work?"

"Just as soon as I get an assignment," I replied, sick of repeating that to everyone who asked.

Bykov sounded surprised. "But you've been assigned to our directorate!"

"What!?"

"Didn't you know? You're the new head of Directorate RT's American department."

That's how I finally found out about my new position as chief of the FCD wing that conducted operations against Americans on Soviet soil. The news stung. Whatever happened, I never thought I'd be thrown out of foreign counterintelligence. Having worked on external intelligence operations for twenty-five years, I was being dumped into an internal directorate whose work was obviously far less important. It was unquestionable that someone wanted me completely out of the KGB—or at least relegated to a building far from the heart of foreign intelligence. If the message weren't clear enough, the FCD leadership hadn't even officially informed me of the decision.

My disappointment notwithstanding, there was nothing to do but chalk up the unpleasantness to the vagaries of fate and get on with my new work. Nothing lasts forever, I told myself. My career in foreign intelligence would have to end sooner or later.

4

RT operatives worked undercover in the Foreign Ministry, the Academy of Sciences, the Novosti press agency and other organizations that officially dealt with foreigners in the Soviet Union. Officers weren't permitted to break cover even with the most trustworthy agents and contacts. That meant the directorate was a political intelligence branch more than an operational one. Since it didn't come close to meeting my professional qualifications, the decision to shunt me there clearly constituted the first stage of my dismissal from the KGB.

A conversation with Directorate RT chief Victor Petrov several months after I began work in 1987 removed any lingering doubt. Petrov and I liked each other and got on well, so he came straight to see me after a particularly pointed conversation with Kirpichenko.

"What kind of relations do you have with Vadim Alexeevich?" Petrov asked me.

"*Nekakiie* [none]," I said. "I've never reported to him. I've never even formally met him."

"Well, I just met with him and he asked me how you were working out in the directorate."

"Oh?"

"He said that if there were any problems, if I wanted to fire you for any reason, I should be assured the FCD leadership would agree." Petrov added that he, outraged at the suggestion, told Kirpichenko he saw no reason to sack me. Distasteful as it was, the episode further clarified my standing in Kryuchkov's FCD.

But dwelling on my circumstances would do me no good. I had to get on with my new assignment. The department I headed was housed on Vernadsky Prospekt in the city's southwest. It comprised several lines running tens of subordinate sections in various institutions throughout the Soviet Union. Contacts included members of almost every U.S. organization whose members set foot in the country. As a rule, the arrival of every foreigner created counterintelligence work.

In 1990, Igor Gulyaev, an officer working undercover as a researcher at the USA and Canada Institute—a think tank dealing with foreign and military policy issues—told me that one of his targets, a member of the Center for Strategic and International Studies (CSIS) in Washington, had asked him to arrange a meeting with Politburo member Alexander Yakovlev. The American, whom we code-named MOLE, was staying in the Sovetskaya Hotel on Leningradskaya Highway in northwest Moscow. We strongly suspected MOLE was a CIA agent.

Alexander Yakovlev wasn't just any Politburo member. As Gorbachev's right-hand man, he became known as the "father of glasnost" for his influence on the new policy of openness. MOLE told Gulyaev he had important information for Yakovlev, but his high position made him inaccessible. After considering the options, I gave Gulyaev the go-ahead to set up a meeting in the Kremlin. I also detailed the case in a letter to Kryuchkov, who had ascended to the post of KGB chairman following Chebrikov's retirement in 1988. Informing the chairman was a matter of course for any operation involving Politburo members. In such cases, the presumed CIA target would be warned well in advance of any potential security threat.

A week later, I received my letter back from Kryuchkov. I expected to see his signature as acknowledgment of having read it. But there was nothing to indicate that either he or Yakovlev had seen it, which I took to mean Kryuchkov had no intention of informing Yakovlev, his fellow Politburo member and ideological enemy—and didn't want to leave any proof that he'd seen the letter himself. I later guessed Kryuchkov already suspected his rival of involvement with the CIA. He failed to inform Yakovlev about MOLE in order to veil his own hypothesis—and continue collecting evidence to support it.

Meanwhile, the meeting between MOLE and Yakovlev went ahead. Having decided to meet the American myself to try to discern his real intentions, I introduced myself as a USA and Canada Institute member. We spoke about U.S. policy toward the Soviet Union, ostensibly his main field of inquiry. Since he clearly didn't know much about it, I decided the main purpose of his visit was to meet Yakovlev.

After their first meeting, MOLE continued to travel to Moscow regularly. Gulyayev informed me about the frequency of his talks with Yakovlev, but MOLE never indicated to Gulyayev what he and Gorbachev's top adviser discussed. Kryuchkov, meanwhile, did nothing. Together with other hard-line Politburo members, he would soon help lead an attempted coup d'état against Gorbachev to put an end to the reform policies Yakovlev was helping implement. After the Soviet collapse, Kryuchkov accused Yakovlev of collaborating with the CIA as an agent of influence, the term for someone in a consequential position secretly working to affect policy. Yakovlev has denounced Kryuchkov's accusations as baseless.

5

Gennady Vasilenko was posted to the Center after leaving Washington in 1981, when he said good-bye to his friend Jack Platt at Dulles airport. Two years later, Vasilenko was assigned to the South American backwater of Guyana.

Back in Washington, Platt was running the Internal Operations training program instructing young CIA officers to work in Soviet Bloc countries. Receiving news of Vasilenko's new posting,

Platt started lobbying for permission to visit him. SE chief Gerber was against the idea, so Platt pitched his proposal to Bearden, the SE division deputy with whom he had a special rapport. In May 1986, with Gerber out of the office, Bearden gave him the go-ahead to meet Vasilenko.[2] Platt retired from the CIA in May 1987 but returned temporarily to work on the case. In October he boarded a plane to Georgetown, the Guyanese capital, toting a Winchester hunting rifle as a gift.

Vasilenko was happy to see his old friend. He assumed his association with the CIA officer could cause unpleasantness for him in the KGB—a reprimand at most, certainly nothing he couldn't handle. He continued secretly meeting his pal over his wife's objections but never became an American agent. Platt stayed in Guyana for several days. Back in Washington, he reported on his meeting. A copy of his account was sent to the FBI.

6

Two months after meeting Platt, on January 11, 1988, Vasilenko was on a plane to Cuba, accompanied by the Soviet ambassador to Cuba, with whom he got on well. The two ordered drinks during the flight. By the time the plane landed, Vasilenko was heavily intoxicated. He'd arranged to be picked up at the airport by a colleague with whom he usually stayed during his trips to Havana. But this time, another KGB officer greeted him. He told Vasilenko his friend was attending a reception he couldn't miss.

It was dark when they arrived. As soon as Vasilenko entered the house where he would be staying, two men grabbed him on either side. The beefy security guards wrestled him to the ground, violently twisting his arms behind his back.

Is this a bad joke? Vasilenko thought. "Let go of my arms!" was all he could manage to say. "You're going to break them!" Despite his drunkenness, the pain was incredible. One of his arms felt dislocated. Dragged into a side room, he was stripped and made to put on a track suit. A KGB investigator was waiting in the room. He seemed small compared to the hulking guards. "Do you know Jack Platt of the CIA?" he asked.

"I met him two months ago in Guyana," Vasilenko said. "So what?"

"You had no right to do so," the investigator snapped. "Are you an American agent?"

"*Nyet*," Vasilenko replied. Desperate for sleep, he wondered what Platt could have done to compromise him.

Several days later, Vasilenko was on a Soviet freighter heading for the Ukrainian Black Sea port of Odessa. He thought of plunging into the dark Atlantic waters, but would that be tantamount to admitting guilt? Would his family really be better off and less ashamed of him if he killed himself? Probably not, he decided.

The ship arrived in Odessa two weeks later. Deeply depressed, his arms still aching, Vasilenko boarded a train to Moscow and Lefortovo prison. He knew that colleagues of his, including Martynov and Motorin, had recently been executed. What was the nature of their espionage? he wondered. The only conclusion he could reach regarding his own predicament was that his friend Jack Platt had somehow framed him. Vasilenko faced grueling interrogations over the next six months. Because his investigators didn't have enough evidence to try him, they relentlessly pressured him to confess.

Two months after his arrest, the lead investigator summoned me to Lefortovo for questioning. I told him it was highly unlikely Vasilenko was an American agent when he worked under me in Washington running Ronald Pelton. Had he been a spy, the FBI would have found out about the former NSA employee sooner than it did—in 1985, when he was exposed by Yurchenko. In the end—in June—Vasilenko was released. But he was also stripped of his rank, fired and deprived of his pension. The only charges against him were conducting an adulterous affair and illegally owning firearms. The KGB confiscated ten knives and sixteen guns, including the Winchester he'd received from Platt.

7

When Vasilenko first spoke to Platt after his release, the latter did his best to convince his friend he'd done nothing to harm him. Vasilenko believed he'd been the victim of a mistake—that there had never been enough evidence to arrest him. Platt says he and Vasilenko eventually agreed that the Russian's failure to report their meetings would have provided adequate reason, however mistaken. The KGB's heightened suspicions following the arrests of the agents Ames betrayed made it even less likely that he'd be believed.

It was 1987 when the Center first learned that Vasilenko had disobeyed the orders of Washington *rezident* Dmitri Yakushkin almost a decade earlier to drop his contact with Platt. The news came in a package of materials left in a Virginia dead drop by the Source. Among the other items was the FBI copy of the report Platt had written after his trip to Guyana. The following February, the Center dictated a message to the Source asking for more information about Vasilenko—who was jailed in Lefortovo. Ransacking his belongings over the next six months, the SCD could find no signs of espionage—no communications, equipment, instructions or anything else damning.

What was in Platt's report that got Vasilenko arrested? Platt maintains his description of his last meeting with Vasilenko was pro forma, clearly stating, as he recalled, that the target wasn't recruited. But it's highly doubtful that the KGB arrested Vasilenko just because he met Platt to talk about women, go hunting and fishing and cook out—and only to release him six months later. It's more likely that Platt's report really did compromise Vasilenko. Either he acted suspiciously or the report incorrectly represented his words. Vasilenko and Platt deny both possibilities, but until the report is declassified, the question will remain unanswered.

The FBI discovered that the KGB possessed a copy of Platt's report in 1998. Since it was clear the information hadn't come from Ames, another mole hunt was launched. Two possibilities explain the tip-off. The most likely is that Vasilenko told Platt about it following his release. (The retired Platt, in turn, informed the FBI.) But it's also possible that the FBI found out about the KGB's possession of the report through an agent inside the KGB.

8

Directorate RT was staffed by many officers deemed unfit to serve abroad. Disciplinary trouble, alcohol, family problems or other difficulties blotted their records. Such factors had an impact on morale, which in turn made it even less likely that contacts with foreigners would develop into anything serious.

Toward the end of 1987, a section head in my department named Leonid Beresov asked me to intervene in the looming dismissal of a young officer, Yuri Shvets, who'd just been sent back from Washington. Shvets had been assigned to Washington in 1985 under cover as a Tass correspondent. I barely remembered him because he was hardly ever in the *rezidentura*.

"He had drinking problems," Beresov said. "That's why he's being relieved. But he has very good writing skills," he added. "At the very least, we could use him to do analysis." That was indeed true—we were always short of capable staff.

I convinced the skeptical personnel deputy to assign Shvets to my department on condition that I'd be responsible for his behavior. Shvets began work soon after—and did well in his writing reports for the KGB information service. I liked the pleasant, dark-haired officer and congratulated myself on doing a good deed.

Six months after he joined the department, Shvets told me an American journalist he'd met in Washington was due to visit Moscow. The man, John Helmer, was sympathetic to the Soviet Union; Shvets suggested it might be a good idea to see him again. Helmer had been an adviser in the Carter administration and wrote critically about the Vietnam War. I agreed with Beresov that Shvets could meet him again, this time posing as a Foreign Ministry official responsible for Soviet–American relations.

The meeting took place in a downtown hotel, and Helmer soon returned to the United States. He reappeared in Moscow sometime later, and I asked Shvets to speak to him again. This time, informers among the waiters in the restaurants and cafés where the two met complained that Shvets seemed drunk and out of control. Confronted with the reports, I asked Beresov to accompany Shvets on his next date with the American.

When they had a moment alone, Helmer told Beresov that Shvets was difficult to communicate with. He was rude and almost always drunk. The next day, I took Shvets off the case, forbidding him to see Helmer again. Although Beresov continued meeting Helmer, he soon reported the journalist wasn't a good prospect for recruitment. When Helmer left Moscow, I thought the case was over.

In 1990, I attended an international conference in the Georgian capital Tbilisi, taking Shvets with me. As soon as we arrived, he got drunk and remained in his room until the event ended several days later. On returning, I admitted my mistake and told Beresov to convince Shvets to quit before he was fired, which would enable him to keep his pension. He indeed left the KGB soon after.

Shvets moved to the United States in 1993 and published a book about his KGB career, claiming to have recruited Helmer as KGB agent SOCRATES in Washington. In the account, he met

Helmer through his journalist wife, Claudia Wright, whom he also recruited, as agent SPUTNITSA. Using pseudonyms for both in his book, Shvets wrote that SOCRATES proved to be a valuable agent but criticized jealous KGB superiors of failing to capitalize on his good work. The book contained many other exaggerated claims and caused a stir, not least with Helmer, who was then working in Moscow as correspondent for *The Australian*. Contacting Yuri Kobaladze, spokesman for the SVR, he complained bitterly. Helmer said he had no idea that Shvets had been a KGB officer. Although I was by then retired from the KGB and in the hospital recovering from a minor illness, Kobaladze insisted on seeing me. When he appeared at my bedside with Helmer, I assured the American he'd never been considered an agent or even a target.

9

The Soviet Union was changing fast. Newspapers published critical stories about the government and television programs dropped their rote recitation of the day's official news in favor of real debates about the state's plight. Western companies began setting up offices in Moscow. Increasing numbers of foreign cars sped along the streets. When a McDonald's opened on Pushkin Square, the entire city buzzed. But the outward signs of openness signaled something much more significant—and dangerous.

As it turned out, the dynamic unleashed by Gorbachev eventually turned against him. Saying he never wanted the Party to collapse, he did everything to ensure it would lose its grip on power. During a visit to Bonn in May 1989, he told West German Chancellor Helmut Kohl that he wouldn't block reforms in Warsaw Pact states, effectively ending the so-called Brezhnev Doctrine under which Moscow put down the Prague Spring in 1968.

That gave a green light for opposition forces in Eastern Europe to stage open confrontation. The Polish Solidarity movement emerged from underground, demanding a hand in government. Gorbachev refused to intervene, leaving Polish communist officials to hold elections that swept Solidarity into power. Following the example, Hungary scheduled elections for 1990, and in September 1989 opened its borders to thousands of vacationing East Germans to flee to West Germany through Austria. Following massive protests in Leipzig and other cities, the East German government also gave in, opening the Berlin Wall on November 9, 1989.

In Czechoslovakia, weeks of protest in Prague by hundreds of thousands forced the fall of the communist regime, also in November 1989. Bulgaria followed in the same month. In December, angry mobs executed longtime Romanian leader Nicolae Ceausescu and his wife. Once started, the collapse of the Warsaw Pact took less than six months. The following year, the unthinkable took place: Germany was unified.

The frenzy of 1989 unleashed an anti-Soviet campaign. I watched in dismay as decades of hard work and sacrifice by dedicated Eastern European communists were cast aside like dirty laundry. But none of that came as a surprise to the KGB. We knew better than most exactly what was affecting the Soviet Bloc: a disease spread by Gorbachev, his close adviser and ideologue Yakovlev and Foreign Minister Eduard Shevardnadze.

Simultaneous institutional dissolution within the Soviet Union resulted from a deliberate effort by Gorbachev and his team to bring the system down in the name of reform. In the first open election in decades, the Congress of People's Deputies, a new legislature set up by Gorbachev, was chosen, partly as a bulwark against Kryuchkov and other hard-liners in his government. Meanwhile, to turn society against the KGB, the self-professed democrats claimed that Soviet intelligence supported corruption in the Communist Party.

Unpopular economic decentralization led to shortages of sugar and other staples. With that came Gorbachev's drive to wipe out alcoholism by slashing alcohol production, a campaign immeasurably harmful to the Soviet state. Decreasing state vodka production meant more people would die from drinking *samogon*, moonshine, while slashing the government's top domestic source of income.

The country was also suffering the devastating effects of the war in Afghanistan. The decision to invade a decade earlier had exposed the convoluted psychology of the aging Brezhnev elite, which was too involved in its own petty interests to reflect on the effects of its policy. The Politburo members who pushed for invasion had learned nothing from the Vietnam War or from attempts to impose communism on tribal groups like the Mongolians, who continued to live as nomads in their traditional yurts despite the best efforts of urban planners in Moscow. The Kremlin fantasy was that a great breakthrough would demonstrate its effectiveness, showing the world that communism was the ascendant political system.

After Washington began to train and supply the Afghan rebels with shoulder-launched Stinger surface-to-air missiles, the conflict turned decisively against our troops. The protracted hostilities began demoralizing Soviet society. After much debate, Gorbachev overcame hard-line opposition and started pulling out our forces in May 1988. The humiliating decision drew attention to the Soviet Union's weakness—but it was necessary.

10

With the birth of my grandson Ivan—named after my father—seven of us were living in my apartment. In early 1991, having tried to find a new place for more than four years, I turned to an acquaintance on the Party's Moscow city central committee. Following an appeal from him, the committee's housing chief told me I'd be considered for a new apartment provided I produced a

request from my bosses. That took months to acquire, but I persevered. In April 1991, my family was allotted a new, bigger place,
where it still lives. I was also able to keep my old KGB-allocated
apartment for my son Alyosha, his wife and his son.

I also had my dacha, which I'd built after wrangling a new plot
of land in the KGB dacha compound. We spent our first summer
there in 1988 and returned each subsequent summer. On week-
days, I'd wake early to drive into the city to work.

On Monday, August 19, 1991, I left the dacha as usual to
drive toward Kievskoe Highway, which would take me northeast
into Moscow. Merging onto the thoroughfare, I was surprised to
see a column of tanks rolling toward the capital in what I took to
be a military exercise. Whoever ordered them out was an idiot, I
thought. They were churning up so much asphalt that the road
would have to be repaved. Entering the city, I saw tanks on the
streets. It began to dawn on me that something serious was taking place.

At work, about ten of us—department bosses and deputies—
assembled. We were informed that Gorbachev, who was vacationing in Crimea, was sick, that a state of emergency had been
declared and an emergency committee (GKChP) was running
the country. A wave of joy washed over me. Finally something
was being done to stop Gorbachev's destruction. "Maybe it's for
the best," I told the group. Most nodded in agreement. No one
believed Gorbachev was really sick.

In a couple of hours Muscovites were calling the developments
a coup d'état. I never really saw it as such. It was a last attempt to
keep the Soviet Union together despite Gorbachev's moves to dismantle it. As the 1980s drew to a close, his decentralization of the
economy and political system had caused a breakdown in management. Instead of working more productively, economic managers
and regional political bosses grabbed control for themselves. As

the economy crumbled, Gorbachev shored up his position against emerging liberal critics by appointing hard-liners to positions of power, including Kryuchkov as KGB chief, Valentin Pavlov as prime minister and Dmitry Yazov as defense minister.

A typical Party apparatchik, Gorbachev had few ideological goals of his own. Unable to find a quick fix to resolve the state's looming chaos and overcome by praise from Reagan and Thatcher, he surrendered communism without a real fight. Miners began staging strikes and Mafia-style protection rackets took over in the nascent private sector. The political situation followed suit as some of the Soviet Union's fifteen republics called for greater independence. In January 1991, blood was spilled in Lithuania and Latvia after Soviet troops seized media outlets and the Interior Ministry headquarters, respectively, to repress secessionist agitation. Meanwhile, Gorbachev allowed tens of thousands of demonstrators to protest in Moscow.

He pinned his hopes on a referendum to preserve the Soviet Union. It took place in nine of the union's fifteen republics in March. Over 76 percent of participants supported the union. The people's overwhelming support of the USSR's continued existence was clear, but that didn't stop Gorbachev from announcing plans to draft a new union treaty in direct defiance of the vote. The proposal would have put an end to the USSR by setting up a confederation in which each republic would exercise separate rights.

In August, Gorbachev met with Yeltsin and Kazakhstan's Party boss, Nursultan Nazarbayev, to make a last push to launch the new treaty. They scheduled Russia and Kazakhstan to sign on August 20. Gorbachev then left for his dacha in the Crimean Black Sea resort town of Foros. The details of the union treaty were kept secret, but the KGB had surreptitiously recorded the talks. On August 17, Kryuchkov gathered eight men, who soon became known as members of the GKChP, for a secret meeting in Moscow. The

following day, a delegation went to Foros to persuade Gorbachev
to abandon the treaty and agree to a state of emergency. Gorbachev refused. The tanks rolled into Moscow two days later.

11

General Leonid Shebarshin, my old colleague from India, learned
about the GKChP on August 18, while the delegation was in
Foros pressuring Gorbachev. Shebarshin had been appointed
FCD chief in 1988, when Kryuchkov took up the KGB chairmanship. Kryuchkov now summoned Shebarshin to ask whether he'd
take part in the emergency committee. Shebarshin shared many
of his boss's sympathies, but didn't want to compromise the FCD's
future by cooperating too closely with the possibly rash actions of
a few leaders. He politely declined, saying he would instead put
the FCD's intelligence at Kryuchkov's disposal. He also agreed to
deploy a crack KGB combat unit called Vympel in central Moscow that night. His decision to largely sideline the FCD helped
save Soviet intelligence.

Others cooperated with the GKChP, including Shebarshin's
deputy, Major General Vladimir Zhizhin. He helped draft the directive signed by Kryuchkov calling for the emergency committee's
assumption of power. It blamed the national crisis on Gorbachev.

Officially, Vice President Gennady Yanayev led the GKChP.
As I was driving into Moscow past the tanks on August 19, the
country was waking up to the news on Channel 1, the main state
television station. It announced that new leadership had taken
over to prevent "chaos and anarchy" and save the Soviet Union.

The effort began failing from the start. Yeltsin and his like-
minded colleagues and supporters weren't arrested. Instead, they
were allowed to gather at the "White House," the Russian Republic's 1980s-style parliamentary building on the Moscow River. No

measures were taken to prevent deputies from entering or leaving the building. The telephones lines weren't cut. Yeltsin read a public appeal denouncing the putsch. "Storm clouds of terror and dictatorship are gathering over the whole country," he said. "They [the GKChP] must not be allowed to bring eternal night."

Yeltsin supporters gathering outside the White House stopped the tanks advancing on the building. The site soon became the center of protest against the GKChP, whose members holed up in the Kremlin. The protesters littered the streets with the carcasses of gutted buses, iron rods, concrete blocks and anything else that could be ripped up to construct flimsy "barricades" that were significant symbolically but couldn't stop a single armored vehicle. Persuaded to "join" Yeltsin, a division of unarmed tanks stood with their guns pointing away from the building. In what became the incident's enduring image, Yeltsin climbed onto one, from which he made an appeal to the "citizens of Russia" (as opposed to the Soviet variety).

The handful of men who'd seized power weren't acting decisively. Shebarshin was getting no orders from the GKChP, which clearly signaled a leadership crisis. In an absurd reflection of their indecision, the tanks belching black diesel fumes on Moscow's streets were stopping at red traffic lights. Even the television programming was wrongheaded—ballet instead of military marches and war films that would have rallied the people by reminding them of the Party's illustrious past. Late in the morning on August 19, Shebarshin ordered his Vympel paramilitary unit to stand down.

When Yanayev, the self-proclaimed acting Soviet president, addressed the people during a live news conference, I realized the GKChP was doomed. Four other GKChP members took part. At one point during the conference, a young *Nezavisimaya Gazeta* reporter disdainfully asked Yanayev, "Could you please say whether or not you understand that last night you carried out a coup d'état?" As Yanayev mumbled an incoherent reply, a Channel 1 camera lingered on his shaking hands. They became a key symbol of the bungled attempt to take power.

Throughout the first night and into the next day, more people came to defend the White House. Prior to the second night, the GKChP imposed a curfew. Rumors leaked from the KGB that the parliamentary building would be stormed and those inside began to fear the worst. That night, three men were killed near the U.S. embassy while trying to stop the armored vehicles moving through the city. The civilian deaths shocked even GKChP members. The following morning, Defense Minister Yazov ordered troops to begin pulling out of the city. By the evening, the GKChP was on the run.

I showed up for work each day of the attempted coup. My department continued its work as usual, and we stayed late. Most KGB people reacted calmly to the events. The prevailing view, which included my own, was that the GKChP wasn't actually staged against Gorbachev, but, perversely, in concert with him. It seemed naive to believe that Gorbachev would leave Moscow on vacation at such a sensitive moment as the eve of the new treaty signing. Most likely, it was a cunning maneuver, part of a double-sided game he was playing to keep his presidency alive. He must have known a coup d'état would be doomed. However, he went along with it, apparently to appease the plotters—but really to frame them. He knew Yanayev, Kryuchkov, Pavlov and the others wouldn't have the guts or the backing to take the decisive measures needed to carry out such a scheme. Instead, they walked into a trap and did nothing for three days beyond ordering those tanks into the streets.

The day after he returned from Foros, Gorbachev summoned Shebarshin to the Kremlin to make him temporary KGB chairman and ordered him to prepare reports on the week's events. In the shortest chairmanship in KGB history, Shebarshin occupied the post for a single day, until Kryuchkov's permanent successor was appointed.

On Thursday, August 22, criminal charges were filed against Kryuchkov and the other GKChP members. That evening, a crowd collected outside the statue of secret police founder Felix Dzerzhinsky at the KGB's old central Lubyanka offices. As night fell, under the glare of television cameras that broadcast the indelible images around the world, city authorities delivered a crane to the site. To the joyful shouts of onlookers, a man climbed up the statue and attached a cable around its neck. The crane pulled Iron Felix down.

I was at work at that moment. Watching the event on television later, I realized I was seeing the symbol of Soviet power topple. I knew it meant the end of my career and my old way of life. It was a senseless act—no better than the destruction of churches after the 1917 Revolution. The Soviet Union had to change, but I couldn't accept the destruction of my country's heritage. Thank God at least the mobs didn't tear down the famous statue of Karl Marx near the Bolshoi Theater.

The following day, Yeltsin called a session of Russia's Supreme Soviet and forced Gorbachev to condemn the Communist Party. With a theatrical flourish, ignoring Gorbachev's entreaties, Yeltsin signed a decree suspending the Party in the Russian Republic and confiscating its property. Gorbachev stayed on as Soviet president, but the state of which he was head disappeared from under him on December 21. That day, the leaders of the republics of Russia, Belarus and Ukraine met in Belarus to replace the Soviet Union with the toothless Commonwealth of Independent States.

After the failure of the GKChP, it was clear to me that things would get worse. Now the collapse of Soviet society was inevitable. The KGB would, of course, be among the first to change. Public opinion had shifted, so that officers who'd spent their careers serving their country were now seen as enemies of the people. If the KGB was considered an immoral organization, I no longer wanted to be part of it. Ten days after the end of the so-called coup d'état, I cleaned out my files, tied up loose ends, and told my deputy I wouldn't be showing up for work the next day.

Then I went to see the deputy head of Directorate RT—a man I'd known for forty years—to hand in my letter of resignation.

"Do you think you're the only person who feels that way about the KGB?" he demanded. "You can't resign. We all feel this way!"

"In that case, you should all resign too," I said. "Why would you remain part of an organization that can no longer function properly?"

The deputy was outraged. "Do you really think you're smarter than everyone else? This is a political statement you're making."

"What do I care about political statements? What do you want me to do? Submit another letter that simply states I want to retire, without giving my reasons? Please—I'm happy to do it." I took out a piece of paper and wrote "I've reached retirement age and would like to leave." Signing my name, I left it on the deputy's desk.

"How dare you!" he hissed.

"Okay then, since I haven't taken a holiday yet this year, think of my absence as an extended vacation."

Then I walked out.

12

Loud chest thumping resounded in the United States about winning the Cold War. In the sense that the American system emerged as the world's single superpower while the Soviet Union crumbled, it was justified. But even though Washington pressured Moscow in various ways, the Soviet Union ultimately collapsed under its own weight.

The CIA conducted many successful operations against the KGB and the Soviet Union, among them TAW and IVY BELLS. But they were exceptional, if vastly interesting. Monitoring naval communications between Vladivostok and Kamchatka exposed only a tiny part of the whole system. Among many other channels of communication, the most sensitive messages were relayed by telegrams in sealed envelopes. And although the CIA network of agents was impressive, the information they betrayed hardly brought Moscow to its knees.

Although the general public clamors for plots about vital issues of national security, most spying has actually made little difference. More significant were the CIA agents of influence in the democratic movement in the Soviet Union's last years. CIA funding and training of mujahideen in Afghanistan also helped turn the tide of the war against us. The economic and human losses struck hard at the Soviet Union's prestige. But that didn't bring the system down any more than the Vietnam War brought down American democracy.

The Soviet Union collapsed because it could no longer support itself. The end was largely triggered by the corruption and mistakes of leaders who didn't try to solve problems lying in plain sight. Responsible for running everything, the Party wasn't held accountable for anything. When Gorbachev came to power, the system was too leaky to withstand his shaking the boat. Once the administrative control of its vertical power structure was undermined, the whole deck of cards collapsed.

_11_

WILD CAPITALISM IN NEW RUSSIA

1

On August 23, 1991, Yeltsin appointed Vadim Bakatin KGB chairman, ending Leonid Shebarshin's day-long tenure. Bakatin was a liberal, a former interior minister whom Gorbachev had recently fired. No one I knew in the KGB took his elevation to the head of the organization as a good sign. His first move, an order to leave the KGB archives untouched, bore out most fears. It prevented officers from destroying highly classified information that could potentially compromise sources and operations. No doubt a lot of dirty laundry was also being removed, but that was secondary to security. The archives contained the names of agents and operations that had remained secret for decades. Keeping them classified was imperative.

Bakatin set about stripping the KGB's services and firing members of the top leadership, who were denounced as communist ideologues. Decades of hard work were thereby wasted. Perhaps the most visible blow concerned a 1980s operation to install hundreds of eavesdropping devices in a new building the Americans were building in their Moscow embassy complex. The construction crew had riddled the structure with highly sophisticated bugs where they'd be hard to detect, such as inside prefabricated concrete slabs and steel beams. The State Department found the bugs during a security check and halted construction on the building in 1985, leaving its red brick exterior to stand forlornly over the complex.

In September, newly appointed U.S. ambassador Robert Strauss asked Bakatin to turn over the blueprints indicating the bugs' locations. The KGB chairman agreed. Ironically, the request was first suggested by Aldrich Ames to Milt Bearden, by then the CIA's SE chief, who was in Moscow for the meeting with Bakatin. The KGB's acquiescence was a stunning, highly unnecessary move. It reflected the mistaken feeling many Russians now held that the demise of the Cold War signaled the end of geopolitical competition between Moscow and Washington. How naive to believe the fall of the Soviet Union meant foreign intelligence would no longer be needed! Bakatin's idiotic decision told the Americans how we operated and what technology we used for eavesdropping. That information, once exposed, could never be made secret again. In return, he got nothing.

Stepping down as acting KGB chairman, Shebarshin retained his position as FCD chief. He held the post for almost a month, until Bakatin announced on September 18 that an SCD colonel named Vladimir Rozhkov would be nominated as the FCD's first deputy director—Shebarshin's number two. Shebarshin, who wasn't consulted, promptly wrote two resignation letters—one to Gorbachev and another to Yeltsin. Two days later, Gorbachev issued a decree dismissing him from his post.

On October 1, Yeltsin appointed Yevgeny Primakov to head the FCD—this time a brilliant choice. Primakov was a longtime

intelligence veteran and Middle East expert who worked as a
Pravda correspondent before heading the prestigious Institute of
World Economy and International Relations. He spearheaded
Soviet efforts at shuttle diplomacy in the Middle East in the
1960s and 1970s. Primakov managed to preserve the structure of
post-Soviet foreign intelligence, saving the organization by keeping it apart from politics. He would go on to become foreign minister and then prime minister.

More changes were coming. On October 24, Gorbachev signed
a decree nominally abolishing the KGB. Yeltsin then set about
splitting the organization, separating the FCD from the SCD, the
border guards, signals intelligence and other branches. The newly
independent FCD was renamed the Central Intelligence Service,
then the Foreign Intelligence Service (SVR). The SCD became
the Federal Security Service (FSB), Russia's internal intelligence
agency. The end of the unified KGB meant the position of chairman no longer existed. In January 1992, Yeltsin finally fired
Bakatin from his second post as head of the FSB, appointing another former interior minister, Victor Barannikov, in his place.
Meanwhile, Kryuchkov was languishing in prison for his part in
the GKChP, but his stamp on the KGB's successor organizations
remained, with Kirpichenko staying on as a top special adviser to
the SVR.

I cut my ties to the KGB residue, only rarely attending meetings
of the intelligence veterans organization. I'd also split with Kalugin, whose open criticism of the KGB in 1989—after he aligned
himself with the new democratic forces—I couldn't condone. By
then, Kryuchkov and Kirpichenko were looking for someone to
directly blame for the agents Ames exposed, and Kalugin emerged
as the easiest target. Soon after his retirement in 1990, he was accused of exposing state secrets. Gorbachev stripped him of his
rank, awards and pension. Kalugin promptly campaigned for a seat

in parliament, the Supreme Soviet, and won. His new post gave him immunity from prosecution, and he continued to criticize the KGB. After the Soviet collapse, the charges against him were dropped, and he became adviser to Bakatin before leaving for the United States in 1995.

Under President Vladimir Putin, however, the accusations against Kalugin resumed with new force. Trying him in absentia in 2002, a Russian court found him guilty of treason and sentenced him to fifteen years in prison. Part of the accusation concerned his testimony against U.S. Army Reserve Colonel George Trofimoff, a former military intelligence officer convicted of spying for the Soviet Union and sentenced to life in prison in 2001. Trofimoff worked in Germany as a debriefer of Soviet defectors. He was exposed after KGB officer Vasily Mitrokhin—who served in the KGB archives for many years—defected to England in 1992, bringing copious notes of KGB documents. In a book based on the "Mitrokhin archive," historian Christopher Andrew described Trofimoff's activities without naming him. The information, however, led the U.S. government to him—and to subpoena Kalugin, then living in the United States, to testify at his trial. Despite his part in the events, Kalugin denied that he'd fingered Trofimoff. Putin has since called Kalugin a traitor.

Meanwhile, Shebarshin teamed up with his friend Nikolai Leonov, the former head of the KGB analytical department, to found a company that would use their knowledge and connections. They joined a group of enterprising young bankers who asked them to provide security. Calling their new organization the Russian National Economic Security Service, they opened offices in the formerly KGB-affiliated Dinamo soccer stadium, where they still operate.

Gennady Vasilenko also landed on his feet. After his 1988 release from six months in Lefortovo, he retreated to his dacha for two months to mull over his future. Some KGB friends who never believed he'd spied for the United States helped find him a job in a KGB cover enterprise, a publishing house run by a former intelligence officer. Soon he reestablished contact with Jack Platt and began picking up the other pieces of his life. After setting up a company that traded in sugar and cigarettes, he went into the security field in 1991.

2

The SVR refused to acknowledge my claim to a pension until April 1993. Even then, the amount wasn't indexed to the skyrocketing inflation, so that by the time the paperwork was processed, it didn't cover the cost of the gasoline needed for the drive to Yasenevo to sign for it. By then, I'd begun making my own difficult adjustment to Russia's new society.

Soon after retiring in 1991, I accepted an offer from the deputy minister for light industry to help open a leather and fur company as part of a plan to spin off private companies from state enterprises. I soon realized that the organization would be run by ministers and their deputies. Having just resigned from a state institution and not wanting to work for another one, I instead joined an acquaintance trying to buy and sell anything he could lay his hands on, including surplus military gas masks and uniforms. We signed contracts worth billions of rubles for the import of containers of cigarette cartons. We never saw the cigarettes and didn't pay any money for them, but continued agreeing to anything that was offered us. In short, we spread our resources too thin to be effective at anything.

My business associate was also setting up a bank with an American partner under the auspices of a nuclear weapons research enterprise. It was in the formerly closed city of Sarov east of Moscow, where Andrei Sakharov helped design the first Soviet atomic bomb. Agreeing to head security for what would be called the First Russian Bank, I joined it in October 1992.

In the lawless conditions of the time, fast-growing organized criminal groups were targeting a vast array of banks established to process the huge profits generated by the give-away sales of state property. Like many other former KGB officers, I exchanged the Cold War cat-and-mouse game for a cutthroat new conflict between hundreds of emerging interests battling to grab a piece of the Soviet infrastructure. Bankers were regularly gunned down in the struggle for control. Successful organizations relied on information that former intelligence personnel were well positioned to procure.

The First Russian Bank became one of the country's largest. Its security service for guarding the main office and various branches eventually grew to 150 men. We found ourselves targeted by the Izmailovo criminal group, one of the country's most notorious, named for a sprawling suburban area in northeastern Moscow. We often feared for our lives, especially after a man we hired to help negotiate with criminal groups was found shot dead in his office. Shaking banks down themselves, police solved almost none of the assassinations. Perversely, criminal groups were the only organizations capable of providing any kind of real "protection." I eventually called on the services of the SVR's Alpha special forces group, originally set up by the KGB for special foreign operations.

In 1995, the First Russian Bank ran into serious trouble. Money was being siphoned out of its accounts; news broke that $70 million invested by an oil company was missing. It was clear the bank would collapse. When one of the founders died in a suspicious car crash, I decided to leave. By then—in January 1996—I'd completed the registration of my own private security company, which I named Alpha-Puma, after the special forces squad. Soon I had a string of clients, including banks, food markets, offices, shopping malls and film studios. I hired former KGB and military officers and trained guards—over one hundred people in all, who watched over fourteen locations.

Now, as Vladimir Putin serves his second term as president, the country continues to adjust after almost a decade and a half of chaotic post-Soviet development. But stability doesn't necessarily mean rule of law. In this case, it comes more from Russia's new political bosses, who are increasingly calling the shots. Once an intelligence officer himself, Putin has elevated many former KGB officers to positions of power. However, it isn't entirely correct to talk about ex-KGB personnel as part of a unified community that has adapted to Russia's new conditions. Many former Soviet intelligence officers condemn Putin for the way he came to power—as a tool to protect the interests of the close-knit Yeltsin-era elite. Although he has done much to shut down individual purveyors of influence under his predecessor, corrupt insider politics have grown.

It's more accurate to see ex-KGB officers as a social group—a collection of former Soviet citizens generally picked for their promise, educated better than most, and given an opportunity to study human nature, a central part of intelligence work. Former KGB officers just happened to be better positioned to provide services that were in demand. It's true that some used their positions to profit handsomely from the state financial structures under their command as government control disintegrated. But that's a minority that had counterparts in each state sector. Although much of the population denounced the KGB in 1991, even some prominent liberals have since agreed that intelligence officers were actually among the least corrupt members of Soviet society. It's ironic that after having been so thoroughly criticized, former KGB officers have ended up in demand in the very private sector they were accused of trying to thwart.

3

In 1997, I made my first trip to the United States since leaving my post as Line KR chief a decade earlier. I'd been invited by one of the men I operated against in the 1980s: Jack Platt, now vice president of a company called Hamilton Trading Group. He asked Vasilenko and me to attend a conference on nuclear waste security at Washington's Georgetown University.

Returning to the United States presented a kind of psychological barrier I was eager to cross. I no longer worked in intelligence. Indeed, I felt I was living a completely new life, this time traveling solely for my private interests. But knowledge of top secret information keeps former intelligence officers from being like ordinary retirees. That was why I called SVR spokesman Yuri Kobaladze to make sure the foreign intelligence service had no problems with my going, despite the many years that had passed since I'd been involved in highly classified work. Although Ames had been exposed three years earlier, other agents I knew about hadn't, including the Source. After speaking to Kobaladze, I drove out to Yasenevo to emphasize my concern that since U.S. newspapers had reported my involvement in the Ames case, there was a distinct possibility I'd be a target for recruitment. But an officer told me I wouldn't be able to compromise any active cases and there was no reason I shouldn't go.

Washington was even more beautiful than I remembered. Although happy to be back, I couldn't shake an upsetting feeling that I was no longer part of the city. At the conference, I was introduced to Brent Scowcroft and Ray Mislock, who headed the national security section of the FBI's Washington field office. I found out later that it was Mislock's computer Robert Hanssen had hacked in 1992 to prove the FBI system wasn't secure. Mislock was chief of counterintelligence operations against Russia at the time.

Now he didn't appear interested in my conversation with Scowcroft—but did chime in with support for Scowcroft's suggestion that the three of us have dinner. I wasn't particularly thrilled at the prospect of being grilled about my knowledge of Ames but agreed to go along. I was eager to talk to Scowcroft, who'd done his part in the American fight against the Evil Empire.

At the table, the conversation was friendly; Scowcroft seemed genuinely interested in finding out why Ames had decided to spy for Moscow. But I realized my invitation had one main purpose: to allow the coy seeming Mislock to get to know me. Afterward, he drove me to my hotel. When I told him I probably wouldn't be seeing him again, he insisted on picking me up the next morning. I called Platt to remind him of his promise that I wouldn't be subject to any pitches. Platt assured me he'd take care of my concern and I wasn't approached for the rest of my trip.

I had a feeling the conference wouldn't be my last brush with the FBI. A year later, I was back in the United States for another symposium, this time on tactics to combat organized crime. The affair was held in Virginia Beach. Vasilenko and I again flew to Washington, where Platt put us up in his house for two days before the conference.

I agreed to go on the trip partly because I wanted to visit my daughter Alyona. She was studying at the Defense Language Institute in Monterey, California, on a two-year exchange program run jointly with Russia's most prestigious university, MGIMO, from which she'd just graduated. Surely the FBI had considered and sanctioned the enrollment of the daughter of Aldrich Ames's handler in an American institution. While I was happy for her chance to experience another culture, I couldn't help worrying that the bureau might lean on her.

During the closing dinner of the conference, I began feeling shooting pains in my right side, so I excused myself and went to my room. The next morning, the pain was worse. Platt drove me to be diagnosed at a local hospital, where I found it curious that doctors gave me an injection without examining me first. Back in my hotel room, I fell asleep for the rest of the day and through the night. I could barely rouse myself the following morning.

It wasn't until I became aware of an unpleasant taste in my mouth that I slowly began to suspect what had actually happened. The taste was similar to the kind I knew accompanied psychotropic "truth" drugs. Having used the chemicals myself more than once during my career, I knew the physical signs that accompanied them. Swallowers quickly entered trancelike states. They remained conscious and responded—earnestly—to all questions, but as if talking in a dream. When given antidotes, they'd snap out of the daze, thinking they'd nodded off by accident. Usually, the telltale signs went unnoticed: headaches, tiredness, depression— and the unmistakable taste.

I reviewed the previous day. Could a drug I'd been slipped during the banquet have given me enough pain to ask to be taken to the hospital, where I was administered psychotropic drugs? I knew the KGB and FBI used similar methods. Why had I slept so long, which was unusual for me? And had I really been asleep? Platt firmly denied my accusations, blaming my pain on kidney stones. I'd indeed suffered from them before, but this time there were too many unexplained circumstances. I decided to take precautions. Buying bottled water, I refused to drink anything in the hotel.

The day after my hospital visit, I took a book to read at the beach, where I found an empty chair. A pleasant breeze blew off the water. Feeling better, I closed my eyes and listened to the lapping waves. In my relaxed state, I ignored a young man with dark hair walking toward me from the direction of the hotel. He was smiling when he reached my chair.

"Victor Cherkashin?"

"Yes?"

"My name is Michael Rochford," he said casually. "I saw you at the conference. I thought the Russian participants spoke well." I thought the Russians had contributed little of interest, but nodded. After a brief talk about the conference, Rochford changed his tone.

"I have to tell you that I'm an agent of the Federal Bureau of Investigation." I said nothing. He continued. "I work casing the Russian embassy and know a lot of people posted there over the years. I want to talk about your time in the United States."

I tried to betray no reaction. The Ames case was closed. I couldn't add very much to what had been made public. Besides, I felt sure I could tell Rochford nothing that would be of much use, as the SVR had assured me before my 1997 trip. I didn't think the FBI would be much interested in the routine of my work in Washington—about which it already knew quite a bit, thanks to Martynov. I'd later learn my confidence was misplaced.

"I don't think I can be of much use to you," I said. "I've been retired for seven years. If you want to talk about Aldrich Ames— well, all I can say is that I learned about what happened to him from newspapers."

Rochford had clearly read my FBI files. I found out later that he'd helped debrief Yurchenko in 1985, along with Ames. "We're looking for someone who delivered information even more useful than Aldrich Ames's," he said. "We believe you were involved in the case." He listed names of KGB officers involved with handling the Source. The information was accurate, and I suspected the FBI got it from high-level Russian informants. On the other hand, I thought, all the names had been made public in the aftermath of Ames's exposure, so it was difficult to tell what Rochford actually knew and what he was making up.

"We know the agent informed Soviet intelligence about the U.S. agents Valery Martynov, Sergei Motorin and Boris

Yuzhin," Rochford continued. "He's also compromised our satellite programs.

"The FBI needs your help in getting more information about this agent," Rochford went on. "We know he voluntarily offered his services to Soviet intelligence in the 1980s, either leaving a letter with a Soviet representative office in Washington or sending it by mail."

"Look," I said slowly, "we received very many letters from various people. If you're asking me to help you with something that happened fifteen years ago, I'm afraid I won't be of much use to you. It's difficult for me to remember that far back."

Rochford was persistent but also polite, even while making veiled threats. He was obviously a professional who knew what he was doing. "Victor Ivanovich," he said, "we've collected almost enough evidence. He'll be arrested within the next two months, I assure you. The only thing we need from you is a little help sorting the case out."

The longer Rochford went on, however, the more I realized he was making up stories. He was trying too hard to convince me the FBI already knew almost everything about the unidentified agent's activities. If the bureau really had that kind of information, it wouldn't allow him to advertise it.

"Of course we don't expect you to help us for free," he said. "The FBI is ready to pay you $1 million."

Having been offered that amount before while serving in Washington, I didn't have to think about my answer. "A million dollars is worth little compared to my honor, Michael. I've been made offers before, as you probably know. But I should tell you that I have enough money—I don't need any more. What I want most is for my children and my grandchildren to be proud of me. Besides, do you think I'd have worked in Soviet intelligence my whole life only to turn now?"

"We know you had contact with the agent in 1984," Rochford insisted. That assertion couldn't have been true, of course, but it piqued my curiosity. "You rode out to meet him on your bicycle," he specified.

So that was it—incredible. Rochford was right about riding my bicycle around Washington, but that had nothing to do with my cases. He must have been referring to a fall I suffered in July 1984. Alyona and Elena were on vacation in Moscow and, as on most Sundays when I was alone, I went for a ride along a former towpath next to Washington's old C&O canal. (The path was too crowded with joggers and bicyclists to be suitable for conducting operations.)

At one point, something must have stuck in my spokes. The front wheel jammed and I flew forward over the handlebars, onto the ground. My back was hurt and my face bleeding, but I'd narrowly missed a ditch that would have caused worse injuries. A passerby who saw the accident offered to drive me to the hospital, where I was given eleven stitches. No doubt the FBI found out about the accident from the hospital report, I now thought.

But perhaps the bureau's involvement was less innocent. Elena was convinced that the FBI was responsible for the accident, which I found laughable. But Rochford's claim that I'd met Ramon in 1984 made me think maybe Elena was right. Maybe the bureau thought I conducted operations on bicycle and tried to foil me that time.

I couldn't rule out that the information in the Source's letter had somehow leaked out of the *rezidentura* in the 1980s. I knew that at least two officers had secretly opened it and read the contents. I finally settled on trying to throw Rochford off the same way I tried to prevent a security breach in 1985—by bringing up my invented story that the letter was simply part of a ploy to help the Bulgarian secret service protect one of its agents.

I finally excused myself and went back to my room. My head was spinning. I needed time to recover from the continuing pain in my side, my bad mood and tiredness. Most of all, I had to think over what had happened.

Rochford tried to speak to me several more times. Still suffering physically, I decided to cut my trip short. I telephoned Alyona to tell her I wouldn't be flying out to see her, then booked a Moscow flight for Saturday. On Friday, my pain stopped as suddenly as it had started four days earlier.

Back home, I mulled things over again. Clearly the FBI was looking for a volunteer who'd sent us a letter exposing Motorin, Martynov and Yuzhin and disclosing intelligence on spy satellites. Although I knew much of what Rochford told me had been made up, the information that was true could only have been provided by an informer. If the Source was still active, he was in danger.

My main concern, however, wasn't what the FBI did or didn't know. It was why the SVR didn't warn me about ongoing cases before I traveled to Washington the previous year. Why wasn't I told that the agent who volunteered to me in 1985 still worked for Russian intelligence? My knowledge about the Source posed him great potential danger. To allow me to travel to the States without even telling me to be careful was inexcusably negligent.

The SVR probably expected me to deal with any danger myself. I'd had no information about developments in any of my agents' cases since being isolated from Yasenevo's corridors of power in 1986. I didn't know Ramon's real name or identity, so I couldn't expose him directly. Still, I knew a great deal. If I'd been given psychotropic drugs as I suspected, there was no way of telling what I might have revealed about KGB operations.

I told Shebarshin about the entire episode as soon as I returned to Moscow. We agreed that the FBI had very likely found out about the Source and was digging to flesh the story out. I wrote a full report and submitted it to SVR chief Vyacheslav Trubnikov. Several days later, Shebarshin and I made an appointment to meet him at his house outside Moscow. The meeting was friendly. I described my trip to Virginia and FBI attempts to pitch me. He agreed with my view that the Source was in danger. Some measures were taken—but it's clear they weren't nearly enough. It took a little over two years for the FBI to nail down the target. All the while, the bureau continued to pitch me.

4

In June 1999, Alyona, returning from Monterey to spend the summer at home, told us she'd fallen in love with an American. That wasn't good news. My first thought was that her love interest might be an FBI agent. I convinced Elena to help me try to temper our daughter's feelings. We stayed up until three o'clock in the morning, trying to persuade her that Americans differed from Russians in culture and mentality. "It would be best for *you* if you forgot him," I said. "You've one more year to go. Then you'll be back in Moscow and everything will be fine."

Alyona said she met her new boyfriend during their second semester in German language classes. They became friendly after he told her he'd been to Moscow and studied Russian. He invited her out for coffee and a talk about Russia. Then he drove her around sightseeing. They became involved a week before Alyona was due to come home.

There was a good chance the FBI had set the whole thing up. I'd hoped the Americans would leave Alyona alone. The unwritten but strict code among the intelligence officers of opposing services was that while they pitched one another, children were kept out of it. If Russian children were targeted in the United States, there was nothing to stop us from approaching the sons and daughters of our counterparts here in Moscow. Nonetheless, I couldn't rule anything out.

In July, I took Elena, Alyona and my grandson Ivan on vacation to Cyprus. One afternoon, a young man wearing shorts approached me as we returned from the beach.

"Victor?" he asked politely. It was Michael Rochford.

"Michael!" I said, feigning pleasure. "What are you doing here?"

Elena and Alyona went inside while Michael and I found a bench to sit on. It wasn't a complete surprise to see him, although I'd never expected it would be in Cyprus. These FBI agents are serious guys, I thought. They don't give up easily.

Rochford's answer to my question about how he found me was laughably predictable: "We have ways of finding out such information."

When Elena emerged to call me in for lunch, Rochford asked me to meet him again in his hotel. I doubted he was alone on his trip but agreed nevertheless. Knowing everything would be recorded, I decided to try to play a psychological game as best I could. Arriving at Rochford's hotel the following day, I offered to drive him around. The question caught him off guard, but he agreed.

We spent two hours in the car, talking about nothing of substance. Rochford knew what he could get from me and I knew what he wanted from me. Back at his hotel, we took a table in a restaurant. Rochford had performed well the last time I saw him in Virginia. Now that he was no longer on home turf, he was having trouble. Meanwhile, I was learning the FBI had nothing new on Ramon. Rochford repeated the same names and stories—and the same offer to me. I refused, leaving him on the same terms.

5

Rochford tried to dismiss my question about how the FBI located me in Cyprus. Surely, it could have found out in Moscow, but I suspected another source. When Alyona admitted her boyfriend had asked for her summer address to send flowers on her birthday, I had little doubt what that was.

So the following September, when Alyona called us from Monterey, I was shocked to hear her say the boyfriend had proposed and she'd accepted. I could do nothing. The decision was Alyona's to make. Since she was resolute, I could only be happy for her and hope for the best. We accepted her invitation to travel to California for the wedding.

Both Elena and I took an instant liking to Alyona's fiancé. He knew who I was and didn't seem to care. The oceanside wedding was a beautiful affair. Elena and I felt as if we were taking part in a Hollywood film. After the reception, we drove out to Alyona's apartment. Half an hour later, there was a knock at the door. It was Michael Rochford. I cursed him under my breath for not picking a better time but agreed to meet him in a bar the following day. I didn't want to cause trouble for my family.

Arriving fifteen minutes early the next day, I waited with a beer, rehearsing my replies to the questions I anticipated. When Rochford showed up, however, he didn't ask for my help or mention our previous meetings. Instead, he said he was concerned that I'd persuade Alyona's new husband to work for Russian intelligence. I replied that he was now a member of my family. I wouldn't do anything to harm my own daughter.

I left the bar feeling—perhaps for the first time in forty years—that I was no longer an intelligence officer. I was a pensioner who had traveled to the United States as a tourist to visit his daughter and new son-in-law. I no longer felt the shadow of a massive secret organization. No one was watching over me any longer. And if they were, I no longer cared. It was a rare sense of liberation.

Soon after graduating from their two-year program the following June, the newlywed couple gave birth to a son, Victor—named after me—and flew to Moscow to spend the summer with us. They planned to return to California in August. Then our beloved dacha caught fire. Workmen putting up a new roof wired a cable badly, causing sparks. We were outside grilling kebabs as the entire structure burned to the ground. The incident prompted Alyona and her husband to stay in Russia to help us rebuild. My son-in-law now works in Moscow, while my new grandson, Vitya, and I are inseparable.

6

Many stories have emerged about how the CIA tracked down Ames and Hanssen. One theory was that it happened after Bakatin ordered an investigation into the FCD's finances to try to ascertain whether the directorate had been involved with the GKChP. No improprieties were found, but some thought investigators could have stumbled on records of money paid to Ames and Hanssen and possibly figured out where the transfers were going.

In fact, it would have been almost impossible to do that. When I ran the agent I knew as Ramon Garcia, I'd propose a payment amount for him along with a report about his latest operation. I'd cable the information to the chief of Directorate K, who would in turn take it to Kryuchkov for approval. If he agreed, Kryuchkov would write "approved" on my report, which would be sent back to the *rezidentura*. I'd then apply for the payment to the KGB financial department, which would send the *rezidentura* an invoice to fill out. Neither the agent's code name nor the country in which he operated would be written down. The only evidence would be that "according to the approval of the head of the First Chief Directorate, we would like to receive payment of $1 million." I'd sign the paper and send it back with no reference to my location. The financial department would then receive cash from the treasury, package it carefully—removing all fingerprints—and send it to the *rezidentura* via diplomatic pouch. There would be no paper trail indicating where the money was disbursed—other than that I'd asked for it. A cable would be sent confirming the agent received payment, but there would be no formal receipts. To some degree, the system operated on trust.

In November 1997, three years after AVENGER exposed Ames, Kirpichenko made his accusation that I'd been the cause of his betrayal—a view that still holds currency for most Russians who know anything about the case. In his article, Kirpichenko accused Kalugin of betraying Ames to the Americans after obtaining his information from a "friend" named Victor who'd been assigned to handle Ames. The text was riddled with inaccuracies, including a claim that Kalugin brought me into the FCD in addition to its flawed basic premise. In his rush to smear us, Kirpichenko didn't even bother to find out that I'd worked for the FCD since 1963, when Kalugin was stationed in the United States. Despite my outrage, however, I followed Shebarshin's advice and did nothing about the accusation.

Two years later, a former KGB officer named Alexander Sokolov published a book called *Superkrot* (Supermole). It was subtitled "The CIA inside the KGB: General Oleg Kalugin's 35 Years of Spying." Sokolov trotted out the same story about Kalugin, identifying me for the first time by my surname.

Other versions of the accusation against me surfaced. One, published in June 2000, came from a young reporter named Alexander Khinshtein, whose good connections to the intelligence services were often wasted in sensationalistic writing. He accused me of fingering Hanssen through a former KGB colonel called Valentin Aksilenko.

Aksilenko, whom I liked, had worked as a political intelligence officer in the FCD's American department. I met him when he was stationed as a Line PR officer in the Washington *rezidentura* in the early 1980s. After he returned to Moscow in 1983, however, an extramarital affair with a woman who also worked for the KGB caused him problems with his bosses. Aksilenko was eventually demoted to the American department of Directorate RT, which I took over in 1987. He later divorced his wife and married his mistress. In 1991 he retired and two years later moved to the United States along with Yuri Shvets.

In 1999, I was surprised to learn that the intelligence officers veterans association planned to hold a meeting to discuss Sokolov's book, recently released by a publishing house connected to the SVR. I decided to attend. Kirpichenko was there and gave an emotional talk supporting the book. That was the last straw. I stood up to say the book contained lies about me originated by Kirpichenko himself. I promised to go to court to defend my name.

Many members of the veterans association telephoned during the following weeks asking me to reconsider. I was told the accusations against me shouldn't be construed as insulting, that it was well understood they reflected only their authors' opinions. I found those entreaties almost as insulting as the accusations themselves. Several months later, I filed a case against Sokolov and his publisher in a Moscow court.

During the litigation, no one from the SVR or its publishing house contacted me to try to settle the matter out of court. No one apologized. It was more than clear that the intelligence establishment supported Kirpichenko. Sokolov, however, did apologize. He said he'd conducted additional research and was ready to publish a new version of his book minus the accusations against me.

Ruling in my favor, the court found Kirpichenko guilty of negligence for publishing groundless accusations. The verdict said that my reputation had unjustifiably suffered, and it fully cleared my name. I forwarded a copy to the SVR, but again received no response.

I would have preferred to ignore Sokolov's book, dismissing it as ranting that would be proved wrong in time. But I wasn't so sure my children and grandchildren would react the same way. Why should their name too be sullied for something that had nothing to do with them? So I went to court to provide a record. I'd never spoken much about my work in intelligence—perhaps wrongly, I now felt. Why should those who spilled dirt on my work be allowed to give lies as the last word?

EPILOGUE

Lessons of Cold War Espionage

1

Yeltsin and the leaders of the new, supposedly democratic Russia that emerged in 1991 knew that the KGB was the country's most disciplined institution, with the most potential to influence internal affairs. After all, it had kept tabs on society. Therefore its leadership knew perhaps better than anyone the full extent of the state's decay. However, far from helping drive policy, as some thought, the KGB was utterly loyal to the political administration—the Party's Central Committee. That perception remained true in 1991 and shouldn't be diminished by Kryuchkov's part in the coup. Ideological faithfulness to the Party underpinned the very foundation of that main pillar of communist rule.

When Yeltsin and the other "democrats" suddenly found themselves in power, they didn't expect the Soviet institutions they'd worked against to seem so politically powerless. Bakatin wasn't appointed because he was the most qualified to run the KGB. Indeed, he had almost no experience. His task was to destroy the intelligence service, starting by disbanding the Fifth Directorate, which had cracked down on internal dissidents. (The former head of the Fifth Directorate, General Fillip Bobkov, took a job as head of security for Most Bank, founded by tycoon and former Fifth Directorate target Vladimir Gusinsky.)

The new leaders wanted to show their American allies that they no longer posed a threat. Hence the decision to hand over the plans for bugging the U.S. embassy in Moscow. The SVR leadership set another major precedent by opening its archives to two authors writing a book about Cold War espionage from the 1930s to the 1950s: American historian Allen Weinstein and Alexander Vassiliev, a former KGB officer.

In Moscow, the writers negotiated through the foreign intelligence veterans association, represented by Kobaladze and Kirpichenko, who helped push the deal forward. They said Random House ended up paying the association $1.2 million. Kobaladze believed the project would become a major contribution to understanding Cold War history. Like many of his colleagues, he felt that since the United States and Russia were no longer enemies, they should cooperate on key issues such as antiterrorism, narcotics smuggling and proliferation of weapons of mass destruction. Kobaladze was SVR spokesman and knew very well that both sides still conducted intelligence operations against the other. But he saw no reason why facts about important historical events, such as the Cuban missile crisis, shouldn't be made public as a way of increasing the atmosphere for cooperation.

SVR chief Yevgeny Primakov gave Weinstein and Vassiliev unprecedented access to a number of KGB archives in 1993. By 1995, however, things began to sour. As the writers pored over KGB documents, it turned out that the American intelligence community had no intention of opening up its files beyond the results of an NSA signals intelligence operation called VENONA, which lasted from 1946 to 1980 and deciphered Moscow's communications to

Soviet representative organizations in the United States intercepted from 1942 to 1946. Ames's exposure in 1994 effectively put a stop to the public pretense that both sides were cooperating. The American government acted outraged, as if it truly believed espionage between Moscow and Washington had ended—even while CIA operations in Russia were continuing at full steam. The perception of betrayal was heightened by Russia's economic aid from the International Monetary Fund, the World Bank, and other U.S.-dominated organizations. Americans naively felt duped by a country they thought they were helping.

By 1995, the SVR, realizing the project wasn't going to be a joint SVR-CIA effort after all, decided to abort. But it was too late. The writers had collected enough material for a book, *The Haunted Wood*. According to Kobaladze, Vassiliev simply disappeared with his research materials in 1996, taking off to live in London and cutting his contact with the SVR. In fact, there was no reason for him to stay in Russia. He'd been given permission to do his work. Now that the SVR had reconsidered, he knew he'd be made a scapegoat. In fact, the blame lay with Kirpichenko and the SVR leadership. Providing information that revealed details of agents that should never have been declassified—like Bakatin's decision to hand over the blueprints for the U.S. embassy bugs—dealt Russian intelligence an irreparable blow. It was absurd to think we'd entered a new era of brotherhood and cooperation with the United States. The fact that the CIA didn't cooperate with *The Haunted Wood* project showed the Americans weren't ready for such friendship.

2

With Russian and American intelligence agencies again gearing up after the brief if partial truce following the Soviet collapse, what lessons can be learned from the Cold War espionage game?

Anyone who has read this far knows my conviction that intelligence work is less politically important than it may seem. During the Year of the Spy, CIA and KGB operations represented little more than intelligence games. Their connection to real issues of national security, such as stealing military/technological secrets—let alone to the larger national interest as a whole—was often peripheral. Mostly they tried to ferret out moles and recruit enemy intelligence officers.

Perhaps nowhere has the subordination of intelligence to politics recently been more clearly demonstrated than in the current war in Iraq and in CIA claims (or lack of them) about weapons of mass destruction development during Saddam Hussein's regime. Since the fall of the Soviet Union and the emergence of a single superpower able to exert its will almost anywhere on the globe, a vital geostrategic balance has come undone. During the Cold War, American decisions to go to war had to be weighed against a response from Moscow, which maintained close relationships with many countries, including Syria, Egypt and Cuba, as well as Iraq. While we didn't approve of Saddam Hussein's treatment of the Kurdish population or his 1990 invasion of Kuwait, we had many economic interests in Iraq (as did the Americans). In today's monopolar world, a mighty United States finds itself alone in a world of states with massive economic, social and political problems. No wonder it often does the wrong thing by them.

In this environment, the CIA became a political tool for the White House as perhaps never before. Despite the many claims to the contrary, I strongly believe the CIA and the administration of President George W. Bush must have known there were no weapons of mass destruction in Iraq. Much of the so-called intelligence about it came from analysts in the Pentagon Office of Special Plans, set up by neoconservative Douglas Feith, third ranking official in the Pentagon, to bypass the CIA and the Pentagon's own Defense Intelligence Agency. Its feeble and flawed "evidence" of WMD served as the publicly declared basis for war.

Nonetheless, the Bush administration had enough good intelligence to ensure that the invasion of Iraq went well. Agents infiltrated Iraq to help orchestrate the betrayals and desertions that made the campaign a relatively quick and bloodless affair. It's certain that the United States also received information about the lack of WMD from the same sources. Why didn't the White House use the information? Because it went against the strategic plan to invade Iraq—which would "stabilize" the oil market, a central part of the Bush national security doctrine, whose main objective has been America's status as sole superpower. Whether or not CIA Director George Tenet agreed, he did nothing about the claims because his job was at stake.

When it became clear to the public that the claims were false, was Tenet fired for providing bad information? He was not, although the CIA was criticized for that and he eventually resigned. It wasn't Tenet who provided the claims. Instead, he served his political bosses by becoming a scapegoat for the White House, which accused the Central Intelligence Agency of the scandalous act of providing false information—about which it then did nothing. It was all a political game.

The CIA shouldn't be blamed for the problems that beset the American occupation of Iraq soon after the spectacularly successful invasion. The fault lies with the Bush administration for making up excuses to go to war—first WMD and then the laughable "liberation" of Iraq—while failing to grasp the real sentiment among demoralized Iraqis, who of course didn't welcome a heavy-handed occupation. The White House conducted not a liberation but a revolution—a coup—by applying external force against a sovereign state. The CIA was used as a pawn in that goal, just as it was used during the Cold War against the Soviet Union. (The KGB was no less guilty of the same political manipulation.)

How to tackle the problem now? The main lesson goes beyond the CIA or the SVR. States must somehow ensure that their intelligence services direct their activities toward achieving properly defined strategic goals instead of following their leaders' political intentions. Aldrich Ames, for one, realized the perils of intelligence—that its priorities were dictated by the desires of its managers, who misled the public by exaggerating the Soviet threat. In fact, as I've stressed, during the last years of the Cold War, intelligence became a game of penetrating the adversary's service. It was expensive and superfluous.

Which strategic goals should define current priorities? Economic development should be near the top of the list, as well as combating organized criminal activities such as drugs and human smuggling. Fighting terrorism is perhaps most important. But that goal can't be achieved using force alone. Above all, terrorism reflects socioeconomic problems. Prosperous societies produce bad candidates for terrorism. Western states should be thinking about how to help regions in the Middle East, Africa and elsewhere overcome their dire financial problems. Most important, the international community must seriously address the Israeli–Palestinian conflict. It remains a major problem, destabilizing the entire Middle East by perpetuating a Palestinian underclass.

Intelligence can help by locating and working with healthy forces in dysfunctional societies instead of solely hunting for terrorist leaders to arrest or kill. In the end, that only creates more converts to terrorism. Greater cooperation among agencies can help achieve the larger, more promising goal.

3

Russia has its own deep-seated intelligence problems. The SVR has more difficulty gathering information than did the KGB. Officers are paid on average several hundred dollars a month, providing bad motivation and boosting reasons to spy for the United States and other countries. Russia still lacks a coherent development strategy. As our people watch a handful of insiders profit from fleecing the country's economic assets, the overriding goal of most, including SVR officers, is to take what they can grab; otherwise, someone else will. "Market economics" has taken on a distinctly criminal meaning in Russia. People are ready to do just about anything for money. But although many, including Gennady Vasilenko, now say corruption looms large in the SVR, I don't believe all is lost.

One of the largest problems for Russian intelligence is the lack of a clear foreign policy. The government has yet to formulate a consistent set of goals beyond claiming that Russia should once again be a great country. Is NATO an enemy or a friend? Does Russia want to return to its Soviet-era opposition to the western world or become a full member of capitalist and democratic society? Those questions haven't been fully answered. Under Putin, policy is largely based on tactics, not strategy—and contradiction is often the result. As long as the state fails to define its priorities, so will intelligence.

One hope for the SVR is to cooperate with the CIA and other agencies on mutual objectives. Russia and the United States will always retain a geostrategic opposition—that's inevitable and natural. Some Russian politicians are heralding the likelihood of long-time instability in Iraq. While Washington wants low oil prices, Russia—which earns most of its hard currency from oil—wants exactly the opposite. Still, in the fields I've outlined above—terrorism, narcotics, WMD and other areas—there should be cooperation. I don't mean simply an exchange of information, which is what often passes for cooperation now. The CIA and SVR should conduct bona fide joint operations to detect likely sources of terrorism and prevent them.

Both the CIA and the SVR/KGB have experience with terrorist groups and their predecessors. The Soviet Union backed many
liberation movements in the Middle East, Latin America and
Southeast Asia—before some evolved into terrorist groups. So did
the CIA. One case in point is the Afghan mujahideen, which produced Osama bin Laden, American public enemy number one.
Despite massive cutbacks in human intelligence following the end
of the Cold War, agencies still recruit agents and generate intelligence. Much of the knowledge base remains unused. It exists in
the form of retirees who, like Jack Platt, leave the CIA without so
much as an exit interview to glean thirty years of accumulated experience and wisdom. But perhaps the attitudes of the younger
generation are to some extent inevitable. If veterans of the CIA
and the KGB know one thing in common, it's that you can't get
around human nature.

NOTES

CHAPTER 2

1. Rem Krassilnikov, *KGB protif MI–6, okhotniki za shpionam* (Moscow: Sentrpoligraf, 2000), p. 207.

2. Oleg Penkovsky, *The Penkovskiy Papers*, trans. Peter Deriabin (New York: Doubleday, 1965), p. 12.

3. Krassilnikov, *KGB protif MI–6*, p. 211.

4. Penkovsky, *Penkovskiy Papers*, p. 3.

5. Christopher Andrew and Vasili Mitrokhin, *The Sword and the Shield: The Mitrokhin Archive and the Secret History of the KGB* (New York: Basic, 1999), p. 399.

6. *Sydney Morning Herald*, July 27, 2002.

CHAPTER 4

1. Pete Earley, *Confessions of a Spy: The Real Story of Aldrich Ames* (New York: Putnam's, 1997), p. 120.

2. Milt Bearden and James Risen, *The Main Enemy: The Inside Story of the CIA's Final Showdown with the KGB* (New York: Random House, 2003), p. 21.

3. Earley, *Confessions*, p. 232.

CHAPTER 5

1. Christopher Andrew and Vasily Mitrokhin, *The Sword and the Shield: The Mitrokhin Archive and the Secret History of the KGB* (New York: Basic, 1999), p. 209.

2. "Oleg Kalugin: Man in the News Again," *Radio Free Europe/Radio Liberty Business Watch*, April 9, 2002.

CHAPTER 6

1. Sherry Sontag and Christopher Drew with Annette Lawrence Drew, *Blind Man's Bluff: The Untold Story of American Submarine Espionage* (New York: Public Affairs, 1998), p. 177.

2. Milt Bearden and James Risen, *The Main Enemy: The Inside Story of the CIA's Final Showdown with the KGB* (New York: Random House, 2003), p. 46.

3. David Wise, *Nightmover: How Aldrich Ames Sold the CIA to the KGB for $4.6 Million* (New York: HarperCollins, 1995), p. 127.

4. Bearden and Risen, *Main Enemy*, p. 87.

5. Bearden and Risen, *Main Enemy*, p. 9.

6. Bearden and Risen, *Main Enemy*, p. 37.

7. Bearden and Risen, *Main Enemy*, p. 34.

8. Pete Earley, *Confessions of a Spy: The Real Story of Aldrich Ames* (New York: Putnam's, 1997), p. 151.

9. Bearden and Risen, *Main Enemy*, p. 72.

10. Wise, *Nightmover*, p. 126.

11. Bearden and Risen, *Main Enemy*, p. 80.

12. Earley, *Confessions*, p. 157.

13. Bearden and Risen, *Main Enemy*, p. 121.

14. Bearden and Risen, *Main Enemy*, p. 121.

15. William Safire, "The Farewell Dossier," *New York Times*, February 2, 2004.

16. David Hoffman, "Reagan Approved Plan to Sabotage Soviets," *Washington Post*, February 27, 2004.

17. Bearden and Risen, *Main Enemy*, p. 51.

18. Bearden and Risen, *Main Enemy*, p. 139.

19. Earley, *Confessions*, p. 164.

20. Earley, *Confessions*, p. 165.

21. James Kelly, "The Spy Who Returned to the Cold," *Time*, November 18, 1985.

22. Bearden and Risen, *Main Enemy*, p. 92.

23. Bearden and Risen, *Main Enemy*, p. 112.

CHAPTER 7

1. Pete Earley, *Confessions of a Spy: The Real Story of Aldrich Ames* (New York: Putnam's, 1997), p. 181.

2. Milt Bearden and James Risen, *The Main Enemy: The Inside Story of the CIA's Final Showdown with the KGB* (New York: Random House, 2003), p. 46.

3. Bearden and Risen, *Main Enemy*, p. 47.

4. Bearden and Risen, *Main Enemy*, p. 48.

5. Sherry Sontag and Christopher Drew with Annette Lawrence Drew, *Blind Man's Bluff: The Untold Story of American Submarine Espionage* (New York: Public Affairs, 1998), p. 248.

6. Earley, *Confessions*, p. 139.

7. Bearden and Risen, *Main Enemy*, p. 120.

8. Bearden and Risen, *Main Enemy*, p. 98.

9. In 1996, five years after I retired from the KGB, a member of President Boris Yeltsin's Security Council asked me to help in Yeltsin's reelection campaign. It was before the presidential elections of that year—and since I thought Yeltsin was the best candidate at the time, I agreed. I was also asked to publicize my own importance by discussing some aspects of the Ames case. He'd been arrested two years earlier and it was already known that I had something to do with his handling. Soon after, a young journalist from *Nezavisimoe voennoe obozrenie* (Independent Military Analysis) called and asked to interview me. When I met him, I tried to skirt talking about Ames as much as I could, but I did say that the agents he exposed shouldn't have been executed. Then we went on to talk about Yeltsin and the elections. I said Russia needed stability—thereby indirectly supporting the incumbent. A week later, I was speaking to Security Council staff members who asked me if I knew who'd interviewed me. I didn't—he never introduced himself and I never asked. It turned out to have been the son of Leonid Polishchuk.

10. Bearden and Risen, *Main Enemy*, p. 30.
11. Earley, *Confessions*, p. 118.
12. Earley, *Confessions*, p. 118.
13. Bearden and Risen, *Main Enemy*, p. 168.
14. Bearden and Risen, *Main Enemy*, p. 155.
15. Earley, *Confessions*, p. 196.
16. Earley, *Confessions*, p. 234.
17. Bearden and Risen, *Main Enemy*, p. 178.

CHAPTER 8

1. Milt Bearden and James Risen, *The Main Enemy: The Inside Story of the CIA's Final Showdown with the KGB* (New York: Random House, 2003), p. 150.

CHAPTER 9

1. This and other information about the Robert Hanssen espionage case comes from an FBI affidavit filed in support of an application for Hanssen's arrest warrant and subsequently made public. The document contains excerpts from correspondence between Hanssen and the KGB and details of his handling that I quote in this chapter.

2. Ronald Kessler, *The Bureau: The Secret History of the FBI* (New York: St. Martin's, 2002), p. 385.

3. Milt Bearden and James Risen, *The Main Enemy: The Inside Story of the CIA's Final Showdown with the KGB* (New York: Random House, 2003), p. 527.

CHAPTER 10

1. Pete Earley, *Confessions of a Spy: The Real Story of Aldrich Ames* (New York: Putnam's, 1997), p. 199.

2. Milt Bearden and James Risen, *The Main Enemy: The Inside Story of the CIA's Final Showdown with the KGB* (New York: Random House, 2003), p. 180.

INDEX